CHEAP BASTARD'S® SERIES

THE CHEAP BASTARD'S® GUIDE TO

Seattle

Secrets of Living the Good Life—For Less!

Second Edition

David **Volk**

gpp®
travel

Guilford, Connecticut
An imprint of Globe Pequot Press

All the information in this guidebook is subject to change. We recommend that you call ahead to obtain current information before traveling.

To buy books in quantity for corporate use
or incentives, call **(800) 962–0973**
or e-mail **premiums@GlobePequot.com.**

Project Editor: Lauren Szalkiewicz

Text design: Sheryl P. Kober

ISSN: 2158-5903

ISBN: 978-0-7627-9230-6

Printed in the United States of America

10 9 8 7 6 5 4 3 2 1

To Jerry Katz (1930–2013), a great father and the nicest
father-in-law a guy could have asked for.

CONTENTS

ABOUT THE AUTHOR

David Volk is an award-winning humor writer and the author of *The Tribe Has Spoken: Life Lessons from Reality TV*. He has written for national and regional publications including *Seattle Magazine, Alaska Airlines, AAA Journey*, and *Koi World*. He has called Seattle home for more than 20 years. When he isn't writing, he can be found searching for urban adventures, odd experiences, and kitschy places to take his family and for locals to take out-of-towners. He has a serious side, but often has trouble locating it. Volk also writes humorous rants on his website, davidvolk.com. Contact him via the website to join the rant list. You can also find additional deals on his website cheapbastardseattle.com

ACKNOWLEDGMENTS

Thanks so much for reading this modest volume, which I like to call "The Cheap Bastard's Guide to Seattle II: Revenge of the Bastards." I know the title will never make it to the book cover, but it amuses me just the same. Come to think of it, there are lots of things that amused me this time around, and Gordon Ramsay's *Hell's Kitchen* wasn't even on the list this edition. Having Scott Cohen lobby to be acknowledged as my muse was one of them. (Sorry, Scott, the job is already taken by my wife and kids, but I am flattered that someone would actually campaign for the job.) Another amusing moment was Richard Isaac's discovery of a Filipino restaurant where a waiter in drag performs a Friday night floorshow. I also got a big chuckle from a sign posted outside the Wedgwood Alehouse, the neighborhood bar where I play pub trivia. The sandwich board advertising a weekly family special said simply, 1 Kid Eats Free. It didn't say which kid or how he or she was chosen. When I went in to investigate, I also asked one of the managers of the alehouse if his establishment had a happy hour, and he responded, "Yes, but it isn't very happy."

Local writer Annika Hipple got me into this mess in the first place when she gave Globe Pequot editor Kevin Sirois my name because she couldn't do the book herself. By now, she should probably be absolved of all responsibility beyond that minor detail, however.

You might think updating a book like this one would be an easy task that just involved a lot of phone calls, but when you're also a stay-at-home dad to two active kindergarten-aged kids, the lovely Hana and the amazing Nathan, it can be more of an uphill battle than you might expect. In fact, the book wouldn't have been possible without my long-suffering wife, Cindy (whatever you do, don't call her Mrs. Bastard), who provided love, support, and encouragement, even when I didn't deserve it. She was also thoughtful and kind enough to line up playdates, babysitters, and special guest star visitors who came by to put the kids (whatever you do, don't call them the bastard children) in bed before she left for her annual Army Reserve training. The group included Sue Bae, Chris, and Austin Lee; Abby Bernhard; Kyra Butzel and Ayla Martell; Don Doering; Myriam and Maya Frieder; Jessica and Adam Graybill; Andrew and Elie Hess; Kim and Sophie Isaac; Julie Katz; Marc, David, Ilana and Evan Jacobson; Renee Katz; Kathy and James

Link; David Loren; Julie Lyss; Aviva Lyss-Loren; Lisa, Chris, and Harper Matsumoto; Ira Mehlman, Peta Kerabus-Mehlman and Mia and Simone Mehlman, Amital Orzech; Eric Radman; Myndee and Waverly Ronning; Gena Shapiro; Jack and Julia Snyder; Deborah Sopher; Alys Yablon Wylen and Avi; as well as Lauren Kurland; Scott Cohen; and Micah and Hannah.

I also can't forget my researchers in the field and many Facebook friends who mentioned places I might have missed. The crew includes brothers-in-law extraordinaire Andrew Hess and Eric Radman and friends from all walks of life including Shirley Abreu, Steve Adler, Kirsten Andresen, Luna Bee, Rob Bhatt, Deborah Binder, Amanda Castleman, Gail Coskey, Brett Fetzer, Philip Gustavson, Erin Goodman, Ronald Holden, Richard Isaac, Lauren Kurland, David and Marc Jacobson, Julie Johnson at Visit Rainier, Heather Larson, David Loren, Julie Lyss, Julie Mains, Tori McIntyre, Emmett Montgomery, Ginny Morey, Dana Neuts, Mary Schweickl, Janna Silverstein, Grant Thornley, and everyone else who sent me an e-mail suggestion or picked up a phone to return my calls. I even got a few pointers from the folks at Savor Seattle. If I've forgotten to mention your name, please forgive me; I was a bit distracted at the end.

I also appreciate the advice provided by Tony Berman at Berman Entertainment and Technology Law (BEAT-LAW) in San Francisco.

As always, thanks to editor Kevin Sirois who let me be as snarky and silly as I wanted to be.

The writing of any book is an emotional period for any author, but this one was especially so because my father-in-law, Jerry Katz, died just weeks before the book was finished. He was a quiet, gentle soul who was loved by people throughout the community and the best father-in-law a guy could ask for. He not only helped me find a car when mine was totaled in an accident, he let me take him out to lunch after I bought the 2000 Toyota Corolla from a car dealership in a neighborhood near where he used to run his own drugstore, Jerry's Garden Pharmacy. He had his choice of any restaurant he wanted, but he requested a Grand Slam Breakfast at Denny's. My only regret is that I happened to be out of town when he died and I didn't get a chance to say goodbye.

He will be missed.

This edition is dedicated to his memory.

INTRODUCTION

Most people would be insulted to be called a cheap bastard, but not me. I consider it a compliment, especially these days. While others have been opening their wallets over the last three years and worrying how they were going to make it from paycheck to paycheck, I have happily taken time out of my busy day to go out and get ice cream, eat yogurt, watch movies, take in plays, attend music shows, eat out, and even take the occasional trip . . . for next to nothing and in many cases for absolutely nothing. And it's not because I have a better paycheck than they do. In fact, this is probably one of the few times a guy is willing to go on record saying mine is probably smaller than yours, but I'm happy to do it. Because I'm a cheap bastard. And proud of it.

That doesn't mean being the CB doesn't have its embarrassing moments. Like the time a woman I know yelled, "Hey, cheap bastard" as I walked into a room filled with people. Since I didn't hear the comment, everyone stared at her because they thought she was insulting me and I was too dignified to acknowledge the slight.

Me? Dignified?

You're talking about a man who goes to tomato battles and snowball fights for a living. I'm the kind of guy who thinks nothing of skipping down the sidewalk with his children while wearing a suit. I'm also the kind of guy who isn't embarrassed to dance with his son in the middle of a grocery store aisle to the accompaniment of really bad Muzak. "Karma Chameleon" done by Mantovani anyone?

At this point I feel it's only fair to mention that I use the phrase "cheap bastard" with tongue firmly planted in cheek. While I wear the title with pride, that doesn't mean I believe in being stingy for its own sake or being rude to get a deal. All of the methods I suggest (and use) are legal, moral, ethical, and a heck of a lot of fun . . . except maybe for my insistence on changing my appearance to get seconds on samples at Trader Joe's. In addition, none of my methods involve negotiating or figuratively beating someone over the head just to save a few cents. But they all involve finding ways to beat the system and enjoy yourself along the way.

This guidebook will show you how to become a cheap bastard, too, in a good way. *The Cheap Bastard's Guide to Seattle* is your secret weapon for improving the quality of your life in the Emerald City because it shows you how to do many of the things you already pay to do, for free. It covers everything from the obvious, like the Ballard Locks and New Year's Eve fireworks at the Seattle Center, to opportunities you never even knew existed, like summer concerts at the Olympic Sculpture Garden. It shows you places you've overlooked and the secret strategies to do things you didn't know you could afford.

Did you ever want to sail Lake Union, but thought it would cost too much? The Center for Wooden Boats offers a free public sail of Lake Union aboard a classic sailing ship every Sunday. Wish you could have attended the opening night gala at the Seattle International Film Festival, but couldn't afford a ticket? If you lived life the cheap bastard way, you could have gotten in for free. All you had to do was volunteer as an usher and you could have stuck around for the big soiree.

The best part is that the cheap bastard approach will make your memory even sweeter and truly make getting there more than half the fun. Sure, you could just go to the box office and buy tickets to see a ballet . . . or you could go behind the scenes to see the show come together. Of course, you could call up Ticketmaster and purchase theater tickets . . . or you could become an usher and maybe seat a few famous folk who paid hundreds of dollars to see the same play you're seeing for free. Doing it the cheap bastard way will allow you to do more than just talk with your friends about the newest big blockbuster movie everyone's seen; it might just give you the opportunity to impress them by telling them what the star said about his role or the director said about her experience.

The book contains three kinds of listings to help you do just that. There are truly free opportunities, those that are free with a catch, and the ridiculously cheap. Truly free items require little additional effort on your part other than calling, making a reservation, or just showing up, such as visiting the Frye Art Museum or taking a tour of Mighty O Donuts. Free with a catch listings require a little more effort, whether it be volunteering as an usher to see a play or helping set up before a show to see a dance performance. As the name suggests, ridiculously cheap items do require you to dip into your wallet, but the financial impact is so light you barely feel it . . . unless you decide to pinch yourself to make sure you heard right.

As with anything free or cheap, there may be a few provisos along the way. For example, some free outdoor movies have suggested donations, and some bars that offer free entertainment may have a minimum drink purchase. In addition, some performing groups prefer only to use volunteers who are willing to make a season-long commitment instead of a person who only wants to help out at one performance. In such cases, I've added the phrase "The Catch" to a listing and then I explain other conditions you'll need to know about before you go.

I've done my best to sniff out and hunt down every free opportunity in the Seattle area, but it's important to remember that things change. All of the information was accurate at press time, but it's always best to check before you go, especially with free events. Places close, prices change, events that were once free suddenly add fees, comedy and open mic nights come and go, and in the current economic climate, programs disappear when government funding dries up. Heck, in the last edition, one of the places I referred to as not being a fly-by-night operation suddenly closed without warning and seemed to move under cover of darkness. That's a mistake I'll never make again. That's also why I've added as much contact information as possible so you can call ahead, check the website, or even stop by just to make sure it's all still current. After all, we may be cheap bastards, but we aren't stupid.

SECTION 1:

Entertainment in Seattle

THEATER:
FREE SPEECH

"Drama is life with the dull bits cut out."
—Alfred Hitchcock

If it's true that "All the world's a stage, and all the men and women merely players," why the heck do plays cost so much? If we're all actors, how come we don't get a professional discount? True, we don't have union cards, but I don't see why that should stop us, especially since there's so much to see in the Emerald City. Mainstream, fringe, ethnic, youth, community, and even clown theater are among the many options available all year long.

Until we can convince box office managers that we're with the cast, however, we'll have to find other ways to get in free. Or at least avoid paying retail. Here are a few ways that work well.

THE **RISE** OF **THE** HOUSE **USHER** (WITH **APOLOGIES** TO **EDGAR** ALLAN **POE**)

Today's usher is a man (or woman) of many contrasts. Although he may seem to lead a carefree existence, happily tearing tickets, passing out programs, answering patrons' questions, and showing people to their seats, he's got a lot on his mind. These days, there are times when he likely finds himself concerned about a variety of issues. "Am I getting the right crowd count?" "Am I prepared to help out in case of an emergency?" "Do I need to report the guy using the laptop during the play to the house manager?" and, even more importantly, "Will I get the seat I want or will I end up standing?"

We're kidding, of course, but only partly so. Although ushering is one of the best ways to see a show for free, there's a bit more to it than showing up at your favorite theater on the day of a performance holding a WILL WORK FOR ADMISSION sign.

The best way to start is by contacting the theater of your choice and beginning the actual volunteering process, which is far less painful than it sounds. Prospective ushers typically fill out an application and wait for a response. The larger the theater is, though, the more formal the process and the longer the wait. A Contemporary Theatre, for example, requires prospective ushers to e-mail a request for information about ushering. At the opposite end of the spectrum, if you want to volunteer at Annex Theatre, all you have to do is call.

Some companies also require volunteers to attend usher training. The sessions aren't long or involved, but they do explain the job's responsibilities. While some are shocked to learn there are actual responsibilities, they aren't terribly onerous. You just have to know how to interact with the public and tear ticket stubs so the company knows exactly how many people are attending a particular performance. Also, you will need to be trained in what to do in the event of an emergency, in case there's a need to evacuate the building. Apparently, running around screaming like a girl is not the appropriate response . . . even if you're a girl given to screaming.

Once you've made it through those hoops, you're ready to work. And once the work is done, there's a play. As long as there's an empty seat for you to sit in. Fortunately, there are usually enough no-shows that there are some pretty good seats left over. And when there aren't, most theater companies will give you a ticket for a performance on another date during the play's run.

One last note: While some smaller companies are grateful for any help even if it's only for one show, larger theaters prefer people who are willing to volunteer on an ongoing basis over those who want to usher just so they can see one particular show. As with any job, the longer you hang around and the more seniority you gain, the better your choices.

A Contemporary Theatre
700 Union St.
(206) 292-7660
www.acttheatre.org
Ushers per performance: 2 to 12

As the name suggests, ACT focuses on new plays that push the envelope. Originally founded as a fringe theater, ACT now attracts what could be described as a better-dressed, less-pierced crowd. It's still doing edgy stuff, though. Years later, I'm still scratching my head over a play in which a man leaves his wife because he's fallen in love with a goat. The building has five performance spaces ranging from a small cabaret to a large theater in the round, so the number of ushers needed can vary wildly. To get on the usher list for mainstage plays, you must send usher coordinator Christine Jew an e-mail at cjew@acttheatre.org requesting ushering information. To volunteer for plays in all other performance spaces, e-mail volunteer@act-theatre.org. The theater also offers day-of-show rush tickets and discounts for people under 25. And it offers pay-what-you-can (PWYC) shows every day for its mainstage performances and select Central Heating Lab shows. The tickets are available in person day of show starting at 1 p.m.

Annex Theatre
Corner of E. Pike Street and 11th Avenue
(206) 728-0933
www.annextheatre.org
Volunteers per performance: 3

One of Seattle's oldest surviving fringe-theater companies, Annex's regular shows focus on new works and what it calls "radical reinterpretations of classic scripts . . . and non-linear wild-ass spectacles." It also hosts "Spin the Bottle," a late night variety show on the first Friday of the month, and the comedy variety show "Weird and Awesome with Emmett Montgomery" on the first Sunday of the month. Annex's performance space is so small there's no need for ushers, but it does need a volunteer to run the box office each show. There's no waiting list to sign up. Just call the main number to volunteer. All Thursday shows are pay what you can. All late night and weekend shows are $10. Student price for all shows is $5.

ArtsWest
4711 California Ave. SW
(206) 938-0963
www.artswest.org
Ushers per performance: 8

The theater may be popular with West Seattleites, but many folks who don't live in this out-of-the-way neighborhood haven't heard of it. That's good news because it's easier to get tickets, but bad news for ArtsWest because it means fewer patrons, though more people are discovering it. It still has a long usher list, so there will likely be some jockeying for popular performances. Ushers can see performances free, but they must complete usher training before they can work their first shift. To volunteer, call or e-mail volunteer coordinator Myron Jenkins (206-938-0963; myronj@artswest.org) or go to the website, fill out the form, and mail it in or drop it by. The company usually holds a pay-what-you-can preview the night before a show opens. Suggested donation is $5. Theater buffs under 25 pay $15 and seniors get a 10 percent discount.

The Great Pay-What-You-Can Debate

There appear to be two schools of thought on what pay what you can really means. While administrators at some companies feel that PWYC shows allow people who couldn't otherwise afford it to attend live theater, others say they believe some in the theatergoing public are abusing the special shows by attending those performances when they could easily pay for a regular ticket. It's easy to tell where the company falls on the issue by looking at how they charge for the shows. All theaters that offer them know they won't break even on the show, but some actually post a suggested donation.

Olympia's Harlequin Productions just leaves a box in the lobby and asks audience members to put in whatever they want to. The amounts are usually pretty small, but someone once left a $100 bill.

"Pay what you can is what it is," artistic director Scot Whitney says. "What's it worth to you? What can you pay? We don't set any guidelines. They're such fun performances. Often they're our best audiences. I would rather have some people take advantage of it than be a hard-ass. Who am I to judge what people can pay?"

At the same time, A Contemporary Theatre has a suggested minimum donation of $5 and Taproot Theatre Company charges $10. All of which prompts us to wonder, is it really pay what you can if

Bainbridge Performing Arts

200 Madison Ave. N
Bainbridge Island
(206) 842-8569
www.bainbridgeperformingarts.com
Volunteers per performance: varies

A sort of one-stop shop for many of your lively arts needs, BPA is where you go on Bainbridge Island to hear the symphony, see plays, visit an art gallery, catch a musical performance, or take in a dance show. The organization uses volunteers in many areas, including ushering, box office, and concession sales just to name a few, and all get to see the event they're working on for free. There's also a PWYC performance of each mainstage someone is telling you how much to pay?

At this point it may be worthwhile to note that the whole idea of pay what you can performances didn't start out as a way to bring in folks who weren't already fans of the lively arts, according to Shane Regan, a programs and members associate at Theatre Puget Sound. Instead, it was partly created as an industry night so that cash-strapped actors could see their friends perform. As Regan sees it, the approach is the perfect compromise between letting people get in free or having them pay full price.

"From what I've seen, it doesn't really bring new people in all that much. It's more people that can't afford it or cheap actors like me," Regan said.

It also helps explain why many of the lower-priced performances tend to be on off-nights so that other actors can attend.

For a list of theaters that offer the discount, check the appendix at the back of the book.

Want another secret? If you're looking for a PWYC performance and don't have the book handy, you can find a short list of upcoming discounted shows by going to www.seattleperforms.com, clicking on the MORE tab, and selecting Pay What You Can. It's not a comprehensive list, but it's a start.

show the Thursday before opening night. The organization also does occasional buy-one-get-one free tickets and will announce when it plans to do rush tickets on its Facebook page.

Balagan Theatre
Various locations
(206) 718-3245
www.balagantheatre.com
Volunteers per performance: varies

Thank goodness for a change of heart. There was a time when Balagan didn't use ushers, but that's no longer the case. Ushers now get to see the show for free, and volunteers get discounted tickets. The theater also offers a PWYC performance on one Monday night during a play's run, usually right before closing weekend. Balagan also has occasional late night fare with tickets selling for $10 to $15. Recent shows have included *Kill Shakespeare* and *Blood Squad*.

Book-It Repertory Theatre
Seattle Center Theatre
305 Harrison St.
(206) 216-0833
www.book-it.org
Ushers per performance: 4 to 6

If you like seeing books come to life on the stage, Book-It is the company for you. Its shows adapt novels into fully produced plays while still following the author's narrative, even inserting "he said" and "she said" where it appears in the original text. Ushers typically get to see the show unless there are no tickets available. Then they get a voucher to attend another performance. The company holds a volunteer orientation once a year, but can reduce it down to a 30-second run-through for newbies who couldn't attend the session. To volunteer, e-mail info@book-it.com. All shows have at least two PWYC performances per run.

Burien Little Theatre
Burien Community Center Annex
14501 4th Ave. SW
Burien
(206) 242-5180
www.burienlittletheatre.org
Ushers per performance: 2

It isn't in the heart of Seattle's theater-going world, but BLT offers professionally produced shows throughout the year. All volunteers get a free show ticket, including people who work in props, costumes, and set design. Sign up to usher at BLT's website. You might not get the exact date you want, but it will be close. On the first Sunday of every run, all tickets are $7; the first Saturday of the run, tickets are two for one. Still, $20 for the general public and $17 for seniors, military, and students isn't too bad.

The Etiquette of Ushering

As we've mentioned, there's a little more to ushering than meets the eye. It's an easy job and the reward is great, but there are a few things you should remember:

- **Dress nicely:** Formalwear isn't necessary, but usher coordinators say your clothes should be in good condition. It's hard to go wrong in black pants and a nice white shirt. Avoid sloppy clothes or anything that's too revealing.
- **Be polite:** You're dealing with the public, so you should be on your best behavior, even if they aren't. As one volunteer coordinator put it, "You need to be civil to the public, even if the public is inebriated."
- **Be prepared for any task:** You never know what you'll end up doing. ArtsWest wants its volunteers to be able to calm the audience in the event of an earthquake or other emergency. At the same time, Harlequin asks one usher to stand at the front of the theater during intermission to make sure people don't walk onto the stage and start picking up props. It may sound strange, but artistic director Scot Whitney doesn't think so. "You'd be surprised" what people do, he said.

Centerstage Theatre

3200 SW Dash Point Rd.
Federal Way
(253) 661-1444
www.centerstagetheatre.com
Ushers per performance: 10

In its publicity materials, the company always follows its name with an exclamation point. Centerstage! serves the South Sound! and specializes in producing musicals and comedies! To volunteer, e-mail mail@centerstage theatre.com. Exclamation points not required.

Copious Love Productions
Locations vary
www.copiouslove.org
Volunteers per performance: varies

Given the company's name, it's not surprising that it loves volunteers; it loves a lot of things, but it doesn't need ushers. It could use backstage and tech-types, though. It also has PWYC performances on two Thursday nights during a play's run.

Driftwood Players
950 Main St.
Edmonds
(425) 774-9600
www.driftwoodplayers.com
Volunteers per performance: 6

Edmonds' 53-year-old community theater group is still going strong with a variety of presentations including mainstage shows, Theatre of Intriguing Possibilities alternative stage productions, and Special Presentations. Driftwood generally uses six volunteers per performance (including one or two concession workers) who can stay and see the evening's show. Dress rehearsals aren't publicized, but are open to the public. Its occasional First Draft program allows patrons to sit in on a reading of a work in progress and ask questions after the performance. First Draft admission is free.

Ear to the Ground Theatre
(206) 432-4824
www.eartothegroundtheatre.org
Ushers per performance: 6

It's about time that clowns had their own theater company. But not the bad kind of clown like the scary Stephen King clowns or the goofy guy you'd hire to perform at your three-year-old's birthday party. Instead, theatrical-style clowns. Think commedia dell'arte or corporeal mime. We're not sure what that is either, but this fringe company's work has increased the amount of physical theater in its productions. To volunteer, e-mail eartotheground-theatre@yahoo.com. The company does workshops on clowning and physical theater every February and offers a limited number of scholarships and work-trades for people who would like to participate.

Eclectic Theater Company

1214 10th Ave.
(206) 679-3271
www.eclectictheatercompany.org
Volunteers per performance: 3

Originally named the Green Theatre, the company that once focused on eco-friendly productions now focuses on producing "original, contemporary, and classic works for the stage and screen" including improv, stand-up and sketch comedy, screenplay readings and films. ETC allows front-of-house volunteers to see the show they're working for free. To volunteer, e-mail rikdeskin@gmail.com. The organization typically needs three volunteers a night, or two a night when its theater is hosting a guest show. Pay-what-you-can previews are the Thursday before opening night, and dress rehearsals are free. Students, seniors, and union members get in for $12.

5th Avenue Theatre

1308 Fifth Ave.
(206) 625-1900
www.5thavenue.org
Volunteers per performance: varies

Staring at the Imperial Chinese–influenced 5th Avenue is as entertaining as the live musical productions that echo through its halls. There are dragons here, a bas-relief of the Forbidden City there, and there might even be angels in the architecture. Many of the shows are either touring Broadway musicals or bound for Broadway. There's no volunteer ushering, but there are many volunteer options including data entry, event staffing, and other administrative tasks. Would-be workers who e-mail the 5th Avenue to volunteer receive notice of opportunities as they come up. Day-of-show tickets are available to patrons under 25 for $20 for most local productions.

Ghostlight Theatricals

2220 NW Market St.
(206) 395-5458
www.ghostlighttheatricals.org
Ushers per performance: 1

Ghostlight generally needs volunteers to build sets or folks with liquor licenses to tend bar. After working a few hours, those volunteers will be able to see a show for free. It also has PWYC performances every Monday and Thursday during a play's run. The company's website also lists opportunities for cheap tickets and other PWYC performances. To volunteer, contact info@ghostlighttheatricals.org.

Harlequin Productions

202 4th Ave. E
Olympia
(360) 786-0151
www.harlequinproductions.org
Ushers per performance: 6 to 8 ushers

The actors may not like it, but this Olympia-based theater's season lasts a full year. While that may mean no summer vacation for them, it means more volunteer opportunities for us. Its productions run the gamut from musicals and classics to new works. Ushers can see the show they work for free. To get on the usher list, go to the website's volunteer page and fill out an application. PWYC performances are on the Wednesday evening after opening weekend. Rush tickets sell for $12 to $20.

Intiman Theatre Festival

201 Mercer St.
(206) 441-7178
www.intiman.org
Ushers per performance: 12

After being forced to cancel much of its 2011 season and lay off many staffers, Intiman has substantially scaled back. Instead of offering a full season of plays, it now stages a festival during the summer months. In 2013, that meant a short season of four shows running from June through September. It still needed ushers, and ushers could still stay to see the show. To volunteer, e-mail volunteers@intiman.org. The organization also planned to offer PWYC shows on the first preview night of each show.

Jet City Improv

Jet City Improv Theater
5510 University Way NE
(206) 352-8291
www.jetcityimprov.com
Ushers per performance: 3

The Catch: All prospective volunteers must complete a training course and the company doesn't take people who plan to volunteer only once.

Quick, give me a word for unscripted fun. The Jet City Improv group serves it up every weekend with a loosely scripted improv show based on audience suggestions and a more adult-themed midnight show on Saturdays. On the last weekend of the month, the group also does "Twisted Flicks," where improvisors turn the sound down on a B movie and dub it live using ideas from the audience. Volunteers can see shows for free. To volunteer, go to the website and fill out a volunteer form.

Kirkland Performance Center

350 Kirkland Ave.
Kirkland
(425) 828-0422
www.kpcenter.org
Ushers per performance: varies

The 13-row, 402-seat center hosts a wide variety of performances. It's possible to see an Indian jazz show one night and a classical guitar concert the next. Patrons who volunteer to usher or work concessions can watch the performance they attend. The best way to express interest is to go to the website and fill out the sign-up form. There are occasional PWYC performances, which are advertised on the center's website and via e-mail.

Mirror Stage

Ethnic Cultural Theatre
3940 Brooklyn Ave. NE
(206) 686-1280
www.mirrorstage.org
Volunteers per performance: 2

A theater company whose mission is to "challenge assumptions, bias and prejudice" based at the University of Washington's Ethnic Cultural Theatre? Who'd have thunk it? The theater is a UW facility, however, and Mirror isn't a UW-affiliated group, so the arrangement could change. Box office volunteers can see performances free. Subscribe to the volunteer e-news to get first shot at upcoming volunteer spots. Ten PWYC tickets are available at the box office an hour before each performance (minimum cost $1). Half off for students and seniors, as well as a limited number of half-price tickets through Goldstar.

New Century Theatre Company
Various locations
(206) 661-8223
www.wearenctc.org
Ushers per performance: varies depending on theater space

New Century is to theater what the Justice League of America is to superheroes: a group of established Seattle actors banding together to save humanity . . . er . . . the humanities. After seeing several medium-size theater companies close, these folks joined forces to create the city's first new professional theater company in more than a decade. Their mission: present edgier work and newer plays that just aren't being performed in Seattle and bring fresh, modern perspective to older plays. The first preview of a run is a PWYC performance. New Century currently produces its plays at a variety of venues, but plans to move into the 12th Avenue Arts Building in fall 2014.

Northshore Performing Arts Center
18125 92nd Ave. NE
Bothell
(425) 408-7997
npacf.org
Ushers per performance: 6 to 10

The Catch: You have to pay $20 for the privilege of volunteering.

The NPAC is an eastern suburb community theater that offers a wide range of family entertainment from concerts to Broadway shows. The Northshore Theatre Guild provides most of the center's volunteers, and the only way to get on the usher list is to join the guild for $20. Ushers can see the performances at which they volunteer. To find out more about volunteering, go to the website and fill out a guild sign-up form.

Phoenix Theatre Edmonds
9673 Firdale Ave.
Edmonds
(206) 533-2000
www.phoenixtheatreedmonds.com
Ushers per performance: 1

Rising from the ashes of the Edge of the World Theater, the Phoenix focuses on humorous productions to dramatize our common humanity and to help foster a love of the magic of live theater. PWYC performances are held on the Thursday before opening night of a production.

Pork Filled Players
Various locations
www.porkfilled.com
Ushers per performance: 1 to 2

Even if you're Jewish, it's still okay to see the Pork Filled Players. They may not be hungry, but they are homeless. The gypsy company puts on shows wherever it can find a performance space. The players do a racy, four-letter-word-laden late night music/comedy cabaret once every two or three months and less risqué prime time presentations a couple of times a year. Some of the prime time shows are straight theatrical productions, while others are sketch comedy shows with guest artists. The group welcomes ushers.

Printer's Devil Theater
Various locations
(206) 860-7163
www.printersdevil.org
Ushers per performance: 1 to 2

This nomadic theater company is always looking for ushers. It also offers PWYC performances the first two Thursdays of a production's run. And it's got a really great name.

ReAct
Various locations
(206) 364-3283
www.reacttheatre.org
Ushers per performance: 1 to 6, depending on venue

ReAct Theater specializes in doing classic plays with non-traditional casts to increase awareness of the arts and humanitarian causes. There's not much of a waiting list, so would-be greeters and seaters will likely get their pick of performances, or at least something relatively close. All they have to do is e-mail react@reacttheatre.org. There are also one or two PWYC performances per mainstage show. It's best to call the theater to find out more about when those shows are scheduled.

Redwood Theatre
Redmond Municipal Campus
8703 160th NE
Redmond
(425) 522-3730
www.redwoodtheatre.org
Ushers per performance: 2

A community theater in the heart of Microsoft country, Redwood is always looking for volunteers. The best way to sign up is to contact the theater through its website. Redwood now has a PWYC performance on the first Saturday of a show's run where all of the money collected goes directly to the actors. The first Sunday matinee is also PWYC.

Seattle Children's Theatre
Seattle Center
201 Thomas St.
(206) 441-3322
www.sct.org
Ushers per performance: varies

When it comes to volunteering, local theaters don't get any more accommodating than SCT. To begin with, the volunteer coordinator takes requests and tries her best to meet them. First, she finds out what play a prospective usher wants to see. If there's space available, she'll then do her best to find a spot that matches the day they want to see the play. Of course, it is possible to schedule a shift as soon as the season is announced, but she has found slots for kids who call just days before the show they wanted to catch. Usher tasks aren't terribly taxing. They involve taking tickets, passing out programs, making sure no one's taking food into the theater, and watching the stage to make sure no one tries to climb up . . . which, come to think of it, isn't all that different from ushering at a regular adult theater. In fact, the only thing that's different is that ushers here can be as young as eight years old (as long as the worker is accompanied by an adult). The only challenge for a first-time usher is getting there on time. Of course, the usher's family has to be equally accommodating. If it's a young volunteer's first shift, they must show up 90 minutes early to go through an orientation session. There is one other bargain to be had if ushering is too much of a hassle, though. Rush tickets are available for Friday, Saturday, and Sunday performances and go on sale an hour before each show for $15 a piece. Unlike most other theaters, you can also call before you go to make sure the tickets aren't sold out. Teen Tix members can see SCT plays for $5. To volunteer, contact the volunteer coordinator.

Seattle Musical Theatre

7120 62nd Ave. NE (in Magnuson Park)
(206) 363-2809
seattlemusicaltheatre.org
Volunteers per performance: 10 to 12

As you might guess, this theater company is all musical, all the time, with a growing focus on contemporary productions like *Legally Blonde* and *Young Frankenstein*. Ushers are just a small part of SMT's needs during a typical performance. It also uses two volunteers in the lobby, two at will call, two at the concession stand, two at the wine bar, and if the crowd is big enough, two at the wine bar upstairs. All can stay to see the show. PWYC performances are the Thursday night preview before the Friday opening. Contact the volunteer coordinator for more information.

Seattle Public Theater

7312 W. Green Lake Dr. N
(206) 524-1300
www.seattlepublictheater.org
Ushers per performance: 2

Having dinner and seeing a play is so yesterday. Why not a walk and a play on the way to see a Seattle Public Theater production at the Bathhouse Theater at Greenlake? Ushers can stay to see the show. SPT's mainstage program typically has a PWYC dress rehearsal the Wednesday before the start of a show's run. It also offers free admission to youth education productions, which are quite good and have included *The Importance of Being Earnest* and *Romeo and Juliet*. To volunteer, contact FOH@seattlepublictheater.org.

Seattle Repertory Theatre

155 Mercer St. (northwest corner of Seattle Center)
(206) 443-2222
www.seattlerep.org
Ushers per performance: 4 to 5

Theater just doesn't get any more mainstream here than the Seattle Rep. The fare leans toward Broadway hits and classic comedies with a smattering of new drama. It has two performance spaces, with the Bagley Wright serving as the company's main stage and the Leo K. its more intimate auditorium. The Rep uses volunteer ushers in Leo K. and allows them to stay and see the show if seats are available. If there's no seating, volunteers are given a voucher to see a performance later in the run. To volunteer, call (206) 443-2202 or e-mail liza.gonzalez@seattlerep.org. Keep in mind, there's a pool of 250 volunteers and there was a waiting list at press time.

The Bagley Wright has PWYC previews the Tuesday before opening night. Tickets go on sale at noon, and the theater asks a minimum donation of $1, cash only. You can also buy rush tickets over the phone with a credit card on the day of the show with a minimum donation of $5. Patrons 25 and under pay $12 for best seat available. Rush tickets are $22 and are released 30 minutes before the start of show. Teen Tix are available for $5.

Seattle Shakespeare Company
Center House Theater
Seattle Center
www.seattleshakespeare.org
(206) 733-8222
Volunteers per performance: 4 to 5

Don't let the name fool you. This troupe does more than Shakespeare. It also presents classical plays year-round with additional help during the summer from its sister company, Wooden O Summer Outdoor Theater. Ushers and other volunteers can see the show if seats are available. Pay-what-you-will performances are held early in a show's run, usually on a Tuesday or Wednesday. Rush tickets are available to a group called Groundlings for $10 on the day of show. You can become a Groundling by applying at the box office. Membership is free.

Seattle Theatre Group
(206) 682-1414
www.stgpresents.org

Paramount Theatre
911 Pine St.
Ushers per performance: 18 to 25

Moore Theatre
1932 Second Ave.
Ushers per performance: 6 to 8

Neptune Theatre
1303 NE 45th St.
Ushers per performance: 4 to 6 (for seated shows only)

STG may have added the Neptune Theatre to its mix of venues, but one thing hasn't changed: It still has a backlog of volunteers. At press time, the organization had 145 applicants waiting for the next training date to be announced by the theater managers. The wait time to become a volunteer can be anywhere from six months to two years. On the plus side, if you do become an usher, you can stay to see some pretty cool shows. Apply to become a volunteer by going to STG's volunteer page at stgpresents.org/get-involved/volunteer.

Second Story Repertory
16587 NE 74th St.
Redmond
(425) 881-6777
www.secondstoryrep.org
Ushers per performance: 2

A shopping center isn't the likeliest location for live theater, but these are the eastside suburbs we're talking about . . . where shopping *is* entertainment. So, Second Story Rep has found a home on the second story of Redmond Town Center next to an Aeropostale shop. Now, if the company could just convince shoppers it isn't a movie theater. That's the next building over. Small ensemble musicals are Second Story's specialty, and the company splits its productions between mainstage shows and productions for children. Ushers can stay and see the show, but they are asked to do some light work before and after the performance. Fortunately, the tasks don't include dusting or windows, just a little tidying up here and there. Call early as ushering slots fill quickly. There's a PWYC preview the Thursday night before opening night.

Sound Theatre Company
Venues vary
(206) 856-5520
www.soundtheatrecompany.org
Ushers per performance: 2

Sound Theatre features works that focus on language and music, often with a political bent. The company typically announces what shifts are available via e-mails to volunteers. To volunteer, contact tthuman@yahoo.com. PWYC performances are held almost every Thursday night during a play's run.

Stone Soup Theatre
4029 Stone Way N
(206) 633-1883
www.stonesouptheatre.org
Ushers per performance: 2 to 3

Stone Soup is a small community theater that also offers drama programs for children. All Thursday evening performances are PWYC, and the final dress rehearsal is half off. The company also offers several two-for-one deals per production to people on its mailing list. To volunteer, call the company.

Tacoma Little Theatre
210 N. "I" St.
Tacoma
(253) 272-2281
www.tacomalittletheatre.com
Volunteers per performance: 5

If it's true that there are no small parts, just small players, what does that say about a place called Tacoma Little Theatre? Either it means it's really tiny or that the name Tacoma Big Theatre was already taken. Volunteers can see the show they volunteer at for free. To sign up, call or write in advance to get on the schedule. TLT has a preview the Thursday night before the opening performance and the PWYC performance is the Thursday after the preview.

Taproot Theatre Company
204 N. 85th St.
(206) 781-9707
www.taproottheatre.org

Taproot's mission is to "create theatre that explores the beauty and questions of life while bringing hope to our search for meaning." Ushers get to stay to see the show when they volunteer. Members of the Citiroots Team who put up posters and flyers to publicize upcoming plays get two free tickets. To volunteer, call the volunteer hotline at (206) 529-3646 or e-mail sonjal@taproottheatre.org. Patrons 25 and under can get tickets for $15. There is one PWYC performance per production with a minimum suggested donation of $5. Students and seniors get $4 off the $20 to $35 ticket price. There's also one discounted senior matinee per run of each play, cutting the price to $15 to $20.

Theater Schmeater
1500 Summit Ave.
(206) 324-5801
www.schmeater.org
Volunteers per performance: 1

Submitted for your approval, a fringe theater company that has risen to prominence on its faithful to the original script, if somewhat campy, revivals of *Twilight Zone* episodes. Even The Schmee's Rod Sterling look-alike manages to be spot-on while still being just this side of over-the-top. The Schmee's classic theater and edgy original productions are all presented out of a subterranean garage on Capitol Hill. Volunteering is easy and all volunteers get to see the show they work on for free. Ushers take tickets. To volunteer, send an email to md@schmeater.org. Shows typically run Thursday, Friday, and Saturday. All Thursday performances are PWYC and some dress rehearsals are open to the public. Anyone under 18 can attend a production for free. The company also does a free Classic in the Park production every summer.

Theatre22
Locations vary
(206) 257-2203
www.theatre22.org
Ushers per performance: 2 to 3

We don't know what the ushering policies of theatres 1-21 were, but this company typically uses up to three each show. It is willing to add another volunteer, however, if a show already has the requisite number of volunteers, but the only way a person can afford to see the show is by volunteering and seeing it free. There's usually no wait list, however. To volunteer, e-mail info@theatre22.org. Thursday nights tend to be PWYC performances and the organization also sells half price tickets on GoldStar. Three shows a year in season, one mainstage musical, one local playwright, and one classic American or British theater. Senior military and educator discounts. PWYC performances every Thursday night of a run.

Twelfth Night Productions

Youngstown Cultural Arts Center
4408 Delridge Ave. SW
www.twelfthnightproductions.org
Ushers per performance: varies

What started as a summer drama camp program has grown into a West Seattle–based production company that does a play each summer and an annual production of *Amahl and the Night Visitors*. To volunteer, contact info@twelfthnightproductions.org. Twelfth Night offers free tickets to ushers and people who work the concession stand during performances.

UPAC Theatre Group

United Evangelical Free Church basement
1420 NW 80th St.
(206) 375-5057
www.upactheatergroup.org
Ushers per performance: 2 to 4

No, it's not a repertory theater for UPS and FedEx employees. It's the United Performing Arts Company, a non-religious acting group that just happens to stage its plays in a church basement. It performs a mainstage show in August and a one-act play in the spring. Ushers must agree to work at least three mainstage shows and can see the show free on their second shift. They are also invited to the dress rehearsal. To volunteer, download an application from the website and return it via regular mail or e-mail. The mainstage show has a PWYC performance the first Thursday of the run and a two-for-one matinee for seniors on the second Saturday of the play's run. There are no discounts for the one-act, but admission is only $10.

Village Theatre

303 Front St. N
Issaquah
(425) 392-2202

Everett Performing Arts Center
2710 Wetmore Ave.
Everett
(425) 257-8600
www.villagetheatre.org

The Catch: There's a waiting list for usher openings.

Village Theatre has the benefit of having two places to call home—one in Everett, the other in the eastern suburb of Issaquah. When one production wraps up in Issaquah, it often goes to Everett. The company's focus may be on musicals, but it also produces non-musicals. Most plays are suitable for the entire family. The theater also produces its own original musicals. Ushers may be able to see the shows they work for free, subject to availability. Rush tickets are available to students and members of the military 30 minutes before curtain.

WARP (Writers and Actors Reading and Performing)
Eclectic Theatre
1214 10th Ave.
(206) 229-7919
www.warptheater.org
Volunteers per performance: varies

This odd hybrid cuts out the middleman between playwright and audience by presenting free readings of original scripts every Tuesday to anyone who will listen. It's more than just a critique group, though, as some of the scripts are incorporated into the shows WARP produces several times a year. Tickets to the plays are $10 at the door, but volunteers are admitted free and tech volunteers who work the entire run will get two comp admissions. Students and seniors pay $5. To volunteer, e-mail warp@warptheatre.org.

Washington Ensemble Theatre
608 19th Ave. E
(206) 325-5105
www.washingtonensemble.org
Volunteers per performance: 1

The Catch: *The company prefers to establish an ongoing relationship with a volunteer rather than using someone only once.*

Given that WET has 49 seats with festival seating, there's no need for ushers. The company does use volunteer house managers, however, who get one free ticket per house management shift. To volunteer, e-mail admin@washington ensemble.org. PWYC performances are sporadic.

Youth Theatre Northwest

8805 SE 40th St.
Mercer Island
(206) 232-4145
www.youththeatre.org
Ushers per performance: 2 to 3

The Catch: *Background check required for people who plan to usher on a regular basis.*

YTN produces 12 shows a year for kids that are performed by kids of all ages. Although its main volunteers are the parents of children performing in the shows, the company does round out the ranks of its ushers with people from the community and does have one-day volunteer opportunities. People who are interested in volunteer ushering on a regular basis, however, require a background check because the job involves regular contact with children. To volunteer, contact the theater. YTN does offer some half-off and two-for-one ticket deals through its e-mail list.

ALWAYS **FREE**

GreenStage

Venues vary; for information, check the website
(206) 748-1551
www.greenstage.org

There really is no better place to put on a play than a park when your mission is to "inspire audiences to engage with live theater as part of their recreation." And GreenStage has been doing just that with its theatrical productions of classic theater for the last 20 years. The company describes its productions as "fun and family oriented," but may have pushed it a bit with 2009's presentation of *Titus Andronicus,* in which, its Facebook page gleefully proclaimed, "4 gallons of stage blood spilled so far, 5 people walked out because of blood and violence, 1 passed out in his seat." Of course, it was Titus and it was a special Halloween-oriented production. At least you can't say they didn't stay faithful to the original.

Arts Crush

What started as the National Night of Free Theater has evolved in Seattle to an event called Arts Crush. Both events happen in October and their goal is essentially the same—getting folks interested in the lively arts—but the methods markedly differ. Where the national event focuses on getting butts in seats at local playhouses, Arts Crush takes a more offbeat approach that includes performances and art workshops.

That's why the Seattle Opera decided against offering free tickets to a performance and opted instead to teach a class on how to make realistic-looking stage blood, suitable for use in a live performance.

The reason is simple really, according to Shane Regan, programs and members associate at Theatre Puget Sound (TPS).

"Our mission is to expand the reach of the arts and bring in people who might not be interested in seeing [plays]," Regan said.

The annual celebration starts with a kick-off party where attendees can go to tables run by local performing arts organizations to find out more about them and then register for free tickets to events offered by their new favorite group. People who can't attend can also register for ticket drawings, but opening night participants get priority codes that give them a better chance of getting tickets to events where there's more demand than supply. Fortunately, since most people register for three shows, they usually get at least one of the ones they wanted, according to Regan.

At press time, the program was going through a transition while the organization looked for a new Arts Crush coordinator, Regan said. He said TPS planned to continue the program while increasing the number of events that take audiences behind the scenes at local arts organizations.

It makes sense, given the whole point of the exercise, he said. "Our mission [is] to have more people have a crush on the arts."

Seattle Outdoor Theater Festival

Volunteer Park
1247 15th Ave. E
(206) 748-1551
www.greenstage.org/sotf

Much more successful than the Winter Outdoor Theater Festival, the summer celebration of the lively arts hosted by GreenStage is held at Volunteer Park and features at least 14 performances by eight companies over two days. So, you can pack a lunch, dinner, and evening snack and a blanket and watch to your heart's content—or until your butt grows numb. The players include such outdoor regulars as Wooden O Theatre, GreenStage, and Theatre Schmeater as well as such dabblers as Open Circle Theatre and improvisation group Wing It Productions. If you miss the show you wanted to see, don't despair. The event is usually a launching point for the season and most of the shows will be performed again in parks throughout the area.

Wooden O Summer Outdoor Theater

Locations vary
(206) 733-8228
www.seattleshakespeare.org/WoodenO/

The local company known for presenting Shakespeare in parks throughout Seattle and King County may have merged with the Seattle Shakespeare Company in 2008, but the show goes on to much critical acclaim. Each year, two productions play in various parks stretching from Lynnwood and Issaquah to SeaTac and Sammamish. There really is no more civilized way to spend a weekend night than a picnic dinner under the stars surrounded by theater-goers of all ages trying to figure out what it was that someone just said in Shakespearean English.

DRAMA **DEALS:** DISCOUNT **TICKETS** & **MORE**

Goldstar.com

The Catch: Tickets are up to half price off, but there is a service charge from $2.50 to $9.

Last-minute rush tickets may be great for single folk and people with lots of time on their hands, but for parents and folks who don't want to risk getting the night off and not being able to get into the show they want, there's Goldstar. Thanks to the online service, you don't have to wait until the day of show to buy tickets. Now you can get tickets far enough ahead that you might actually have time to hire a babysitter and have a full night out complete with dinner using the money you saved. You do have to become a member, but it's free and it gives you the ability to buy tickets for everything from plays and concerts to sporting events and other diversions. The site does have a service charge, but it also gives helpful pointers including what to wear, how to get to the venue, and where to find parking. It may sound odd, but the company believes people who have free tickets are more likely to show up if they pay a small amount than if they paid nothing at all. Another cool, new feature, "Sit With Friends," allows you to buy tickets and then forward a unique URL to your friends so they can buy their own tickets and be seated with you.

Seattle Opera
Seattle Center
McCaw Hall
321 Mercer St.
(206) 389-7600
www.seattleopera.org

What's that I hear? It's the fat lady singing about your chances of volunteering and staying to see a show for free. The opera doesn't use volunteer ushers and the people who do volunteer there don't get free passes to performances, either, but there are so many ways to see shows at a discount that they fill a whole page on the opera's website. For starters, there are a select number of tickets on the second balcony that sell for $25 a show. There are also rush tickets for students ($20) and seniors ($30) available at 5:30 p.m. for evening shows and noon for afternoon shows. Standing room tickets are available for Wednesday and Friday shows for $12 on the day of show. Teen Tix are available for $5. Volunteering doesn't get you any special consideration at the box office for regular shows, but you may be able to get tickets to certain dress rehearsals for free. Regularly scheduled family day performances are $15 for the under-18 set. Members of the young professionals group Bravo! save 50 percent on all tickets, and members of the military save 15 percent.

Teen Tix
www.teentix.org

Look who's getting an upgrade. The Teen Tix program, one of the best bargains in town for kids aged 13 to 19, has gone independent from the Seattle Center and built a spiffy new website. The program was designed to foster interest in the arts and create future audiences by giving teens inexpensive access to cultural and creative experiences all over town. Tix members can buy $5 same day tickets to a variety of organizations and events ranging from exhibits at the Seattle Art Museum to the Seattle Symphony, depending on availability. While none of that will change, the new organization will have a website and blog that tells members which tickets are available each week and gives audience etiquette tips as well as directions and maps. The blog will also feature reviews. Membership is free and available through the Seattle Center website.

FILM:
CHEAP SHOTS

*"You know what your problem is, it's that you
haven't seen enough movies—all of life's riddles
are answered in the movies."*
—Steve Martin

When it comes to movies in Seattle, "free" is a relative term. There are a few free screenings to be had, but they come at a price. If you love the full-on, indoor theatrical experience, you may want to opt for cheap theaters, but if you are okay with less than sterile conditions, sitting outdoors, or a little bit of unpredictability, then the free options will likely work for you. Here's a mix of all of the options.

FREE **YEAR**-ROUND

Ballard Pizza Company
5107 Ballard Avenue NW
(206) 659-6033
www.ballardpizzacompany.com

Pizza and a movie are a hard combination to beat, but they're even better when you don't have to clean up after it's all over. Every Wednesday, Ballard Pizza shows two movies: a kids' movie at 5 p.m. and a slightly more mature movie for parents and other adults at 7 p.m. The movies are free, but the pizza is not.

Friday Night at the Meaningful Movies
Keystone Congregational United Church of Christ
5019 Keystone Place N
www.meaningfulmovies.org

Yes, I know it's at a church, but the films aren't church-related and there are no religious messages. If you're an old lefty or you just love movies with a cause, this is the place for you. Every Friday night at 7 p.m. The Meaningful Movies Project screens documentaries about social justice issues followed by open discussion. The gatherings are designed to help foster conversation, build community, allow justice groups to publicize their issues, help people do meaningful social justice work, and allow filmmakers to promote their work. But it's okay to show up just because you want to get out of the house and watch a good movie.

GOFOBO
Gofobo.com

The Catch: Movies are overbooked and you might miss out if you don't show up early.

Although I'm told the puzzling name is short for "Go for Box Office," I'm still not sure what the significance of it is other than that it's an online ticketing website where people can go to find out about advanced screenings of movies in the area where they live. There are two ways to get tickets. One is to get a code for a movie by winning a radio station contest or other promotion. The more direct route is to create an account on the site, search within the zip code where you live, find a screening, and download movie passes. There are a limited number of passes for each screening and the screenings are typically overbooked, so you may have to show up and stand in line an hour and a half before showtime to get a seat. If you don't get in, you'll usually get a code or a pass to another, similar movie.

Harbour Pointe Coffee House
2818 E. Madison St.
(206) 420-1187
hpcoffeehouse.com

This southern branch of a Mukilteo-based coffeehouse was slated to show classic movies on Friday nights. That's just part of the mix offered by the company, though. It also has board game nights on Thursday and open mic nights on Wednesday. All of the events start at 7 p.m.

King's Hardware
5225 Ballard Ave. NW
(206) 782-0027
www.kingsballard.com

You could be forgiven for thinking a local Ace Hardware shop was showing movies in the back, but what can you expect when you start naming bars things like the Loft and King's Hardware? As you probably guessed, it's another bar in Ballard's hopping industrial district. This one rings in the workweek with a Monday movie night on the covered heated patio out back. The movies start at dusk and are usually based around a monthly theme that could be anything from the films of Bill Murray to a high school series that

The Best Bargain in Town:
The Seattle International Film Festival

Why volunteer to usher at a play and only see that show for free when you could usher at a movie and still get a voucher to see another movie free?

Yes, I know there's nothing like free live theater, but Seattle International Film Festival ticket vouchers are better because they're more flexible.

The Seattle International Film Festival (SIFF) has long offered its ushers and other volunteers many ways to go to the movies for free. Back in the day when the CB served as an usher, it was often possible to see the movie I volunteered at for free, depending on what my responsibilities were, and get vouchers to see two more movies. The festival says that's no longer the case, but you will get a voucher for a free ticket for every two hours you work. Given that most shifts require coverage of more than one movie, that could mean vouchers for at least two movies. Of course, there's always a chance you might work for a soft-hearted house manager who will let you see a movie after you've finished doing your duties on your shift, but the volunteer coordinator says you can't count on it. In fact, SIFF's volunteer benefits page says ushers shouldn't sign up for a shift that includes a film that they want to see because they may end up with duties that need to be completed after the movie has started and may lead to them missing the entire show.

featured *Ferris Bueller's Day Off* and *Revenge of the Nerds*. As a special added attraction, all buffalo wings are 27 cents during the event. At that price, who cares what's showing?

Wayward Coffeehouse
6417 Roosevelt Way NE, #104
(206) 525-5191
www.waywardcoffee.com

What makes the vouchers an even better deal is that they don't lose their value once the festival ends. Instead, they are good for a year and can be used at other movie festivals, series, and screenings at SIFF Cinema for regular-priced screenings where space permits, or can be converted into an Enthusiast membership level of SIFF. If you have five vouchers to spare, the Enthusiast-level membership is a great deal because members are invited to free previews throughout the year.

The best news of all is that you don't have to wait until the festival starts to begin racking up vouchers. SIFF needs so many volunteers in the weeks and months before the event that it's easy to spend the better part of the festival sitting in a darkened theater without a care in the world . . . other than wondering how you're going to spend the rest of your vouchers.

Volunteer jobs before the start of the festival include proofreading publications, distributing movie guides, answering phones, selling tickets, and stuffing gift bags. If your schedule won't permit ushering, but you want to work during the festival, you can work will-call tables, pick up guests at the airport and drive them back, transport films to venues, or do any of the hundreds of other tasks that keep the event going.

To learn more about volunteering with SIFF, visit www.siff.net/volunteer.

New and improved! Now more geekier than ever, the recently relocated science fiction–themed cafe has a sci-fi/fantasy movie every second Saturday of the month starting at 9 p.m. As if that weren't enough, it's also the home of the Seattle Browncoats (fans of *Serenity* and *Firefly*), it holds a monthly Geek Bingo night, and many of its specialty drinks sport names that pay homage to favorite movies. The Iocane latte is the perfect example. Fans of *The Princess Bride* may remember that Iocane was a highly toxic substance that played an important part in one of the scenes. According to the menu, the latte contains "iocane and vanilla."

See Free without Standing in Line (sort of)

If you're a parent of young kids like I am, you don't get much of a chance to see the latest first-run blockbusters because you don't have the time or you can't find a babysitter when you want to go. Even renting a movie is iffy because most rentals only last a few days and there are always late fees to contend with. Fortunately, there's an alternative that not only costs nothing, but also is easily accessible and is something that everyone's heard of: the local library.

Both the King County Library and Seattle Public Library systems lend movies on DVD to their card-carrying patrons for longer than your average rental with far lower late fees (overdue fines) than even the most liberal video stores. The disadvantage is that you might not get to see that hot new flick as soon as it's released on DVD, but at least you can get on a waiting list . . . and you do move up pretty quickly. In addition, the Seattle Public Library also offers downloads and streaming of some movies.

At the King County Library, you can check out a DVD for seven days and renew it up to two times, if needed, and fines are only 10 cents a day (topping out at $3). Don't get the wrong idea, though. The system won't play Mr. Nice Guy forever. Materials out over 28 days past the due date are considered lost and you will be billed. If you accrue fines of over $10, you won't be allowed to check out books. And if your fines reach $25, they'll sic a collection agency on you.

Seattle Public Library loans DVDs for two weeks and allows up to two renewals unless there is a hold on the film. Once a download or streaming movie has been out past its due date, it simply disappears from your computer. Otherwise, fines are 25 cents per day with a maximum of $6. Lending privileges are suspended at $15. Once an account reaches $25 or an item has been out more than 50 days, the account is turned over to Unique Management Service. Go ahead, laugh at the name if you will, but whatever it is, it can report you to credit agencies and charge you a $12 processing fee.

Hey, they may be librarians, but they're not pushovers.

CHEAP

In my early days as a poor, starving freelancer, second-run movie theaters like the Crest Cinema Center were a staple of my entertainment budget. Of course, in those days, they only charged a dollar or two. As I made more money, the Crest remained the heart of my movie priority rating system. Instead of relying on numbers, I based it on cost. The continuum went this way: Long-awaited, hot new release that I absolutely must see—opening night at full price. New release that I really want to see—matinee. Movies that interested me, but were not top priority—Crest. Shows that I'm so-so on—wait for the video. Films that have captured my curiosity, but I'm not terribly optimistic about—watch after it comes off the new-release wall at my local video store. Those were the days before Redbox came on the scene, of course. I will occasionally do an inexpensive Redbox rental, but only if I'm absolutely sure I'll have the time to watch it in one night. Over the years, I've been surprised by how few movies have merited opening night rating. How picky am I? Even *Avatar* didn't make the opening night movie cut. So, if you're patient like me, you may want to consider making these theaters part of your own rating system.

Cinnebarre
6009 244th St. SW
Mountlake Terrace
(425) 672-7501
cinebarre.com

Remember the cinema taverns from years ago? Cinnebarre has upscaled the concept and added liquor to the mix of food and films. On Tuesday, tickets for all showtimes are $5 with a surcharge for 3D movies. No minimum food order.

The Crest Cinema Center
16505 5th Ave. NE
Shoreline
(206) 781-5755
www.landmarktheatres.com/market/seattle/crestcinemacenter.htm

The Catch: Watch where you park. Neighbors living to the west of the theater are quick to tow illegally parked vehicles.

If a first-run movie makes it to this second-run movie theater on the edge of town quickly, you can be pretty sure it's a turkey, but it's so cheap, it's almost worth seeing how bad it is. You might want to bring a cushion though because the seats can be hard. Tickets are $3 for standard projection shows and $4.50 for 3D movies. Of course, it's not always a good idea to see a movie for its cost alone. After seeing *Basic Instinct* here, I realized that was two hours of my life I'd never get back.

East Valley 13
3751 E. Valley Rd.
Renton
(425) 873-2077

If you can't find what you like at the Crest, you might consider checking out this multi-multiplex with 11 out of 13 screens operating at press time. It is $3.50 all seats, all times, but you may have to travel the dreaded I-405 to get here.

Gateway Movies 8
2501 S. Gateway Center
Federal Way
(253) 946-9224
www.starplexcinemas.com

This theater would give the Crest a run for its money, if only it were located in Seattle. It's 22 miles from downtown Seattle, but depending on gas prices and where you live, it could be worth the drive for a $2 movie. Better yet, go on Tuesday when tickets are $1. Hot dogs are also $1.

Grand Cinema
606 Fawcett Ave.
Tacoma
(253) 593-4474
grandcinema.com

The Catch: All volunteers have to attend a training session, and concession stand volunteers need a food handler's permit.

To hear the folks at Grand Cinema tell it, there's only one first-run movie theater left in Tacoma's city limits—this little non-profit art house that also shows new movies. It's also the only place you can volunteer and see a

The Death of the Matinee

Long, long ago in an Emerald City not so far away, there were theaters that offered matinee showings up until 6 p.m. on weekdays, weekends, and holidays. And there was much rejoicing, especially among those who came home to spend Thanksgiving with the family and realized why they moved away in the first place when they needed a place to escape for a few hours. Some theaters were more persnickety and had matinees only for the first showing of the day, but there was still some rejoicing. All that changed recently when most local cinemas decided to roll back matinee times to 10:30 a.m. and there was much sadness. Now, not only do prodigal sons and daughters have to guess whether their relatives will irritate them and take preemptive action, they also lose the joy of dramatically storming out of the house when someone inevitably says something that really ticks them off.

movie. For each two-hour volunteer shift, you get a free pass to see a regular movie any day, any time, first run included (except festival screenings and special events). Before volunteers can work, they have to go through training and get a food handler's permit. Once they've done that, they get a login and go onto the website to find an open shift. That's not the only way to see a free movie, though. At 10 a.m. on the third Saturday of the month, the theater shows a free family film, but there's only room for 100, so it's worthwhile to arrive early. Regular price tickets are $9, but matinees before 6 p.m. on weekdays are $2 off, and you can cut $2 more off if you are a senior, a student, or in the military.

The Historic Admiral Theatre
2343 California Ave. SW
(206) 938-3456
www.farawayentertainment.com/admiral.html

If you live in the south end of town or think the Crest is too far, you can always hit this nautical-themed second-run theater in West Seattle. It'll cost you a bit more, though. Movies at this two-screener are $5.50. On Tuesday, people over age 60 pay $4.50.

SUMMER **SCREENINGS**

Bellevue Summer Outdoor Movies in the Park
Bellevue Downtown Park
10201 NE 4th St.
Bellevue

Family-friendly Tuesday night movies run from early July to late August are presented by Bellevue Parks and Community Services, sponsored by Inome. The films and the popcorn are free, but each has a themed charity benefit. When the city showed *Hotels for Dogs,* for example, the movie helped raise funds for the Hopelink Food Drive.

Seattle on Film

Movies and television shows set in the Seattle area:

10 Things I Hate About You (Movie, 1999)
A Guy Thing (Movie, 2003)
Agent Cody Banks (Movie, 2003)
An Officer and a Gentleman (Movie, 1982)
Battle in Seattle (Movie, 2007)
Black Widow (Movie, 1987)
Dark Angel (TV, 2000–2002)
Dead Like Me (TV, 2003–2004)
Disclosure (Movie, 1994)
Double Jeopardy (Movie, 1999)
Fear (Movie, 1996)
Firewall (Movie, 2006)
Frasier (TV, 1993–2004)
Get Carter (Movie, 2000)
Grey's Anatomy (TV, 2005–)
Harry and the Hendersons (Movie, 1987)
iCarly (TV, 2007–2012)
It Happened at the World's Fair (Movie, 1963)

Carillon Point Outdoor Movies
Carillon Point Plaza
4100 Carillon Point Rd.
Kirkland

These Saturday night movies running mid-July through August come with a beautiful view as the screen overlooks lovely Lake Washington. Suggested donation is $5 with proceeds going to Hopelink. All movies are family friendly. No showings in the rain.

Family Fun and Films
A different park every week
Renton

Kyle XY (TV, 2006–2009)
Life or Something Like It (Movie, 2002)
Love Happens (Movie, 2009)
Mad Love (Movie, 1995)
McQ (Movie, 1974)
Paycheck (Movie, 2003)
Reaper (TV, 2007–2009)
Rose Red (TV miniseries, 2002)
Saving Silverman (Movie, 2001)
Say Anything (Movie, 1989)
Shoot to Kill (Movie, 1988)
Singles (Movie, 1992)
Sleepless in Seattle (Movie, 1993)
Stakeout (Movie, 1987)
The Fabulous Baker Boys (Movie, 1989)
The Hand that Rocks the Cradle (Movie, 1992)
The Last Mimzy (Movie, 2007)
The Parallax View (Movie, 1974)
The Ring (Movie, 2002)
War Games (Movie, 1983)

The city of Renton is taking its outdoor movie show on the road by leaving the friendly confines of Liberty Park and setting up shop at a different city park on Fridays throughout the summer. Seating and family-friendly activities start at 7 p.m. along with family activities. Movies start around 9.

Marymoor Outdoor Movies
Marymoor Park
6046 W. Lake Sammamish Parkway NE
Redmond

The Catch: Suggested donation of $5 per person or $15 per family and a mandatory $1 parking fee.

One of the largest and most popular parks in the King County system, Marymoor hosts family-friendly movies at McNair Field on Wednesday nights. There are some catches, though. It's free, but there's a suggested donation of $5 per person or $15 per family. There's also a $1 charge for parking. Unfortunately, this isn't one of those neighborhood parks where you can go outside the boundaries, find a spot on a side street, and park there free. No, you're stuck, but on the plus side, how many other places can you park for two hours for only $1?

Movies at the Mural
Mural Amphitheater
Seattle Center

One of the best parts of watching a movie while sitting in the shadow of the Space Needle is that if the movie stinks, you can still look up in the sky and marvel over a Seattle landmark. The season starts in late July on the same Saturday night as the Seafair Torchlight Parade and continues on Saturday through August, featuring a mix of popular movies that are rated PG-13 or under. The soft-sloped lawn makes for a more comfortable experience than the asphalt surface found at most outdoor shows and the 45-foot-wide screen means there are no bad seats. Shows start at dusk.

Redhook Moonlight Cinema
Redhook Brewery
14300 NE 145th St.
Woodinville

Is there any way to beat watching *National Lampoon's Vacation* while drinking a beer? Some movies just shouldn't be seen sober. Films are shown Thursday nights from mid-July to mid-August in Redhook Brewery's Outdoor Bowl amphitheater near Redhook's brewpub, the Forecaster's Pub. There's a beer garden and food is available from the pub. No beer service after the start of the movie. Admission $5 per person.

Summer Outdoor Cinema Series
Tukwila Community Center
12324 42nd Ave. S
Tukwila

Movies run Friday from late July through mid-August. Admission is free, but there is a suggested donation of a can of food for a local food bank.

Three Dollar Bill Outdoor Cinema
Cal Anderson Park
1635 11th Ave.

Movies run on four successive Fridays from late July to early August at this popular Capitol Hill Park just a block off Broadway.

West Seattle Movies on the Wall
California Ave.

Films are shown on a wall in a courtyard between Dr. Wolff (4400 California Ave. SW) and Hotwire Coffee (4410 California Ave. SW). Free. Family movies shown on Saturday nights from mid-July to mid-August.

MUSIC:
OF FREE I SING

"You're willing to pay him a thousand dollars a night just for singing? Why, you can get a phonograph record of Minnie the Moocher for 75 cents. And for a buck and a quarter, you can get Minnie."
—Groucho Marx, A Night at the Opera

As a local comedian once said, the great thing about Seattle is that you can go to a garage sale and get a grunge band. Grunge may have come and gone, but the Emerald City continues to be a hotbed for music of all types, whether it's serious groups like Heart, kid rockers such as Caspar Baby Pants and Recess Monkey, or even hip-hopper Macklemore. Once the rain clears, folks are so happy that they're likely to break into song with little provocation, and the abundance of festivals in our few sunny months alone is enough to guarantee a steady stream of free music throughout the summer. And that doesn't even count lunchtime concerts, farmers' markets, restaurants, coffeehouses, and your next-door neighbor's son's garage band.

For more on Seattle's music scene, see Appendix E, "Additional Seattle Music Festivals" on page 262.

JAZZ/**BLUES**/WORLD

Agua Verde Café and Paddle Club
1303 NE Boat St.
(206) 545-8570
www.aguaverde.com

Not only is Agua Verde a kayak rental shop and a great, inexpensive restaurant to take out-of-town guests, it's also a great place to sit on the patio overlooking the Ship Canal, enjoying Baja-inspired Mexican food and whiling away the hours listening to music—if you can get a seat outside. A Latin duo plays some Saturday afternoons from 1 to 3 p.m. and there's jazz from 6:30 to 9 p.m. on the first Tuesday of the month. The schedule is subject to change. Check the website for more details

Antique Sandwich Company
5102 N. Pearl St.
Tacoma
(253) 752-4069

Long a venue for folk music, the Antique Sandwich Company has open mic nights on Tuesday from 7 to 10 p.m.

Aqua by El Gaucho
2801 Alaskan Way, Pier 70
(206) 956-9171
www.waterfrontpier70.com

You might not be able to see the much-vaunted view of Elliott Bay through the floor-to-ceiling windows when you sit at the bar of this high-end waterfront restaurant, but you get what you pay for. If you manage to get one of the barstools, however, you may have a nice view of the Space Needle while you listen to Ben Fleck play soft jazz on the piano. The music starts at 6 p.m., but given the fact that it's meant to be background music, you might not notice.

Bake's Place
161 107th Ave NE
Bellevue
(425) 454-2776
bakesplacebellevue.com

Bake's is the type of place that proves Bellevue is coming into its own as a city. Having a jazz club like Bake's Place allows eastsiders to take in jazz without braving the wilds of gritty downtown Seattle to get their fix. A jazz trio plays Tuesday nights, a blues trio Wednesday, and a singer-songwriter trio on Thursday (we're beginning to detect a theme here); no cover charge.

Barca
1510 11th Ave.
(206) 325-8263
www.barcaseattle.com

If only the fourth letter in the name were a hard "c" and not a soft one and you were a regular, you'd be a Barca lounger. Sadly, that's not the case. The Capitol Hill bar/art gallery has free jazz featuring Phil Sparks, Adam Kessler, and guests from 9 p.m. to midnight every Thursday.

Café Racer
5828 Roosevelt Way NE
(206) 523-5282
caferacerseattle.com

Don't Forget to Tip Your Player

Free is a great price, especially when it comes to music, but don't forget that the people who are up on the stage playing their hearts out for you need to make a living, too. Sure, many aspiring musicians take the free gigs just for the exposure, but they wouldn't mind a little cash to help out, even if it just covers the cost of gas or a repair for the van that broke down two blocks away from the venue so they had to carry all their equipment on their backs. One of the nice things about putting the money in a performer's hat or instrument case is that they get to keep all of the proceeds. That isn't the case when you have to buy tickets later on. Then, everyone gets a cut including ticket sellers, club owners, and managers long before the musician sees any of the money.

We're not saying you have to reach into your wallet and give until it hurts or even pay the equivalent of a cover charge, although we're sure the artist wouldn't mind. But if enough people gave a dollar or two, it could make a difference in the artist's bottom line without affecting yours.

Racer is so small that you might miss it while driving past, but it's a popular live music venue with something on the calendar almost every night, except for Monday when it's dark. The Racer Sessions on Sunday at 7:30 p.m. is a jazz-influenced jam session with room for improvisationalists of all sorts.

88 Keys
315 2nd Ave. S
(206) 839-1300
www.ilove88keys.com

I just can't help it. Whenever I hear the phrase "dueling pianos," I think of a scene out of an old western where two baby grands roll down the street, then turn and shoot each other. That's not what really goes on at a dueling piano bar like 88 Keys, but a guy can hope, can't he? Instead, it's a funny musical show where two piano players stand back-to-back and use their instruments to duke it out while entertaining and amusing the crowd. The regular show isn't free, but Blues To Do tapes a live cable access show about jazz in Seattle every Monday night at 7 p.m. A blues jam follows at 8. Both are free, but you may want to get there early to make sure you get a seat. On Wednesday nights, there's no cover to hear a rock-and-roll blues band play. Hotel guests with keys from any local hotel get free admission to the dueling piano show on Friday and Saturday nights.

Hiroshi Jazz and Sushi
2501 Eastlake Ave.
(206) 726-4966
www.hiroshis.com

The name "Jazz and Sushi Fridays" says it all. Enjoy raw fish with a side of hot jazz every Friday night from 7:30 to 10 p.m. in the most unlikeliest of places, a strip mall Japanese restaurant.

La Flora Tapas Restaurant
4500 9th Ave. NE
(206) 632-7135
www.laflorarestaurant.com

The same folks who brought you Bilbao have changed their name and set up shop in a new location, but they still have the same no cover charge policy for their music. There's jazz music on Monday at 9 p.m., flamenco music on Friday from 8 to 10 p.m., and live band music on Saturday from 8 to 10 p.m.

Lucid Seattle
5241 University Way NE
(206) 402-3042
www.lucidseattle.com

A hidden treasure on The Ave in the University District, Lucid is located on the street's far northern reach where businesses thin out, giving way to apartments and mixed-use buildings. It's steadily gained a following among jazz lovers and those who stumble across it. The club has free live music many nights. It also has an extensive seasonal scratch cocktail menu.

New Orleans Creole Restaurant

114 First Ave. S
(206) 622-2563
www.neworleanscreolerestaurant.com

The original owner died recently, but the show goes on with live music four nights a week, much of it free. The tunes serve as a tasty aural side dish to its Cajun and creole cuisine. The house band, the New Orleans Quintet, plays on Monday from 6:30 to 9:30 p.m. On Wednesday, the Legacy Quartet with Clarence Acox plays traditional jazz, and the first Friday of every month is Jam Night. For more details, check the restaurant's Facebook page.

1 Hundred Bistro and Bar

1020 108th Ave. NE
Bellevue
(425) 455-4278
www.1hundredbistro.com

The home of the former Grand Cru Bistro and Bar may have changed owners, color scheme, and overall vibe, but the upscale neighborhood gathering place still has live music with jazz every Sunday.

The Royal Room

5000 Rainier Ave. S
(206) 906-9920
theroyalroomseattle.com

Jazz, country, gospel, Americana . . . about the only type of music The Royal Room hasn't presented is heavy metal. The neighborhood spot originally planned to make certain nights of the week no cover nights, but it has found that it doesn't always work with the booking schedule of some of the artists they bring in. The founders originally planned to have live music with no cover Thursday through Monday and touring acts that charge a cover on Tuesday and Wednesday, but artists' schedules don't always match their plan. So sometimes, there's no cover when you're expecting one and other times there is when you aren't. A quick look at the calendar on its website shows that there are more no cover shows than not.

Seamonster Lounge

2202 N. 45th St.
(206) 992-1120
www.seamonsterlounge.com

With a slogan like "eat, drink, groove," how can you go wrong? There's live jazz/funk music every night and never a cover. As for the food, well, it's not exactly a sushi bar. Instead, it's a bar that serves sushi.

Serafina Osteria

2043 Eastlake Ave. E
(206) 323-0807
www.serafinaseattle.com

The Catch: You don't have to buy dinner, but it does guarantee a better seat if you're there to see the band.

Serafina is a neighborhood Italian restaurant, but it is loved city-wide despite the occasional parking difficulties. The osteria repeatedly shows up on ratings of the city's top eateries for its food, but it gets equally high praise for being a great date spot. Add a jazz combo and the occasional torch singer, and you have the makings of a beautiful evening on a Friday or Saturday night. Who knows? The romance might continue through to Serafina's Sunday Jazz Brunch from 11 a.m. to 1:30 p.m. There's music on the first Wednesday of the month from 8 to 10 p.m. and Friday and Saturday 9 p.m. to midnight. It's free, but keep in mind that the stage is at the back of the dining room and the room is open to diners only until the waitlist has been seated around 10 p.m.

ECLECTIC/**ROCK**/FOLK/**COUNTRY**/ BLUEGRASS

Central Club

124 Kirkland Ave.
Kirkland
(425) 827-0808
www.centralclubkirkland.com

This holdout against Kirkland's continuing move upscale could be called a classic Kirkland place given how long it's been around. The dive bar has free music on Wednesday and Sunday nights. Wednesday nights have an old-school rock-and-roll feel while Sunday is more bluesy. The music plays from 8:30 p.m. to 12:30 a.m. on Sunday and 9:30 p.m. to 12:30 a.m. on Wednesday.

Conor Byrne

5140 Ballard Ave. NW
(206) 784-3640
www.conorbyrnepub.com

There's just something about Ballard's old industrial district along Ballard Avenue that makes it a great spot for live music joints. There's the Tractor, the Sunset (which both have cover charges for all shows), and this place. An Irish pub with food service, the Byrne offers a mix of styles throughout the week including alt country, rockabilly, and Irish, of course. No cover Sunday through Wednesday. Open mic on Sunday, old time social on Tuesday, and a capella pub trivia on Wednesday. Covers range from $5 to $8, so even on nights when you have to pay to get in, it's still relatively cheap.

Couth Buzzard Books and Espresso Buono

8310 Greenwood Ave. N
(206) 436-2960
www.buonobuzzard.com

It's hard to believe a bookstore, an espresso stand, and live entertainment can fit in this small space, but they do week after week at this Greenwood community gathering spot. There's live music Friday and Saturday from 7:30 to 9:30 p.m., Celtic jams every other Saturday, open jazz jams from 1 to 3 p.m. on the third Sunday of the month, and northern tunes (Celtic, Appalachian, and Nordic music) from 6 to 9 p.m. on the fourth Sunday of every month. All free or cheap.

Crossroads Mall

NE 8th Street and 156th Avenue NE
Bellevue
(425) 644-1111
www.crossroadsbellevue.com

Imagine what would happen if the people behind Third Place Books opened a mall, and you have an idea of what this eastside shopping center is like.

They didn't open it, but they helped rescue it from obscurity by taking it over and making it a community gathering point. There's still the standard mix of stores you'd find in a suburban mall—JoAnn's, Bed Bath & Beyond—but there's also plenty going on outside the stores including classes, community events, games, local gatherings, and live entertainment. The first Thursday of the month is open mic night from 6 to 9 p.m., while other Thursdays offer a mix of music from 6:30 to 8 p.m. The music on Friday and Saturday nights can cover the waterfront from jazz and Cajun to big band or reggae and beyond and plays from 7 to 9 p.m. There's a Big Band Dance the first Saturday of each month, and the second Saturday of the month is especially family friendly with music from 5 to 8 p.m. and a range of diversions including jugglers, balloon artists, and tables where families can play board games—also free. Too bad all of the kiddie play areas feature coin-operated rides. All shows are free.

Fado Irish Pub
801 First Ave.
(206) 264-2700
www.fadoirishpub.com

It's part of a chain, but it doesn't feel like an anonymous, interchangeable eatery found in every city. It has good food and offers the look of a slightly dodgy pub not far from gritty Pioneer Square. It has plenty of nooks and crannies for you to hide out in where no one will be able to find you but the waitstaff.

The bands play covers on Friday and Saturday, but at least Fado doesn't charge one. There's also an Irish session where a group of musicians gather to play traditional Irish music with harp, fiddle, and guitar. It's open to all ages and starts at 4 p.m. every Sunday except when there's a big sporting event at one of the nearby stadiums. Weekend shows run from 10 p.m. to 1 a.m., and there's no cover except on St. Patrick's Day.

Georgia's Greek Restaurant and Deli
323 NW 85th St.
(206) 783-1228
www.georgiasgreekrestaurant.com

Greek food just goes down better with a side of ethnic music regardless of whether it's Macedonian, Serbian, Albanian, or Balkan. Music is free and starts at 7 p.m. on Saturday.

Grateful Bread

7001 35th Ave. NE
(206) 525-3166
gratefulbreadbaking.com

This neighborhood bakery has had an on-again, off-again relationship with open mic nights and folk music. Currently, it's on again with a free open mic night from 7 to 9 p.m. on the second Tuesday of the month.

Inay's Asian Pacific Restaurant

2503 Beacon Ave. S
(206) 325-5692
www.inays.com

Cheap eats and kitsch come together at this Filipino restaurant that *The Stranger,* a Seattle-area alternative newspaper, calls "one of the city's most magical outposts of awesomeness." How else would you describe a restaurant where there's a waiter who does a one-person drag show on Friday nights? He doesn't serve tables on Friday, but he does the rest of the week. The fun starts at 7:30 p.m. Reservations recommended.

Kells Irish Restaurant & Pub

Pike Place Market
1916 Post Alley
(206) 728-1916
www.kellsirish.com

The Catch: There is a cover charge on Friday and Saturday, but only if you get there after 9 p.m.

Located on Post Alley at the Pike Place Market, Kell's is decidedly more lively than it was in the building's earlier days when it was a mortuary. You can quibble about the quality of service and food, but all seem to agree on the quality of the music. Not too surprisingly, it's almost all Irish or Irish-themed (think classic rock done in an Irish style). Go figure. Music during the week is free. There may not always be a cover charge for music on weekends, but when there is, you can avoid it by getting there before the charge goes into effect at 9 p.m.

Little Red Hen

7115 Woodlawn Ave. NE
(206) 522-1168
www.littleredhen.com

The Catch: It's not free, but it's cheap and there are free dance lessons.

Seattle may not seem the likeliest locale for a country bar, especially around Greenlake, a park frequented by politically correct power walkers and people who want to discuss their relationships, but the Little Red Hen has been in their midst for years. Its name is painted larger than life on the back outside wall, but it's a safe bet that most non–country music fans don't even know it's there. There's a small cover after 8 p.m. Thursday through Sunday, generally around $3 to $5, but there are free dance lessons on Sunday nights before the dance starts. There are also line-dancing lessons on Monday and regular lessons on Tuesday nights and no cover charge.

Murphy's Pub

1928 N. 45th St.
(206) 634-2110
www.murphysseattle.com

As hard as it is to believe, there was a time when this was one of Seattle's only Irish pubs. Musical offerings include an Irish jam session on Monday at 8 p.m. (along with Irish drink specials), open mic nights on Wednesday, and The Visitors, a blues band, every third Thursday of the month. Heck, the music is even free on the occasions when bands play on Friday and Saturday.

The Ould Triangle

9736 Greenwood Ave.
(206) 706-7798

Considering that one of Seattle's claims to fame is its Nordic heritage, it sure has a heck of a lot of Irish bars. This one has open mic night on Tuesday, a blues jam on Wednesday, acoustic and mellow rock music on Saturday, and an acoustic jam session Sunday—all free. And for you billiards fans, pool is free all day Sunday, Monday, and Tuesday.

Owl and Thistle
808 Post Ave.
(206) 621-7777
www.owlnthistle.com

With at least three Irish pubs between Pioneer Square and the Pike Place Market, it's a wonder that there are enough customers to go around or even enough Irish bands for that matter. There's a free jazz jam on Wednesday nights and free music many other nights as well. There is a cover charge on Friday and Saturday, but it's usually only about $3.

Paragon Restaurant and Bar
2125 Queen Anne Ave. N
(206) 283-4548
www.paragonseattle.com

Music at this cozy Queen Anne eatery with wooden booths and a big fireplace runs from rock, acoustic, and soul to R&B and funk. On the first Tuesday of the month, the band Fiasco does a mini-rock show. Open mic night is the second and fourth Tuesday of the month. There's also live music on Thursday nights, a DJ on Friday, and different live bands on Saturday nights, including Soul Bird and Dynamite Supreme, both of which play soul and rock fusion.

Pies and Pints
1215 NE 65th St.
(206) 524-7082
www.piesandpints.com

Australian-style savory potpies are the signature dish at this friendly neighborhood pub just north of the University District. There are other items including fish, soups, and salads, but let's face it, if you really wanted to eat healthy, you would have gone to Whole Paycheck down the street. The music goes from 8:30 to 11 p.m. Sunday and Wednesday. The Seattle Folk Review holds down Sunday nights.

Salty's

Salty's on Alki
1936 Harbor Ave. SW
(206) 937-1600

Salty's at Redondo
28201 Redondo Beach Dr. S
Des Moines
(253) 946-0636
www.saltys.com

A West Seattle institution with a stunning view of the Seattle skyline, Salty's is so well known for its beautiful seafood brunch buffet with light piano accompaniment that most people don't think of it as a live music venue. Heck, if it weren't for the piano being so close to the buffet, some are so food-focused, they might not even realize the piano music is live. The Alki bar features live music from 5:30 to 8:30 p.m. on Friday and Saturday. The Redondo location has pop music on Monday, Friday, and Saturday from 8 to 10 p.m. There's also live music at the Columbia River location, but the three-hour drive to Portland may be farther than most want to travel.

Skylark

3803 Delridge Way SW
(206) 935-2111
skylarkcafe.com

A popular favorite for live music in an intimate venue even before it was named Skylark. There's a free open mic at 9 p.m. Wednesday and an all-ages open mic at noon on the last Sunday of the month.

Smokin' Pete's Barbecue

1918 NW 65th
(206) 783-0454
www.smokinpetesbbq.com

One of the best things about the live music here is the time of the Thursday night show. While most live music in Ballard doesn't start until 9 or 10, the music starts here at 6:30 p.m. So, you can take in a show without having to stay out late, which is especially nice for reformed singles now raising families of their own. The offerings include blues, bluegrass, jazz, and alternative music. It's so family friendly that a middle school jazz band plays there twice a year.

SoulFood Books and Cafe

15748 Redmond Way
Redmond
(425) 881-5309
www.soulfoodbooks.com

SoulFood's monthly calendar is filled with New Age offerings including tarot readings, drum circles, and Reiki workshops (whatever they are). If you look closely, though, you'll also notice open mic nights on the first Saturday of the month and music on most Fridays and Saturdays, along with the occasional Wednesday. The mix includes jazz, folk and even heavy-metal guitar. The cafe's only requirement is that "you must play the truth." Which is why it recently rejected a band featuring bragging fishermen. Okay, I made that up. The best way to see if you'll like the music is to visit the website, select "SoultribeTV.com," and listen to a few recent shows.

St. Clouds

1131 34th Ave.
(206) 726-1522
www.stclouds.com

The Olive Garden may say "when you're here, you're family," but St. Clouds means it. The restaurant is active in its community and supports many local causes. Bands play in the small bar, but the music can be heard throughout the restaurant from 8 to 10 p.m. Friday, Saturday, and Monday. People who want to enjoy dinner and music can reserve a small table in the bar for an intimate evening. The music runs the gamut from jazz and folk to Latin and blues. There's no cover and the bar seats 20 plus 15 standing. Also worth mentioning: St. Clouds provides a space for area residents to cook for the homeless.

Thirteen Coins

125 Boren Ave. N
(206) 682-2513

18000 International Blvd.
Seatac
(206) 243-9500
www.13coins.com

There aren't many classic Seattle places left anymore, but this is one—a 24-hour watering hole where counter seating is preferred over booths

Singing for Supper (and Breakfast and Lunch)

The street musicians at the Pike Place Market are a motley crew and they embrace almost every musical style under the sun. One has a piano that he rolls out to street corners. There's also a gospel group that always seems to be perched at Starbucks and a continuing cast of thousands scratching out a living an hour at a time.

While we can't tell you who they all are or even where they came from, we can tell you how they get there. Every busker has to pay a $30 annual fee to get a permit to perform, which is valid until April 14 of the following year. (If you're so inclined, you can go to the market website and download an application at pikeplacemarket.org/applications_permits/become_a_busker.)

Once buskers have badges, they are free to perform at one of 15 locations throughout the market designated by a painted musical note on the sidewalk. They can't hog the spot, though. Their performance time at each spot is limited to one hour if another performer is waiting. If no one is waiting, they can keep on playing. The musical notes also have a stenciled number in them to indicate how many performers can play in the spot at the same time. If the stenciled number is pink, no performances are allowed after 7 p.m. Other locations allow playing from 9 a.m. to 9 p.m. daily.

After years, there's finally some good news for balloon artists: The market no longer restricts the number of permits it issues to their ilk each year. Unfortunately, the market does not have a limit on the number of clowns, either, which seems wrong, somehow. Clowns and balloon artists can only accept tips, however, and cannot charge for

because of the show the cooks put on in the kitchen. The food isn't cheap, but the music in the lounge is free on Friday and Saturday nights and starts at 9:30 p.m. There's also a location near Seattle Tacoma International Airport with music on Wednesday and Thursday starting at 7:30 and Friday and Saturday at 8:30. Much of the music at the Seattle location is request play and Jimmy Buffett is high on the listener list. We're not sure why, but we hear there have been many lost shakers of salt.

balloons because of a prohibition against using busker spots to sell merchandise.

If you're up for a musical tour of the market, here's where to look for free live music in its natural setting:

- Under the clock at the entrance to the market
- The corner of Pine Street and Pike Place near Cinnamon Works
- The entry to the North Arcade from the Desimone Bridge (except on Saturday)
- In the courtyard between the Post Alley Building and the Sanitary Market near Copacabana
- Near Left Bank Books and the flower shop at the corner of First Avenue and Pike Place
- The corner of First Avenue and Pine Street
- Next to the metal staircase at the southern end of the Triangle Building just south of Greek Delicacies
- West of the information stand on the sidewalk between Pike Street and lower Post Alley
- On the first lower level near the exit to the Pike Place Hill Climb
- Next to Local Color at the corner of Pike Place and Stewart Street
- On Pike Place near the second home of the original Starbucks
- On the sidewalk in front of the Pear Deli
- First Avenue just south of Virginia Street
- At the bottom of Hill Climb on Western Avenue
- The second lower level between the Pike Street Hill Climb and the bridge over Western Avenue

Triple Door Lounge Musiquarium
Downstairs from Wild Ginger Restaurant
216 Union St.
(206) 838-4333
www.thetripledoor.net

Dominated by a 1,900-gallon glass aquarium, the Musiquarium at the Triple Door isn't just a place to hang out while waiting for the main stage show to start. The bar beneath the Wild Ginger Restaurant and Satay Bar features music from all genres and varies each day of the week. The Musiquarium also features a happy hour from 4 to 6 p.m. and 9 p.m. to midnight.

2.0 Cafe & Wine Bar
1912 201st Place SE, #203
Bothell
(425) 286-2192
www.coffee2point0.com

This small coffeehouse/wine bar in a suburban strip mall features free live music Thursday through Saturday ranging from rock to light jazz.

Wayward Coffeehouse
6417 Roosevelt Way NE, #104
(206) 525-5191
www.waywardcoffee.com

Klingon love ballads, anyone? Wayward moved to the Roosevelt District after a fire shut down its Greenwood location and it couldn't find a suitable location. Not much else has changed at the cafe where everything has a science fiction/fantasy theme except for the music. At least, usually anyway. Most Friday and Saturday night performances lean toward jazz, folk, and acoustic rock, but there is the occasional filk artist (folk song with a science fiction/fantasy theme). Check the website calendar to be sure of the schedule. The Northend Jazz Quintet plays on the first Saturday of the month from 8 to 10 p.m. And in case you were wondering, these aren't the droids you're looking for.

Wilde Rover Irish Pub and Restaurant
111 Central Way
Kirkland
(425) 822-8940
www.wilderover.com

This popular Kirkland bar features music every night of the week except pub trivia night on Wednesday. Musical styles include Irish bands, classic rock, and R&B. There's a $5 cover charge on Friday and Saturday, but you can avoid it by showing up before 9 p.m.

CLASSICAL

Frye Art Museum
704 Terry Ave.
(206) 622-9250
www.fryemuseum.org

The Ladies Musical Club may sound like an organization straight out of *The Music Man,* but the LMC and the Seattle Classical Guitar Society hold concerts at this hidden gem of an art museum on First Hill. Not too surprisingly, the concerts feature classical music. There are monthly concerts, but the day varies, so it's best to check the website's calendar for dates. The performances are free, but tickets are required. Arrive at least an hour early as the 142-seat auditorium fills quickly. There are other free concerts and recitals throughout the year. Check the site regularly for more details.

Seattle Symphony Community Concerts
Various locations
(206) 215-4700
www.seattlesymphony.org/symphony/community/engagement/

Not everything the symphony does is expensive. In fact, it offers several freebies throughout the year. In the early part of the year, it does a small number of free concerts throughout the community to bring music to the masses who might not otherwise experience live orchestral music. Most of those concerts are in January or February and include a lunchtime concert at City Hall. If you prefer the ambience of Benaroya Hall, you can also attend one of the free recitals performed on the 4,490-pipe Watjen Concert Organ. The performances occur about six times a year, start at 12:30 p.m. on select Mondays, and last a half-hour. For dates of the recitals, check the website at www.seattlesymphony.org/benaroya/tour. Then there are the Side-by-Side Concerts that the symphony does with high school orchestras in the fall, which are also free and open to the public. Finally, the organization also occasionally holds a Day of Music at the beginning of its performance season with different groups playing throughout Benaroya Hall and two free concert performances in association with the event.

In a Class by Itself

A cathedral might not seem like the ideal place for a romantic date night, but over the last 50 years the Compline service at St. Mark's Cathedral, 1245 10th Ave. E, has become the church equivalent of a hot ticket. That doesn't mean that the Episcopal church on Capitol Hill is turning people away just yet. Instead, the formal service chanted by a men's choir in a darkened cathedral every Sunday night has quietly grown to a point where it now attracts 500 people week in and week out, with much of the audience being in its teens and early 20s. If you can't make it to St. Mark's, you can still get the idea by turning down the lights in your home, tuning in KING-FM (98.1) or www.king.org at 9:30 p.m., and listening that way. The service only lasts half an hour and is occasionally followed by a free organ demonstration, which you can hear only if you're at St. Mark's.

If Compline is a little too late for your blood, you might also want to consider jazz vespers at Seattle First Baptist Church, 1111 Harvard Ave. The monthly concert on the first Sunday of the month at 6 p.m. is more a community outreach event than a religious service. In fact, there's only a blessing and a freewill offering at the beginning and the rest is pure entertainment featuring a different performer every time, including the likes of the Overton Barry Trio. The event usually attracts anywhere from 200 to 400 people and with 800 seats in the auditorium, there's always plenty of places to sit. Although the event is free, it never hurts to give a few shekels because much of it goes to a $1,000 scholarship for an up-and-coming student jazz musician who plans to study music. There are no jazz vespers in July, August, or September.

SUMMER CONCERTS

Concerts at the Mural
Seattle Center
www.seattlecenter.com

The Seattle Center and public alternative rock station KEXP join forces in August to present four Friday night concerts. Each of the two-hour shows features three indie rock bands and runs from 5:30 to 8:30 p.m.

Downtown Bellevue's Live at Lunch Series
Various locations
Bellevue
(425) 453-1223
www.bellevuedowntown.org

Who says there's no culture on the eastside? Besides Seattleites, I mean. The Live at Lunch series of mid-week concerts proves that local business-folk know how to rock, or tap their wingtips somewhat rhythmically. At least during the day when they probably should be in their offices, but who's counting? The season begins in July and runs through September with shows held from noon to 1:30 p.m. on Tuesday, Wednesday, and Thursday. The Thursday concert is always at the Bellevue Galleria, but other performances are held at office buildings throughout downtown. Not only are the concerts free, but you can also leave a bit richer if you win the season's drawing for a $50 gift certificate from the Tap House Grill that's good each month for a year, or if you come out on top in the concert series' Rockaroke contest held close to the end of the season.

Fountain of Light
Seattle Center International Fountain
www.seattlecenter.com/festival/detail.aspx?id=85

If you thought teaming up with alternative radio station KEXP to do concerts was cool, head on over to the International Fountain for something even more cool. Once the concert ends, the center turns the fountain into a big projector screen by projecting short movies featuring found imagery onto the water. The event runs from 9 to 11 p.m.

Hempfest
Seattle waterfront from Myrtle Edwards Park north to Elliott Bay Park
(206) 364-HEMP
www.hempfest.org

Dude, if the citizens of Washington passed a law legalizing marijuana, why are we still doing this weekend-long concert where the goal is to advocate

the legalization of marijuana? Like, what's next? Come find out at the event.
that's part political gathering, part social justice rally, part weekend-long
concert, and maybe the first public event to have marijuana dispensaries as
its main sponsors.

Kent Summer Concert Series
Locations vary
Kent
(253) 856-5050

Kentonians can see up to three free concerts a week in summer, depending
on their tastes. Tuesdays are the days for lunchtime concerts at Kent Station
(417 Ramsay Way), which make for a nice afternoon break for Regional Justice Center employees, shoppers and people who have the time off. Wednesday concerts also start at noon, but the shows at Townsquare Plaza (2nd
Avenue and Harrison Street) are aimed at the school-aged set and feature
children's performers. Both groups can come together at the Thursday evening concerts at Lake Meridian Park (14800 SE 272nd St.) that go from 7
to 8:30 p.m. and cover a wide variety of musical styles ranging from blues
and jazz to world pop. The season runs from July to August and all shows
are free.

Kidd Valley Summer Concert Series
Gene Coulon Memorial Beach Park
1201 Lake Washington Blvd.
Renton
(425) 430-6700
rentonwa.gov/living/default.aspx?id=74

Driving I-405 is never fun, but at least these concerts make the trip worthwhile and end in a nice mid-week family outing. The Wednesday night series
starts in early July and ends in mid-August with a variety of musical styles
including everything from Celtic and steel drums to polka and rock and roll.
The bands play in front of the Kidd Valley burger stand. Blankets and picnics
are welcome, but, sadly, dogs are not.

Mostly Music in the Park

Mercerdale Park
77th SE and SE 32nd
Mercer Island
(206) 236-3545
mercergov.org/mostlymusic

Mostly Music is Mercer Island's summer concert series, which runs from July to August. Most performances are on Thursday at 7 p.m. and last 90 minutes and take place under the Veteran's Pergola. Occasional special, larger concerts may be held at the Luther Burbank Amphitheatre.

Northwest Folklife

Seattle Center
(206) 684-7300
www.nwfolklife.org

The Seattle Center becomes one giant folk music concert on Memorial Day weekend as folksters from all over gather to take in traditional American music as well as styles that most people have never even heard of. Hungarian Tanchaz. Pirate Pub. Tribal and fusion bellydance. Apparently, Balkan Bridge Dance has absolutely nothing to do with trumps and tricks. Who knew? Although there is an extensive schedule of concerts, some of the best music can be heard outside the venues where impromptu jam sessions come and go. Although there are scattered events held throughout town earlier in the month including the University District Street Fair, Folklife marks the true start of the summer festival season in Seattle.

Out to Lunch Concert Series

Various locations
Downtown
(206) 623-0340
www.downtownseattle.com

Now in its 34th year, downtown's Metropolitan Improvement District–sponsored series runs between mid-July and mid-September with performances from noon to 1:30 p.m. on Wednesday and Friday. There's a different venue for every performance and the venues range from Pioneer Square all the way north to Denny Triangle, helping to ensure that workers from all over downtown will have the chance to see a performance near their offices. Although the styles have included jazz, rock, pop, country, and even a stab at opera, the DSA refers to it as "just fun summer music." If getting out in the sun isn't reason enough to go, contests associated with the series might help sweeten the pot.

Seattle Chamber Music Society
Volunteer Park, 1247 15th Ave. E
Cascade Playground, 333 Pontius Ave. N
Westlake Park, 401 Pine St.
(206) 283-8710
www.seattlechambermusic.org

These concerts may have moved from the parklike setting of Overlake Park to the concrete jungle surrounding downtown's Benaroya Hall, but that doesn't mean you can't enjoy the music in bucolic surroundings. After first piping the music out to families sitting outside Benaroya Hall, the organization decided to continue having the concerts at Benaroya, but pipe the music to one of three area parks. Wednesday concerts will be broadcast at Volunteer Park. At press time, it had not been determined which other park would feature a concert on Monday and which on Friday.

Seattle Peace Concerts
Locations vary
(206) 706-3035
www.seapeace.org

This Seattle institution brings together local musicians and large crowds in local parks for six hours every other Sunday throughout the summer to benefit local foodbanks. The concerts are family friendly and include a wide range of musical styles.

Seattle Presents

Seattle City Hall
600 4th Ave.
(206) 684-7171
www.seattle.gov/seattlepresents

A perfect little getaway in the middle of the day for office workers wanting to escape the grind, these concerts are held in City Hall Plaza at noon on occasional Thursdays in July and August. The series focuses on homegrown talent and includes a variety of musical styles. Check the website to find out what bands are featured. In case of rain, the concerts move into the lobby.

Summer Concerts at the Ballard Locks

Hiram M Chittenden Locks
3015 NW 54th St.
(206) 783-7059
www.nws.usace.army.mil/Missions/CivilWorks/LocksandDams/Chittenden-Locks/CalendarofEvents.aspx

After 20 years, there's a reason people haven't heard of this music series at one of Seattle's top tourist spots: There's no advertising budget. Zero. Nada. Zilch. And that's too bad because it makes for a great family outing on a sunny Sunday afternoon. Concerts in the ongoing summer series are held on weekends from early June through Labor Day, start at 2 p.m., and run at least an hour. The park sets up 150 chairs on the main lawn in the Carl S. English Jr. Botanical Gardens—you know, the place that you rush through to take visitors to see the ships passing through the locks and the migrating fish making their way up the salmon ladder—but there's plenty of room for lawn chairs, blankets, and picnics. Since the concerts have attracted a slightly older crowd, the music tends to fit their tastes, but organizers work hard to include music that appeals to kids and even work in a children's theater group along the way. In past years, the schedule has been jazz heavy, but has also included groups like the Sound Swing Band, the Ballard Sedentary Sousa Band, and the Microsoft Orchestra. As the name suggests, the

A Guide to Tipping Street Performers

Although you know to tip waiters and waitresses at least 15 percent at the end of a meal if the service was good, the most frustrating thing for street performers and onlookers alike is that there are no rules for what to do when one comes across the busker in his or her natural habitat. Should the average citizen turn around and run the other way or hold out money and hope the performer won't attack? And should the performer put up a sign in their instrument case with a sign showing a suggested donation? And what can a performer do at a place like the Pike Place Market where asking for donations is strictly prohibited?

This is where being a cheap bastard who knows a street musician or two comes in handy.

As veteran market busker Jonny Hahn says, "If you stop and listen for any length of time, [a performer] would like to have that type of appreciation in the form of a tip. Tip size doesn't matter." Better still, if you really like the performer, consider buying a CD. That's how my kids became fans of the group Slim Pickins.

Sousa band plays march music while sitting. And there's absolutely no truth to the rumor that the Microsoft band started late because it had to reboot.

Thursdays at the Park
Olympic Sculpture Park
2901 Western Ave.
(206) 654-3100
seattleartmuseum.org/getout

When the Olympic Sculpture Park has a summer concert series, it really knows how to do it up right. Considering the beauty of the setting, organizers could be forgiven for having a band play with a view of Elliott Bay in the background and calling it good, but the Seattle Art Museum branch adds bells and whistles including art activities for kids and adults, Art Hit

Here are a few other handy pointers that will help keep both sides of the equation happy and on good terms:

- Make sure to tip more if you've taken a picture of the performer or posed with them. "They should pay more, especially if they have an expensive camera," Hahn jokes.
- Remember good camera etiquette. It's okay to take pictures, but it's not okay to be intrusive. These are working artists, after all, not your personal models.
- If you've filmed the performer or used your video camera, you should also consider giving more. After all, if you value the performance enough to want to capture it on video, your tip should reflect that value.
- Whatever you do, never take money from a performer's case. It's more than just theft, it's also bad karma.

Other than that, let your conscience be your guide.

As Hahn says, "In general it's nice to get tips for the ego thing and because we are there trying to make a living."

mini-tours that focus on some aspect of the park, and a band of some sort, of course. A rotating selection of Seattle food trucks are also on hand to sell a wide range of foods, but if you want to keep the event free, you can bring a picnic dinner. The music plays from 6 to 8 p.m. and the event is free. The series runs from mid-July to late August. The park also has free yoga and Zumba on Saturdays.

University Village Concert Series

University Village
25th Avenue NE and NE 45th Street
(206) 523-0622
www.uvillage.com

Now a summer tradition, University Village Concert Series includes seven free family concerts on successive Wednesday nights. The short concert season usually starts after July 4. The performances themselves go from 6:30 to 8:30 p.m. and feature local celebrity bands playing tunes everybody knows. The event also features gourmet bites from many Village restaurants, a beer garden on one side of the stage, and a kids' area on the other with sprinklers, face painting, and other fun stuff for the younger set to do.

COMEDY:
FREE-FOR-ALL

"Comedy is the art of making people laugh without making them puke."
—Steve Martin

Despite its reputation for political correctness, Seattle has long been a great town for comedy. Like any city, we have our share of dreadfully earnest people who wouldn't recognize humor if it hit them with a pie in the face, and irony is not spoken here, but there's still plenty to laugh at: Ballard residents who insist on driving at a snail's pace with their turn signals on long after turning, uptight liberals, cranky conservatives, and a professional baseball team that was once so bad one local comedian said the main reason to go to a game was that "sometimes, they let you pitch." There are venues where it's possible to see top-name comics, but you'll have to pay a pretty penny to get in. Or you could always save your money, take your chances, and see young comedians and old pros alike get their acts together at some of these places.

The Capitol Club
414 E. Pine St.
(206) 325-2149
www.thecapitolclubseattle.com

Flamenco and belly dancing may be a thing of the past, but the comedy light still burns bright at this popular Capitol Hill spot. Level Up is presented by local comedy troupe Children of the Atom at 7:30 p.m. every Thursday night, and there's also Candy Basket on the third Wednesday of the month starting at 7 p.m. Both shows are free and coincide with the 5 to 8 p.m. happy hour, but Thursday has an added bonus: $1 tacos. Although it's a proven fact that comedians are funnier when you've been drinking, this place answers the question, "Are they funnier on a full stomach?"

CC Attle's
Beard Practice
1701 E. Olive Way
(206) 726-0565

Professional baseball has spring training, so why shouldn't open mic night have a farm organization of its own? Just hours before the start of Punchline Tuesday at Jai Thai (see below), you can go to this alternative club and hear up to 15 folks tell five minutes' worth of jokes. The event has proven so successful that even some of the regular customers have begun participating. Signup starts at 6:30 p.m. on Tuesday, and the jokes begin at 7 and go until just before the show at Jai Thai.

Comedy Underground

109 S. Washington St.
(206) 628-0303
www.comedyunderground.com

The Catch: There's a $6 cover.

Shhh. Can you hear that? An open mic comedian bombing is so quiet, you can hear a pun drop. It can be especially deafening at one of Seattle's oldest comedy clubs, complete with the obligatory brick wall backdrop. Still, if you had to spend $6 on an open mic night, this might be your best bet because it's long been home to some of the area's best comedians. The Monday Open Mic Night starts at 8 p.m. and usually goes to 11, with each comedian getting three minutes.

Conor Byrne

Jack-A-Napes Comedy Night
5140 Ballard Ave NW
(206) 784-3640
conorbyrnepub.com

We're not sure what Jack-a-Napes is, but there's free open mic comedy at an Irish pub in Norwegian Ballard starting at 7 p.m. every other Wednesday night. It already sounds funny.

Eclectic Theater

1214 10th Ave.
(206) 679-3271
eclectictheatercompany.org

One Sunday night a month, Eclectic hosts a free open mic night. What Sunday night it is depends on when there's a hole in the schedule. The show runs from 7:30 to 9 p.m. and features stand-up as well as improv and sketch comedy.

Grit City Comedy Club

445 Tacoma Ave. S
Tacoma
(253) 961-4262
www.gritcitycomedy.com

With a name like Grit City, you've just got to expect that things will be a little harder-edged here at this T-town titter factory. Free open mic on Monday from 8 to 10 p.m.

The Heartland Café
Knotts Night—Comedy Open Mic and Showcase
The Benbow Room
4210 SW Admiral Way
(206) 922-3313
heartlandcafeseattle.com

An outpost for midwestern food in West Seattle, the Heartland has free open mic nights at 9 p.m. on the first and third Thursday of the month.

The Highline
Patent Pending
210 Broadway Ave. E
(206) 328-7837
highlineseattle.com

What is it about Wednesday that prompts so many clubs to have comedy nights? Is it that it's humpday and we're so desperate for a laugh that we might not make it to the weekend without comedy? Or is it just a coincidence? You be the judge. Regardless, this club has open mic night from 7 to 9 p.m. on, you guessed it, Wednesday.

Magic Monday

The bookstore becomes a veritable cafe of conjuring at 7 p.m. on the second Monday of the month when a trick of magicians (that is the collective noun for magic men, isn't it?) appear to strut their stuff and then seem to vanish as quickly as they arrived. Or not.

Third Place Books Ravenna
6504 20th Ave. NE
(206) 525-2347
www.thirdplacebooks.com

Entertainment's Redheaded Stepchild

Go ahead, laugh all you want . . . for now. Just know that things could change on short notice and that tonight's open mic night could easily become tomorrow's poetry reading. Or jazz show. Or karaoke night. Or anything else you can think of. When it comes to adding entertainment to a club's mix of offerings, comedy tends to be the redheaded stepchild. Many club and restaurant owners turn to comedians in hopes of filling seats on quiet nights only to discover it's not as big a crowd pleaser as they first thought. Sometimes it's hard to attract audiences, while other times comedians are in short supply. Occasionally, it just isn't a good fit. For whatever reason, comedy nights seem to come and go rather quickly. In fact, 11 of the places that offered comedy in the original edition of this book no longer have open mic nights. So it's best to call before you head out looking for an evening of yuks only to discover it's been replaced by a goth poetry slam or a men's drumming circle.

Jai Thai
Punchline Tuesdays and Punchline Fridays Open Mic Standup
235 Broadway E
(206) 322-5781
www.facebook.com/jaithaibroadway

Go ahead, Thai one on in the main part of the restaurant and then move to the bar for open mic comedy every Tuesday and Friday at 9 p.m. It can't hurt. Who knows? It just may make the comedians sound funnier than they are. They don't care—as long as you laugh out loud.

Laughs Comedy Club
12099 124th Ave. NE
Kirkland
(425) 823-6306
www.laughscomedy.com

This suburban comedy club has two things that Pioneer Square's Comedy Underground doesn't: parking and a less scary neighborhood. And there's no admission charge for open mic night, which starts at 8:30 p.m. on Tuesday. It's enough to make you wonder if suburban comedy is different from the urban version.

Tacoma Comedy Club
933 Market St.
Tacoma
(253) 282-7203
tacomacomedyclub.com

One of the advantages of doing open mic night in Tacoma is that if you stink up the place, locals are so used to "aroma of Tacoma" from local pulp mills, that some might not even notice. Open mic night starts at 8 p.m. on Wednesday. Free admission for women on Thursday night.

DANCE:
FREE EXPRESSION

"If I can't dance, I don't want to be part of your revolution."
—Emma Goldman

Contra. Square. Swing. Lindy hop. Seattle has always been a dancing kind of town. In fact, back in the 1950s it was so popular here that it seemed like you couldn't swing a cat without hitting a dance hall. Those glory days are gone, of course, and it's a good thing because cats don't really make good swing partners. As it turns out, they're moody and they prefer to waltz. Who knew? That doesn't mean dance is dead in the Emerald City. There are still places to learn the art or sit back and enjoy watching those who dance, and some of them can be surprisingly inexpensive, if not free.

PERFORMANCE

Coriolis Dance Collective
Westlake Dance Center
10701 8th Ave. NE
(206) 854-1462
www.coriolisdance.com

Coriolis focuses on experimental dance that involves collaboration among artists from many disciplines. Volunteer slots are available during some performances and often involve jobs including venue setup, ushering, and performance teardown. Volunteers get comp tickets.

On the Boards
100 W. Roy St.
(206) 217-9886
www.ontheboards.org
Ushers per performance: 6 to 8

Many of On the Boards' shows feature dance, but not all. Some are theater, some are a mix of both, but all rely on volunteer ushers to keep things going before the curtain goes up. To sign up, e-mail hm@ontheboards.org. Opening night rush tickets sell for $12. There are also senior discounts, tickets for under 25s are $12, and Teen Tix are available for $5.

Pacific Northwest Ballet
Seattle Center
Marion Oliver McCaw Hall
(206) 441-2424
www.pnb.org

You can't usher your way into a performance, but you can volunteer and earn a ticket based on the number of hours you've worked. If you can't wait that long, there are plenty of ways to see a show without paying $25 to $160, however. Patrons 25 and under can see all Thursday and Friday performances of a run for $15 per person or $25 for two, but you must be present and have valid ID to get the tickets (except *The Nutcracker*). Dress rehearsals are $30 the day before a show opens and include a pre-show lecture. If you just want to attend the lecture, it's $12. Teen Tix tickets are $5, depending on availability. Student and senior rush tickets are half off and are also available 90 minutes before each performance. Can't make it to the show, but want a little taste? PNB offers an hour-long Friday preview in its studios for $10, but you have to act fast. Once word of the date hits the website, it sells out quickly. There are also free lunchtime previews at the Seattle Public Library's Central Library the Tuesday before opening night.

Seattle Dance Project
Locations vary
(206) 419-0328
www.seattledanceproject.org

This modern dance company was created in 2007 and features top-notch dancers from the likes of the New York City Ballet and the Pacific Northwest Ballet. Ushers can stay to see the show. In addition, people who volunteer to help out with events after a performance can see the show before the event. SDP also has a pay-what-you-will dress rehearsal as well as discounts for students and seniors. It also does Teen Tix.

Spectrum Dance Theatre
800 Lake Washington Blvd.
(206) 325-4161
www.spectrumdance.org

Spectrum doesn't need ushers for its larger productions. It can use volunteer meeters-and-greeters during its studio performances at its Lake Washington

Boulevard home in late fall. The job typically involves studio setup and ticket taking. Spectrum also offers classes including African dance, children's movement, and creative dance and will trade an hour of volunteering for an hour of class. To volunteer, e-mail shirley@spectrumdance.org.

Stone Dance Collective
The Theater at Meydenbauer Center
Bellevue
(206) 799-6004
www.chopshopdance.org

Stone Dance performs only at Chop Shop: Bodies of Work, which it produces every February. The event is a festival focused on contemporary dance. Prospective dancers can take a free dance class in connection with the event (usually in early January) through the Bellevue Parks Department or take in a free lecture on modern dance and then score a free ticket to a show.

PARTICIPATORY

Balorico
Kenyon Hall
7904 35th Ave. SW
(206) 679-7229
www.balorico.blogspot.com

If you have spare time on your hands, you can volunteer two to four hours doing administrative and/or marketing work, and earn a free session of a dance class. So, now's your chance to take those Afro-Peruvian classes you've been saving up for. Or tango, quickstep, mambo, or salsa.

The Century Ballroom
915 E. Pine St.
(206) 324-7263
www.centuryballroom.com
The Catch: You pay for the lesson, but the dance is free.

The prices have gone up at Century Ballroom, but you can't blame them. How was the owner to know she was supposed to collect sales taxes on cover charges as part of Washington's obscure "opportunity to dance tax?" Like many club owners, she was blindsided by the bill. In her case, it was $92,000. So, swing and salsa lovers can pay between $8 and $17 to attend lessons before dances and get into the dance free. If it's a night when there are multiple dances at the club, you can pay to attend the dance with the highest cover charge and get into all of the evening's dances. It isn't as cheap as it was, but the cheap bastard is keeping this one around for sentimental reasons. Besides, most drop-in dance lessons cost around $15 and don't include a dance. Lessons are usually an hour before the dance. For more details, see the calendar on Century's website.

Dancing til Dusk
Various locations
Mid-July to late August
www.danceforjoy.biz

It's a beautiful summer evening, there's not a cloud in the sky, why not dance the night away under the stars? Even that old excuse about not knowing how to dance won't work here because lessons are offered before each dance in the series. The styles include salsa, swing, cajun, and tango and the events themselves are held in downtown parks including Westlake Park, Occidental Park, Freeway Park, and the Olympic Sculpture Park. Beginner's lessons start at 6 p.m. and dances go from 7 to 9:30 p.m, all free. The schedule varies from year to year, so check the website for details. If the weather's iffy, call the rain hotline before you go at (206) 264-5646.

Little Red Hen
7115 Woodlawn Ave. NE
(206) 522-1168
www.littleredhen.com

The Catch: The live music isn't free, but the dance lessons are.

You don't have to skedaddle out to a roadhouse on the far end of town to learn how to dance the Bootscoot Boogie, line dances, and other country music dances. Instead, giddy up over to the Greenlake neighborhood. The Hen offers lessons Sunday through Tuesday before the music starts. On Monday, the focus is on line dancing. While the lessons themselves are free all three days, there's a cover charge for the Sunday night dance. Fortunately, the cover charges are usually quite small, ranging from $3 to $5 Thursday through Sunday.

Velocity Dance Center
1621 12th Ave.
(206) 325-8773
velocitydancecenter.org
Ushers per performance: 1

Besides providing a home to many other contemporary dance companies, Velocity Dance Center has a company of its own that specializes in, you guessed it, contemporary dance. People who volunteer to usher, work the box office, or serve as greeters can stay to see the show, but they might not have a seat because many shows sell out. While it doesn't have PWYC performances, it has plenty of other non-performance PWYC opportunities including the artist-curated panel discussion Speakeasy Series on a variety of topics, Velocity Open For(u)ms featuring free-wheeling discourse on issues in contemporary art and society, and the quarterly interdisciplinary conversation about the creative process called What We Talk About When We Talk About. . . . Velocity also offers dance classes and offers a work-study program where you clean and help maintain studios in exchange for discounted classes.

Living in Seattle

FOOD:
ON THE HOUSE

"Food is an important part of a balanced diet."
— *Fran Lebowitz*

If you ask me, Costco has the right idea. Hire a bunch of demonstrators to hand out food samples at peak shopping hours. The goal is to either get you to consider trying something you wouldn't otherwise or at least guilt you into it. Fortunately, the crowds are large enough to provide plausible deniability. You can feign interest in the item, ask where it is on the shelf, walk there, and ignore it as you pass. Some call it product demonstration; I call it lunch. You can do something similar at many shops in Seattle and the Pike Place Market, but you might not want to skulk away because if you stick around, you might just learn a little about something you really want to eat. The same is true of happy hours in Seattle. You can eat it and beat it, but if you stick around you just might order something you've never tried before, just because it's free . . . or cheap.

HAPPY **HOURS**

And then there was one.

For years there were a few holdouts who happily gave away finger food during happy hour, but all but one finally fell. Up until right before the last edition of *The Cheap Bastard's Guide,* the steakhouse provided free filet mignon sandwiches to its patrons. Now, it sells them for $6. At the same time, Il Fornaio in Pacific Place had a late afternoon buffet that featured whatever the chef felt like making that day, whether it be pizza squares, chicken wings, or something more adventurous. And then it went to a bar menu with actual prices. Even McCormick & Schmick's $2.95 burger went up to $5.95. Scandalous! Oliver's now remains the lone holdout and given all this talk of the economy, one wonders how long that will last. Sure, you could count Osteria La Spiga, but you have to buy a drink just to get them and there's a limit to what you get. On the plus side, you are guaranteed to get that amount even if you get there at the end of happy hour, so it's not all bad.

Don't get me wrong, I understand all these restaurants have to worry about profits and the bottom line, but it's always sad to see a good deal die. Fortunately, there are still plenty of happy hour bargains left. You just have to pay more for them, is all.

Free Happy Hour Food

Oliver's at Mayflower Park
405 Olive Way
(206) 623-8700
www.mayflowerpark.com/olivers.asp

The cheap bastard can't believe it's finally come to this, but now there's only one happy hour in town with free food and it's at a place that isn't all that cheap to begin with—but it is stylish. While it's best known for serving some of the best martinis in town, the lounge at the boutique Mayflower Park Hotel also offers free appetizers from 4:30 to 6 p.m. Monday through Friday. The offerings vary from day to day, but there are usually two dishes that include food such as egg rolls, spring rolls, chicken wings, and hummus. There are no drink specials during happy hour, however.

Osteria La Spiga
1429 12th Ave., Ste. A
(206) 323-8881
www.laspiga.com
Late Night Happy Hour

It may not be enough to fill you up, but there is free food served during La Spiga's aperitivo hour from 5 to 6:30 p.m. Monday through Friday and 11 p.m. to midnight on Friday and Saturday. The restaurant serves four small plates with a $3 beer or $4 well drink or glass of wine. The dishes include olives, Italian cheese, roasted nuts, and a pâté. Other happy hour menu items range from $3 to $10.

Cheap Happy Hour Food

Art Restaurant and Lounge
99 Union St.
(206) 749-7070
www.artrestaurantseattle.com
Late Night Happy Hour

The Catch: Wait until the late night happy hour for the cheese deal.

Happy Hours: Not Just for Dinner (or Breakfast) Anymore

Leave it to the city that brought you the Wave, the espresso cart, and the first toothbrush for dogs to come up with a new wrinkle on the happy hour: the late night happy hour. If you were at home, you'd call it a midnight snack, but since you're still out, you're hungry, and the restaurant you just passed is still open, those cheap late night specials are a way for eateries to grab a last bit of business and keep you from launching an early morning raid on your fridge. The special menus have worked so well that more and more restaurants are adopting them. And that doesn't even include the places that now offer all-day happy hours, weekend ones, brunch ones, and even a few breakfast versions.

Rather than debate the issue of how any hour can last all day, much less a happy one, we'll just go with the spirit of the thing and say, "Isn't that as it should be? After all, why are we only allowed to get happy right after work when there's so much of the day left?"

Fourteen dollars is a so-so happy hour price for an all-you-can-eat cheese and antipasto bar, but if you can wait until the late night happy hour from 9 to 11 p.m., you can belly up to the same bar for just $7.

The Berliner Doner Kebab

Pioneer Square
221 First Ave. S
(206) 888-0339

South Lake Union
428 Westlake Ave.
(206) 838-5032
www.berlinerseattle.com

B. Kliban was wrong. There are times when it is okay to eat something bigger than your head. These doner sandwiches aren't quite as big as a human's noggin, but they sure seem so when you try to eat one in a single sitting. Even the regular-sized ones, which are all on special for $5 during happy hour from 3 to 6 p.m., Monday through Friday.

The Best Damn Happy Hour
Seattle Center Armory
Seattle Center
Third Thursday of the month

One of the latest entries in Seattle's happy hour scene is in a class by itself because it involves 13 restaurants, several games, three or four signature drinks, and one really large garage. In short, the Seattle Center's food-court-turned-gourmet-eatery-zone-called-The-Armory pulls out many of the stops from 5 to 8 p.m. on the third Thursday of every month and has a party featuring reduced price menus from the likes of Skillet, Bean Sprouts Café and Cooking School, and Bigfood BBQ, along with games including giant Jenga and minigolf, live entertainment, and cool prizes given away every half-hour. And did we mention beer, wine, and specialty drinks? There's no cover and if you play your cards right, you'll pay $2 or less for parking.

Bitterroot
5239 Ballard Ave. NW
(206) 588-1577
www.bitterrootbbq.com

One of the biggest things I miss from living in Kansas City is great barbecue. Seattle's food scene falls flat when it comes to BBQ, and barbecued salmon ain't cutting it. Brisket with pepperoncini on a pretzel roll isn't exactly traditional, but it's the best damn 'cue I've found in the Northwest. And at happy hour the sandwich is only $5. The same is true for the pulled pork sandwich. The happy hour menu even features a few vegetarian entries, which seems wrong, but I'm willing to overlook a lot for good barbecue. Happy hour runs 3 to 6 p.m., Monday through Friday.

Blue Moon Burger
Capitol Hill
523 Broadway E
(206) 325-2000

Fremont
703 N. 34th St.
(206) 547-1907

South Lake Union
920 Republican St.

(206) 652-0400
bluemoonburgers.com

You don't have to wait for the next blue moon to get a deal on a burger here. On Meatless Mondays, all meatless burgers are half price after 4 p.m. and on Wednesday all burgers are half off.

Club Contour
807 First Ave.
(206) 447-7704
www.clubcontour.com

This nightspot has a specials menu that is as extensive as its happy hour is long. It has 18 items going from a quarter-pound provolone cheeseburger with fries for $3 all the way to sautéed scallops for $6. Beers are $3 to $5, and well drinks are $3.75 (menu subject to change). The specials run from 3 to 8 p.m. Monday to Thursday, 3 to 9 p.m. Friday, and 2 to 8 p.m. on weekends.

Dragonfish Asian Café
722 Pine St.
(206) 467-7777
www.dragonfishcafe.com
Late Night Happy Hour

It's hard to go wrong with $1.95 sushi when it's this good. Half rolls range from $1.95 to $2.95, and small plates run $1.95 to $5.95. You can get draft beer, special cocktails, and sake for $2.95 from 3 to 6 p.m., and late night happy hour from 9 p.m. to 1 a.m. Tuesday through Sunday. Happy hour also runs from 3 p.m. to 1 a.m. on Monday.

Elliott's Oyster House
1201 Alaskan Way, Pier 56
(206) 623-4340
www.elliottsoysterhouse.com

Oyster lovers, this waterfront eatery is the place to be at 3 p.m. for the start of the Progressive Oyster Happy Hour when the chef's choice of whatever is being freshly shucked is available for 75 cents apiece. Prices jump 50 cents every half-hour until they're $1.75 per at 5:30. The fun goes from 3 to 6 p.m., Monday through Friday.

Endolyne Joe's

9261 45th Ave. SW
(206) 937-5637
www.chowfoods.com/endolyne
Late Night Happy Hour

There was a time when the Endolyne's happy hour schedule was based on the Vashon Ferry schedule. Now, however, the restaurant has gone with the more typical time of 3 to 6 p.m. daily as well as a late night menu from 9 to close, except on Tuesday when happy hour runs from 3 p.m. to close. Food prices include $4 for mac and cheese, $5 for pork sliders, and $6 for calamari. The eatery even has Not So Early Bird specials for breakfast from 8 to 11 a.m. Monday through Friday when prices on the special menu are $5.75 for such treats as a goat cheese and fresh herb scramble and a halfway caramel apple french toast. At these prices, why not go all the way?

5 Spot

1502 Queen Anne Ave. N
(206) 285-7768
www.chowfoods.com/5-spot

This favorite neighborhood eatery atop Queen Anne Hill is owned by Chow Foods, the folks behind Endolyne Joe's and The Hi-Life, and has many of the same specials, including a happy hour from 3 to 6 p.m. and a late night bar menu from 10 to midnight Monday through Friday. Everything is $5.75 including such items as chili and cornbread, red beans and rice, and a hot turkey sandwich with mashed potatoes and gravy. Pints of Pabst Blue Ribbon are $1. The regular happy hour menu is available only in the bar, but late night deals are available throughout the restaurant.

Hattie's Hat

5231 Ballard Ave. NW
(206) 784-0175
www.hattieshat.com
Late Night Happy Hour

A classic Ballard place, Hattie's continues to hold its own against the Johnny-come-lately joints that have suddenly discovered Ballard, raising rents and taking up all the parking. Gee, cheap bastard, tell us how you really feel. Happy hour at this old school dive bar runs from 3 to 6 p.m. daily and 10 p.m. to midnight Sunday through Thursday. Prices range from $1.50 for house-smoked ribs and $2 braised greens to $5 hot wings. Other deals include $2 off all burgers on Monday, $2 tacos on Tuesday, and $1 ribs on Wednesday.

The Hi-Life
5425 Russell Ave. NW
(206) 784-7272
www.chowfoods.com/hi-life

This Ballard Chow Foods favorite has a regular happy hour from 3 to 6:30 p.m., except on Tuesday when it runs from 3 p.m. to closing time. The late night happy hour goes from 10 to closing time. Pizzas, bread pudding, and other side dishes start at $4; cheeseburgers and chik'n fried portabello go for $5. All of the dishes on the Not-So-Early Bird breakfast menu from 8:30 to 11 a.m. Monday through Friday are $5.75, including the herb and goat cheese scramble and the Ballard Barrio Breakfast Burrito. When did the Norwegian section of town become a barrio?

Il Fornaio
Pacific Place
600 Pine St.
(206) 264-0994
www.ilfornaio.com

One of the last bastions of free happy hour food fell when this Pacific Place eatery eliminated its small buffet and added a regular menu with—gasp!—actual prices. Happy hour eats include $5 pizzas and antipastis.

Kate's Pub
309 NE 45th St.
(206) 547-6832

The tradition continues. Instead of having a special menu, this eatery does it right by serving all regular menu items at half price, even dessert. Microbrews are $3. Happy hour is from 4 to 7 p.m.

List
2226 1st Ave.
(206) 441-1000
www.listbelltown.com

The half-off concept goes upscale in this Belltown eatery near downtown. If you liked half off at Kate's, you'll love it at List where happy hour runs all day Sunday and Monday, 4 to 6:30 p.m. and 9 to midnight Tuesday through Thursday, as well as 4 to 6:30 p.m. Friday and Saturday, especially when it includes grilled Caesar salad for $3.50, cannelloni with spinach and ricotta for $4, and seared ahi tuna for $6.50.

Lost Lake Cafe & Lounge
1505 10th Ave.
(206) 323-5678
lostlakecafe.com

Opened just as the book was going to press, this 24-hour Capitol Hill diner is brought to you by the people behind 5-Point Café. Although it served its first meals in early May 2013, it already looked like it had been there forever, in a good way. The happy hour menu includes a 6-ounce cheeseburger and fries for $2.50, a chorizo quesadilla and many other dishes for $3, and domestic drafts for $2.

Maximilien Restaurant
81A Pike St.
(206) 682-7270
www.maximilienrestaurant.com

Sure, happy hour prices have gone up, but this romantic French eatery in the Pike Place Market makes up for it with a beautiful view of sunset over Puget Sound. Prices now range from $4 for a goat cheese mousse and $6 for escargots a la bourguignonne to the not-so-cheap-bastard price of $12 for foie gras. Margaritas and French martinis start at $6, French beer is $3 or $15 for a bucket of six, and absinthe is $7. Happy hour runs from 5 to 7 p.m. Monday through Friday, 8 to 10 p.m. Saturday.

McCormick & Schmick's
McCormick & Schmick's Seafood Restaurant
Various locations
www.mccormickandschmicks.com

The Catch: *$3.50 minimum beverage purchase per diner.*

Yes, McCormick & Schmick's is a chain, but its four local restaurants have long had one of the best happy hours around. What's on offer varies from location to location, but prices start at $2.95 and go up to $5.95 at all locations. Each menu is anchored by the generous $5.95 half-pound cheese-burger with french fries. Combine that with another side and it's more than enough for a meal.

Moshi Moshi Sushi
5324 Ballard Ave.
(206) 971-7424
www.moremoshi.com
Late Night Happy Hour

Cheap sushi, Pabst Blue Ribbon, and inexpensive sake all in the same place! The selection includes tiger rolls for $2.95, California rolls for $3.95, PBR in cans for $2, and small sake for $1.95. Happy hour runs from 4 to 6 p.m. Monday through Saturday and 3 to 6 p.m. Sunday; late night happy hour is 10 to 11 p.m. Monday through Thursday, and 11 p.m. to midnight Friday and Saturday. Happy hour prices reign supreme in the bar all night on Sunday.

Norm's Eatery and Ale House
460 N. 36th St.
(206) 547-1417

Finally, a happy hour that proves beer isn't man's only best friend. Dog lovers and their pets are welcome as long as they're well behaved and on a leash (the dogs, not the dog lovers). The food isn't free, but portions are generous and you can't beat the company. Specials run from 4 to 7 p.m. Monday through Friday. There's also a brunch happy hour on weekends with $4 Bloody Marys and mimosas.

Peso's Kitchen & Lounge
605 Queen Anne Ave. N
(206) 283-9353
www.pesoskitchen.com
Late Night Happy Hour

When a place bills itself as having "the city's most visited happy hour," it's hard to call it modest, especially when its happy hour menu features around

50 items, with the majority going for $5 or less. The selection includes soups, salads, tapas from land and sea, hot sandwiches, tacos, and desserts. I can't say exactly how many people have visited this happy hour, but folks in the know mention it frequently. Its signature dish is chicken fried steak with spicy jalapeno corn gravy. Some of the more expensive items on the regular breakfast menu are $9, which is still a substantial discount from regular prices. Breakfast specials run 9 to 11 a.m. Monday through Friday. Happy hour (4 to 6 p.m.) and late night happy hour (10 p.m. to 1 a.m.) both are on tap daily.

Sazerac
Hotel Monaco
1101 Fourth Ave.
(206) 624-7755
www.sazeracrestaurant.com

A taste of New Orleans, Sazerac has a much-loved happy hour with appetizers like hearts of romaine "Caesar style" for $5.50, two barbecue pulled pork sliders for $6, and 10-inch wood fired pizzas for $6. Beer, wine, and mixed drinks are $3.50. It goes from 4 to 8 p.m. Monday through Saturday.

Serious Pie
316 Virginia St.
(206) 838-7388
tomdouglas.com/index.php?page=serious-pie

There comes a time in the life of every great city with a great chef when its citizens must ask, "Don't you think you have enough restaurants already? Don't you think we could do without one or two of them?" We thought Seattle's Tom Douglas might have reached this point until he opened Serious Pie along with its happy hour roasted chanterelle, truffle cheese 6-inch mini pizza for $6. Beers are $4 a pint, wines are $5, and other pie options include Yukon gold potato and rosemary olive oil; Penn Cove clams, house pancetta, and lemon thyme; or even guanciale, soft egg, and dandelion greens. (Heck, we don't even know what guanciale is, but we bet it's something good.) Now, we find ourselves realizing we might have been a bit hasty. All we have to do now is convince Douglas to change his happy hour times. It goes from 3 to 5 p.m. There have been times when we've just missed the deadline and it's not pretty. And take it from us, no one likes to see a grown man cry.

Talarico's
4718 California Ave. SW
(206) 937-3463
www.talaricoswest.com
Late Night Happy Hour

Some might ask what's the point of a late night happy hour without drink discounts, but not me. I'm usually in it for the food. And $4 for a 14-inch slice of pizza isn't bad, although I'm still trying to figure out how that's measured. Lengthwise? From side to side? The early happy hour runs from 3 to 6 p.m. Monday through Friday and includes draft beers for $3.50. The late night version runs from 11 p.m. to 1 a.m. nightly and has the same food prices, including $6 for meatball sliders, but no drink discounts.

Tin Hat Bar & Grill
512 NW 65th
(206) 782-2770

The food isn't quite free at this dive bar, but 69 cent hard-shell tacos on Tuesdays and $3.95 for spaghetti and Texas toast on Wednesdays isn't far off. And don't forget pulled pork sandwiches on Monday for $4.95 and $5 cheeseburgers on Thursday for $3.95. In addition to the all-day specials, happy hour runs from 4 to 7 p.m. with $2 PBRs, $3.50 draft beers, and $4 well drinks.

Toulouse Petit
601 Queen Anne Ave. N
(206) 432-9069
toulousepetit.com
Late Night Happy Hour

The Catch: Minimum $3 beverage order per person.

Mexico not your cup of tea? Just up the block from Peso's is this New Orleans–inspired eatery with an equally impressive happy hour menu featuring more than 30 items for $5 or less, including such oddities as fried chicken gumbo and fried green tomatoes with remoulade. The late night menu features eight dessert options for $6 or less. As with Peso's, there's also a breakfast happy hour where most items are $8 from 8 to 11 a.m. Monday through Friday. Happy hour is 4 to 6 p.m., late night 10 p.m. to 1 a.m. On Tuesdays from 10 p.m. to 1 a.m., the restaurant has a special it calls Ménage à Trois with five dishes selling for $3 each.

FREE **SAMPLES**

Beecher's Handmade Cheese
1600 Pike Place
(206) 956-1964
www.beechershandmadecheese.com

The guides at a local walking tour company make great hay out of the fact that this place was founded by Kurt Dammeier. That's Kurt, not Curd. It is pretty funny when you stop to think about it. Even if you don't like puns, there are usually cheddared curds and the flagship cheese out and readily available for sampling. Workers will also let you try anything in the case. The CB's favorite is the Marco Polo with black pepper in it. There are even more samples during the annual Seattle Cheese Festival in May. Oh, what a friend we have in cheeses.

Borracchini's Bakery
2307 Rainier Ave. S
(206) 325-1550
www.nowcake.com

There's more to this South-end bakery than the pastries and cakes that have been a part of many family celebrations for four generations of Seattleites. It's also a deli, Italian market, and importer of Mediterranean foods. Despite its diversity, the store's best samples are from the bakery. Don't miss the shelf featuring cake-of-the-day samples. Kids and adults are mesmerized by the bakery window, where you can watch cakes being decorated.

Britt's Pickles
1500 Pike Place, #15
(253) 666-6686
www.brittsliveculturefoods.com

Some may say that the pickles sold out of barrels may be a little pricey. I beg to differ. Speaking as someone who hits New York's Lower East Side just to get fresh pickles to take back every time I visit the Big Apple, even with parking costs factored in, a visit to Britt's is much cheaper than a plane ticket to Manhattan. What's on offer varies seasonally, but includes fermented Meyer lemon, Market Kimchi, sauerkraut, and pickles, of course. Half sours, full sours, spicy, ginger pepper, and hot and sour.

Central Market
15505 Westminster Way N
Shoreline
(206) 363-9226
central-market.com

It's not as centrally located as the name would suggest, but it is a great Home Depot–sized grocery store that somehow still manages to be a neighborhood supermarket. Friday night summer dinners with live music and other celebrations help. The store has discounts on prepared foods during the concerts, whether it be reduced prices on the salad bar or a few bucks off the store-made pizza. Numerous cooking demonstrations and food sampling events don't hurt, either.

Cheesemonger's Table
203 5th Ave. S.
Edmonds
(425) 640-8949
www.cheesemongerstable.com

What started out as a cheese shop has evolved into a small deli-style restaurant that stocks 100 varieties of cheese and accompaniments including house-made tapenade and hummus. They always have a cheese sample out.

Sample-palooza

The names for the place are as numerous as its visitors. Some tourists call it Pike Street Market, Pike's Peak Market, or simply Pike's Market. Locals call it the Pike Place Market. Me, I call it a ticket to a free lunch. When I first worked downtown, I used to love going from one inexpensive food stand to another assembling an impossibly inexpensive meal. A cheap humbow here, a day-old pastry there, all topped off by a beautiful piece of whatever fruit happened to be in season.

All that changed, however, when I discovered how many places in the market offered samples all day, every day. Heck, considering the sheer variety of foods there for the asking, it's easy to see that Costco's got nothing on this place. In fact, there are times when going to the mega-retailer on a Saturday in search of free bites almost feels like cheating on Rachel the Pig, the farmers, and all the other characters at the market. Oh, Pike Place, we may not always have Paris, but with merchants like these, we'll always have lunch:

Beecher's Handmade Cheese: Offers cheddared cheese curd and the store's Flagship cheese.

Britt's Pickles: Provides a wide range of samples, some seasonal including fermented Meyer Lemon, Market Kimchi, sauerkraut, pickled onions and garlic, and pickles, of couse. The pickles typically include half sours, full sour dills, hot and sour, and ginger pepper. And who can forget the brine shots?

Chukar Cherry Company: Serves preserves and chocolate.

The Confectional: Colombian drinking chocolate and, if you're really lucky, cheesecake, but that's only if a highly skilled cakemaker makes a mistake.

Chukar Cherry Company
1529-B Pike Place
Pike Place Market (in the center of the Main Arcade)
(206) 623-8043
www.chukar.com

DeLaurenti Specialty Food and Wine: Cheese, olive oils, and balsamic vinegars. Also has a weekly wine tasting. Other foods available for sampling on request, including meats.

La Buona Tavola Truffle Cafe and Specialty Foods: Serves potato leek soup with white truffle oil and provides samples of its gourmet oils, pestos, and pasta sauces.

Market Spice: Serves its signature orange-cinnamon black tea, Market Spice tea.

Micks Peppourri: Samples pepper jellies.

Pappardelle's Pasta: Samples its uncooked flavored pastas, 14 balsamic vinegars, and olive oils.

Perennial Tea Room: Has four teas in pots that are available for sampling and may also custom brew one for you from its bulk section.

Pure Food Fish: Serves three of the five varieties of its smoked salmon—teriyaki, pepper, and garlic—smoked scallops, smoked mussels, and smoked black cod.

Simply the Best: Offers five varieties of apple chips from sweet to sour, usually honey crisp apples and other options on a seasonal basis ranging from okra beet chips to green beans.

Sosio's Fruit and Produce: What fresh fruit is on offer varies based on seasonality.

Sotto Voce: Olive oils and vinegars.

Stackhouse Brothers Orchards: Samples a variety of nuts.

Stewart's Meat Market: Offers pepperoni and jerky.

Woodring Orchards: Fruit spreads, pepper jellies, apple butters, and pumpkin butters.

Who knew there were so many things you can do with cherries? This booth samples a wide range of products including dried cherries, peach cherry salsa, and cherry chipotle grilling sauce. Are you beginning to see a theme here?

The Confectional

Pike Place Market
1530 Pike Place
(206) 282-4422

618 Broadway Ave. E
(206) 282-4422
www.theconfectional.com

If you're really lucky, you might be here on a day when someone makes a mistake on a cheesecake that turns it into a factory second ripe for sampling. If not, well, you can always try a sip of its Colombian drinking chocolate.

Costco

Various locations
Costco.com

Don't look now, but I think they're onto us. Why else would they have so many folks offering so many food samples, especially on weekends? People in the grocery industry call it "product demonstration." I call it lunch.

DeLaurenti Specialty Food and Wine

Pike Place Market
Southwest corner of First Avenue and Pike Street
(206) 622-0141
www.delaurenti.com

Hungry, but don't want to wade into the craziness that is the Market on a summer's day? This Italian market is great for a quick slice of pizza, a sandwich for lunch, a cup of espresso, and picking up items for dinner. Although charcuterie may be all the rage, people forget this shop has some of the finest charcuterie and sausage from small, local sausage producers, which you can sample from the deli case. With nine types of prosciutto, you should find something that you like. There's also a table where you can try olive oils and vinegars.

Great Harvest Bread

5408 Sand Point Way NE; (206) 524-4873; www.greatharvestsandpoint.com
2218 NW Market St.; (206) 706-3434

4709 California Ave. SW; (206) 935-6882; www.greatharvestwestseattle.com
Lake Forest Park Town Center, 17171 Bothell Way NE; Lake Forest Park; (206) 365-4778
Bear Creek Village, 17192 Redmond Way, Redmond; (425) 883-6909
3610 Factoria Blvd. SE, Bellevue, (425) 643-8420; www.greatharvestbellevue .com

Sometimes the places that give free samples are so obvious we completely overlook them. Great Harvest is a good example. At most locations, a slice of wheat bread or whatever happens to be on offer that day is yours for the asking, usually along with some butter for you to slather on it. Some locations also give out breadsticks for kids. In my neighborhood, you can have an additional slice for a dollar; other locations may charge less or not at all. Some also have free doggie biscuits as well.

La Buona Tavola Truffle Cafe and Specialty Foods
Pike Place Market (in the Triangle Building between Mr. D's Greek Deli and Mee Sum Pastries)
1524 Pike Place
(206) 292-5555
www.trufflecafe.com

Potato leek soup with white truffle oil, apple curd, lemon curd, almond curd, pistachio cream, flavored oils . . . It's easy to get overwhelmed with all the good stuff that you can try here and almost impossible to get out the door without buying something. A pesto or a black truffle oil, perhaps?

Market Spice
Pike Place Market Economy Arcade
85A Pike St.
(206) 622-6340
marketspice.com

Because of the popularity of its signature cinnamon-orange Market Spice tea, people tend to forget this place also sells over 240 spices and spice blends in bulk. It samples its namesake tea every day and also offers spiced cider in winter.

Son of Sample-palooza:
Markets for Those Who Can't Be Bothered

Although Seattleites love the Pike Place Market, we aren't all that crazy about the traffic, the crowds, or the hassle of looking for parking downtown. Fortunately, there's an option for people who love to try and buy from local producers and those who just can't be bothered to run the Pike Place gauntlet: weekly neighborhood markets. And it seems like new ones are opening every year. Here's a list of some of the top neighborhood markets in the region:

Ballard Sunday Farmers Market, Ballard Avenue and 22nd Avenue NW; (206) 851-5100; ballardfarmersmarket.wordpress.com; Sunday from 10 a.m. to 3 p.m., year-round.

Bellevue Farmers Market, First Presbyterian Church, 1717 Bellevue Way NE; www.bellevuefarmersmarket.org; Thursday from 3 to 7 p.m., May through October; and NE 6th and 106th Ave NE ; Saturday from 10 a.m. to 3 p.m., June through November

Broadway Farmers Market, Broadway Avenue East and E. Pine Street at Seattle Central Community College; www.seattlefarmersmarkets .org/markets/broadway; Sunday from 11 a.m. to 3 p.m., April through December.

Columbia City Farmers Market, South Edmunds Street between 37th Avenue South and the alley at 36th Street; www.seattlefarmersmarkets.org/markets/columbia_city; Wednesday from 3 to 7 p.m., May through October.

Crossroads Farmers Market, NE 8th Street and 156th Avenue NE, Bellevue, in southeast parking lot of Crossroads Mall; www.crossroadsbellevue.com/specialevents/farmers-market; Tuesday from noon to 6:30 p.m., May through October.

Fremont Market, Phinney Avenue and N. 34th St.; (206) 781-6776; www.fremontmarket.com; Sunday from 10 a.m. to 5 p.m., year-round.

Kirkland Wednesday Market, 25 Lakeshore Plaza; www.kirklandwednesdaymarket.org; Wednesday from 2 to 7 p.m, June through September.

Lake City Farmers Market, NE 125th Street and 28th Avenue NE, in front of the Lake City Library; www.seattlefarmersmarkets.org/markets/lake_city; Thursday from 2:30 to 7:30 p.m., June through September.

Lake Forest Park Commons Farmers Market, Lake Forest Park Town Centre, intersection of State Road 522 and Highway 104; www.third placecommons.org/farmers-market; Sunday from 11 a.m. to 4 p.m., May through October.

Magnolia Farmers Market, in the heart of Magnolia Village at West McGraw Street at 33rd Avenue West; www.seattlefarmersmarkets.org/markets/magnolia; Saturday from 10 a.m. to 2 p.m., June through September.

Mercer Island Farmers Market, 7700 SE 32nd St., Mercer Island; (206) 235-1185; www.mifarmersmarket.org; Sunday from 10 a.m. to 3 p.m., June through October.

Phinney Farmers Market, N. 67th Street and Phinney Avenue North, in the Phinney Neighborhood Center's lower parking lot; www.seattle farmersmarkets.org/markets/phinney; Friday from 3 to 7 p.m., June through September.

University District Farmers Market, University Heights Center for the Community, corner of University Way NE and NE 50th Street; Neighborhood Farmers Market Alliance; (206) 632-5234; www.seattle farmersmarkets.org/markets/u_district; Saturday from 9 a.m. to 2 p.m., year-round.

Wallingford Wednesday Farmers Market, Meridian Park, Corner of N. 50th Street and Meridian Avenue North; (206) 781-6776; wallingford farmersmarket.wordpress.com; Wednesday from 3:30 to 7 p.m., May through September.

West Seattle Farmers Market, 44th Avenue SW and SW Alaska Street; www.seattlefarmersmarkets.org/markets/west_seattle; Sunday from 10 a.m. to 2 p.m., year-round.

Metropolitan Market

Kirkland, 10611 NE 68th St.; (425) 454-0085
Uptown, 100 Mercer St., Seattle; (206) 213-0778
Admiral/West Seattle, 2320 42nd Ave. SW, Seattle; (206) 937-0551
Sand Point, 5250 40th Ave. NE, Seattle; (206) 938-6600
Proctor, 2420 N. Proctor St., Tacoma; (253) 761-3663
www.metropolitan-market.com

Have you ever found yourself wanting to spend a ridiculous amount of money for a highly specialized condiment? I mean, why go with ketchup when Dijon ketchup will really set off the flavor? If so, this small regional chain of gourmet groceries with high-quality ingredients you didn't know you needed is the place for you. Or you could just go and see what's being sampled the day you happen to be driving by. It could be anything from cheese and crackers to a food demonstration of some ingredient you've never known how to use. Check the website or bi-weekly ads to find out what's on offer.

Micks Peppourri

Pike Place Market
Next to the Skybridge in the Main Arcade
1531 Pike Place
(800) 204-5679
www.micks.com

If you are sampling your way through the market, stop at this purveyor of peppery treats before Woodring Orchards just across the hall. That way, you can set your tastebuds a-sizzle with samples of pepper jelly flavors like hot cranberry, lime, and ginger (or any of the other 25 flavors available for tasting), then douse the flames with a taste of Woodring's cider (when it's in season). The booth also samples its wine jellies, but you have to request a taste; the jellies aren't on the table because they don't want kids getting into them.

Pappardelle's Pasta

Pike Place Market
1501 #8 Pike St.
(206) 340-4114

Just the thought of dark chocolate linguine was enough to make me curious. It really does taste like chocolate. I had to stop sampling there, though. Otherwise, I would have been there all day trying all 75 flavors, including such oddities as curry angel hair, orange Szechuan linguine, and basil garlic penne. So what if they're not cooked? And when I was through with that, I'd sample their private-label oils and balsamic vinegars.

PCC Natural Markets
Edmonds PCC, 9803 Edmonds Way, Edmonds; (425) 275-9036
Fremont PCC, 600 N. 34th, Seattle; (206) 632-6811
Greenlake PCC, 7504 Aurora Ave. N, Seattle; (206) 525-3586
Issaquah PCC at Pickering Place, 1810 12th Ave. NW, Issaquah; (425) 369-1222
Kirkland PCC, 10718 NE 68th, Kirkland; (425) 828-4622
Redmond PCC, 11435 Avondale Rd. NE, Redmond; (425) 285-1400
Seward Park PCC, 5041 Wilson Ave. S, Seattle; (206) 723-2720
View Ridge PCC, 6514 40th Ave. NE, Seattle; (206) 526-7661
West Seattle PCC, 2749 California Ave. SW, Seattle; (206) 937-8481
www.pccnaturalmarkets.com

This co-op chain isn't as glamorous as Whole Foods and, shockingly enough, can occasionally be more expensive than the privately owned Austin, Texas–based behemoth, but PCC still has one key advantage over its competitor. It's local. PCC gives children a free piece of fruit each visit. It also does some sampling for adults including soups, gelato, and other items, depending on location.

Perennial Tea Room
Pike Place Market
1910 Post Alley
(206) 448-4054
www.perennialtearoom.com

The street is just called an alley, but it isn't one really. Need proof? If tea is the height of civility, why would any tea room set up shop in a dangerous neighborhood? In addition to selling everything you need to brew a cup, Perennial always has four teas in pots that are available for sampling or the store will custom brew one for you from its bulk section on request. Check the board over the counter to find out which ones are available for taste testing when you stop by.

Pure Food Fish

Pike Place Market
1511 Pike Place
(206) 622-5765
www.freshseafood.com

When you're just down the arcade from the guys who throw fish, you have to try a little harder to catch the public's attention. Offering free samples of smoked fish definitely helps. Smoked salmon samples come in garlic, pepper, and teriyaki flavors. They also sample smoked scallops, smoked mussels, and smoked black cod.

QFC

Queen Anne, 500 Mercer St., Seattle; (206) 352-4020
University Village, 2746 NE 45th St., Seattle; (206) 523-5160
Ballard, 5700 24th Ave. NW, Seattle; (206) 297-2150
Wedgwood, 8400 35th Ave. NE, Seattle; (206) 523-5847
Consult the website for additional locations.
www.qfc.com

Samples depend on what departments are at a given location in this Kroger-owned regional chain. At a smaller location like Wedgwood, for example, baked goods, fruit, crackers, and spread are often offered. At a larger store like the University Village location, the nibbles may also include fish, sushi, shellfish, and the occasional beverage. Some claim you could turn a visit to some QFCs into a meal. If you do, you'll probably starve.

Simply the Best

Pike Place Market (under the clock)
(206) 624-8863
esimplythebest.net

If it weren't so close to those fun-loving, fish-throwing guys at Pike Place Fish, the stall selling organic dried Washington-grown apples (plus other non-Washington fruits and vegetables) would be hard to miss. Fortunately, there's nothing like a taste of okra beet chips, green beans, or honey crisp apples to focus the concentration. Although apple chips from sweet to sour are its main samples, you can ask to try just about anything. The products contain no preservatives.

Sosio's Fruit and Produce

Pike Place Market
1527 Pike Place
(206) 622-1370
www.sosiosproduce.com

Not the cheapest place in the market, but it has the best fresh fruit and the most courteous employees, who are more than willing to offer free samples, even if what you're interested in isn't one of the items they are sampling.

Sotto Voce

Pike Place Market
1532 Pike Place
Corner of Pine Street and Pike Place
(206) 624-9998
www.sottovoce.com

Everything's going artisanal these days. Coffee and chocolate were understandable, but vinaigrette? Sotto Voce is known for its hand-crafted, spiced, flavored virgin olive oils, vinegars, and its own spicy vinaigrette. All of the oils and vinegars are made and hand-bottled in Spanaway, not far from Tacoma. All of the oils are on a table for sampling along with pieces of bread for dipping.

Stackhouse Brothers Orchards

Pike Place Market
1531 Western Ave.
(800) 382-7654

Sample nuts including flavored almonds, natural almonds, and a small selection of dried fruits.

Stewart's Meat Market

Pike Place Market
85 Pike Place
(360) 458-2091
www.stewartsmeatmarket.com

Don't let its location in the day stalls fool you, Stewart's is an institution at the market and is known for its jerky and pepperoni samples.

Theo Chocolate
3400 Phinney Ave. N
(206) 632-5100
www.theochocolate.com

The country's first organic chocolate factory gives $6 tours every day complete with plenty of samples, but you don't have to shell out the cash to try such treats as the Bread and Chocolate Dark Chocolate or the Coconut Curry Milk Chocolate bars. Instead, you can hit the lobby where there are usually a few samples of several of Theo's treats.

Trader Joe's
112 West Galer St.; (206) 378-5536
4555 Roosevelt Way NE; (206) 547-6299
Consult the website for additional locations.
www.traderjoes.com

Okay, I know it's wrong, but the samples here are just so good there are times when I try to change the way I look by removing my glasses or taking off my jacket just so I can get seconds. There are only one or two food samples offered at a time, but they're always good. And you can wash them down with the free coffee.

Whole Foods Market
Interbay, 2001 W 15th Ave., Seattle; (206) 325-5440
Roosevelt, Roosevelt Square, Seattle, 1026 NE 64th St.; (206) 985-1500
Westlake, 2210 Westlake Ave., Seattle; (206) 621-9700
Bellevue, 888 116th Ave. NE, Bellevue; (425) 462-1400
Redmond, 17991 NE Redmond Way, Redmond; (425) 881-2600
West Seattle (slated to open in 2015)
www.wholefoodsmarket.com

There's a reason it's nicknamed "Whole Paycheck." The produce is beautiful, but pricey. The organic items are exquisite, but expensive. And don't even get me started on the baked goods. Still, all locations offer a variety of samples including cheese, produce, and tofu-based products. Each offers occasional theme-based freebies as well. Interbay offers a variety of famil-iarization tours of departments with free tastes. Check each store's calendar for more free food opportunities.

Woodring Orchards
Pike Place Market
1529 Pike Place
(206) 340-2705
www.woodringnorthwest.com

Fame hasn't gone to Woodring owner Dale Nelson's head. Not only were he and his Parker Pickles featured on an episode of *Top Chef*, Season 10, but those tasty treats were responsible for one chef being sent packing. If they happen to be in season when you stop by, you can sample them and see what the fuss was about. If not, you'll just have to be content trying any of the 40 fruit spreads that happen to be open for tasting including pepper jellies, apple butters, chutneys, and dessert toppings. There's even cider—in season, of course. The only thing you probably won't see is Nelson himself. He's too busy thinking up new flavors of jams and jellies to tantalize your tastebuds in person.

NOT **FREE,** BUT **PRETTY** DOGGONE CHEAP

Alhadeff Grill
Culinary Arts Building
South Seattle Community College
6000 16th Ave. SW
(206) 934-5817
www.southseattle.edu/alhadeff-grill

The Catch: It's only open from 11 a.m. to 12:50 p.m. when school is in session.

The students at South Seattle Community College's culinary arts program staff and run this inexpensive upscale restaurant that offers gourmet food at casual dining prices, including a prix fixe menu with starter, entree, dessert, and drink for $13.95. There are also special three-course connoisseur lunches with wine and the occasional high tea several times each quarter.

Bakeman's Restaurant
122 Cherry St.
(206) 622-3375

Bakeman's decor may be interesting, but most people don't come to this subterranean restaurant for atmosphere. The lunch crowd lines up around the block for the inexpensive sandwiches served with a side of good-natured abuse from a counterman who keeps things moving along whenever a diner's indecision threatens to slow the pace. There are plenty of combinations to choose from, starting at $3.75. Comparisons to the Soup Nazi on the TV show *Seinfeld* are only natural, but not quite accurate. He's more like a sandwich martinet.

Café Alki
Culinary Arts Building
South Seattle Community College
6000 16th Ave. SW
(206) 934-7952
www.southseattle.edu/cafealki

The Catch: It's only open from 11 a.m. to 12:50 p.m. Monday through Friday when school is in session.

Second verse, same as the first (the Alhadeff Grill, above). Culinary arts students run this one, too. The only difference is it's an inexpensive casual eatery where you get your choice of portion sizes for a song. A half portion of rhubarb salmon with beurre blanc, rhubarb pickle, rice, and seasonal vegetable was just $3.25, a full portion $5.50. The cafe also offers a monthly international-themed buffet at a reasonable price. Too bad the hours are so short.

Canton Wonton Noodle House
608 S. Weller St.
(206) 682-5080

You've got to love it when a restaurant offers most of its dishes in small or large and the price for the large is between $5 and $7. This popular International District spot sells soups, noodle dishes, wonton, and congee . . . all for a song.

Gorditos
www.gorditosmexicanfood.com
213 N. 85th St., Seattle; (206) 706-9352
1909 Hewitt Ave., Everett; (425) 252-4641

Gorditos' menu may seem to violate my goal of keeping listings close to $5, but not when you average it out. Considering that most of the burritos are less than $10 and big enough to feed two people, the price is right. And even when the line is out the door, the service is fast and the food is excellent.

Pho Than Brothers
1299 156th Ave. NE, #133, Bellevue; (425) 818-4905
22618 Hwy. 99, #101, Edmonds; (425) 744-0212
7714 Aurora Ave. N; (206) 527-5973
2309 N. 45th St., (206) 632-7378
Consult the website for more locations.
www.thanbrothers.com

To paraphrase Keye Luke in *Gremlins,* whatever you do, don't order the large. Not before midnight, not after. Like Luke, I know you won't listen, but don't say I didn't warn you. The small pho is so big, you might consider skipping the medium as well. This ever-expanding chain of Vietnamese soup restaurants has it down to a science. They seat you, give you a menu and a cream puff—you've got to love a place that serves dessert first—take your order in less than five minutes, and have your soup and all its accoutrements at your table before you know it. Sure, it's high volume, but it's good, it's filling enough to keep you going the whole day, and a "small" bowl of soup is about $5.

Festivals of Fixed Prices

There are times when even a cheap bastard gets a hankering for the finer things in life. As the saying goes, "Man cannot live on bread alone." (And it's a good thing, too, because it's awful hard to make a sandwich if you're not allowed to put something between the slices.) Fortunately, there are a couple of times a year when it's possible to go to some of the city's top high-end restaurants without paying traditional high-end prices. Although they may have started as a way for eateries to fill seats during traditional slow periods, they've become so popular that they've come to be seen as a way to try out new restaurants for not a lot of money, and space at some places runs out long before the events begin.

   In this case, not a lot of money is a relative term. All of the restaurants involved in a given promotion offer three-course prix fixe dinners for around $30 or so. While that may not be a lot of money to folks who dine out at Tom Douglas restaurants every week, it's about $20 more than most cheap bastards consider to fall under the definition of "not a lot of money." Fortunately, many of the restaurants involved in the promotions offer lunches for half the cost of dinner, give or take.

Saigon Deli
1237 S. Jackson
(206) 322-3700

Whenever I go to Saigon Deli, I feel like I'm cheating on my first love, Seattle Deli, just a little north and across the street, except when I order a sandwich that isn't on the other deli's menu. Like the egg bahn mi. And they also take credit cards, which Seattle doesn't. I know that the *New York Times Magazine* says this place is on the list of the country's top 13 bahn mi stands, but I'm just happy I can get a big sandwich for a small price, usually around $2.50.

Dine Around Seattle (dinearoundseattle.org) typically occurs Sunday through Thursday in March and features a number of popular restaurants throughout Seattle as well as some on the eastside. In 2013, the three-course prix fixe dinners included a starter, entree, and dessert for $30 and three-course lunches for $15.

As strange as it sounds, **Seattle Restaurant Week** (seattletimes.com/seattlerestaurantweek) not only lasts two weeks but also happens twice a year. So it should probably be called Seattle Restaurant Weeks. The event usually involves more than 100 of the city's restaurants and runs Sunday through Thursday over two weeks in April and October. In April 2013, three-course dinners were $28 and lunches were $15.

Tacoma Restaurant Week (www.facebook.com/TacomaRestaurantWeek) is also held in October, but the event is smaller and the three-course menus are less expensive. Like Seattle's event, it's Sunday through Thursday over two weeks in October. Unlike Seattle, there are only 30 restaurants involved.

Not far away, Vancouver, British Columbia, holds a similar event in January called **Dine Out Vancouver** (www.dineoutvancouver.com). In 2013, it featured prix fixe meals at $18, $28, and $38 Canadian per person.

Seattle Deli
225 12th Ave. S, Seattle; (206) 328-0106
22618 Hwy. 99, Edmonds; (425) 776-1788

The International District is filled with inexpensive places to grab a bite, but this could be one of the cheapest. The specialty is bahn mi, a Vietnamese sandwich on a baguette with pickled veggies, mayo, maybe some cilantro, and thinly sliced meat. On the streets of Saigon, it's a treat filled with mystery meat. Here, you'll know what you're getting and at around $2.50, you can be sure it's a really great bargain. The takeout-only restaurant also has a location in Edmonds.

Szechuan Noodle Bowl
420 8th Ave. S
(206) 623-4198

From all accounts, it isn't exactly big on atmosphere or high on decor, but it's great for all things noodle, including wontons and dumplings at prices ranging from $3 to $7.

WINE, BEER & DISTILLERY TASTINGS: CHEAP DRUNK

"I made wine out of raisins so I wouldn't have to wait for it to age."
—Steven Wright

The big news on the free beverage front has been the explosion of micro-distilleries throughout the state. No, we don't mean there have been a bunch of stills exploding in Washington. But the passage of a law creating a craft distillery license has led many unlikely folk to get into the business. In the Seattle area alone, the cottage industry has attracted two doughnut makers, a former U-pick farmer, and a Boeing aerospace engineer to craft spirits ranging from gin, whiskey, and the Japanese spirit Shochu to brandies, liqueurs, and chili-infused vodka. Even better, many of them have opened tasting rooms, which is great news because state law prohibits distilleries from charging for tastes. All of which means that there are now more options for people to get free samples of adult beverages than ever before.

I'll drink to that. Heck, at this point, I'll drink to just about anything.

All Things Wine
4605 NE 4th St.
Renton
(425) 254-8400
www.allthingswineonline.com

Originally the result of a hobby grown out of control, this shop has been so successful that the owner finally quit his day job. That's the good news. The bad news? Now that his mother is no longer helping out, she's taken the store's other employee with her. Customers really miss that toy poodle. The store specializes in Northwest, boutique-style wines and Washington wines you won't find anywhere else. Tastings are available Wednesday and Friday from 5 to 7:30 p.m., and Saturday from noon to 7 p.m.

Arista Wine Cellars
320 5th Ave. S
Edmonds
(425) 771-7009
www.aristawines.com

This wine shop in a northern suburb with a small-town feel offers tastings from 1 to 4:30 p.m. on Saturday and also from 5 to 8 p.m. on the third Thursday of the month in conjunction with the city's Third Thursday Art-walk. Check the store's website for the theme of upcoming tastings. Tastings are free and the shop usually pours four to six wines each time. The staff prides itself on being knowledgeable, but not snobbish.

Bainbridge Organic Distillers

9727 Coppertop Loop NE, Ste. 101
Bainbridge Island
(206) 842-3184
www.bainbridgedistillers.com

If these folks have their way, they could be part of a new tourist attraction on the island. A brewery has opened next door, a winery was set to open soon, and the owners were trying to find a way to provide some sort of transportation from the Bainbridge Island Ferry Dock for thirsty travelers. So, you may want to check before you go to all the trouble of taking your car on the ferry. Bainbridge says it's the only organic distiller in Washington state. It does tastings of its gin from noon to 5 p.m. Monday through Saturday. Another bit of trivia: It makes its gin with Douglas fir needles.

Champion Wine Cellars

108 Denny Way
(206) 284-8306
www.championwinecellars.com

There are so many wines in this little shop that there's hardly any place to walk, but there's still plenty of room to house the owner's expertise. Not too surprisingly, his events aren't designed for big crowds. Instead, the drop-in tastings (Saturday from 11 a.m. to 5 p.m.) are informal with Emile Ninaud explaining the wines as he pours.

City Cellars Fine Wines

1710 N. 45th St.
(206) 632-7238
www.citycellar.com

The Catch: Tastings cost $3 for three wines, but there's no charge if you buy any bottle during the tasting.

This neighborhood wine shop is known for two things: its focus on European wines and its selection of high-value, low-priced wines. Seventy percent of the themed tastings are European-based with the rest focusing on Northwest wines or comparing similar wines from different places. Although most of its wines are under $40, the wall of value near the door features 100 wines for $10 or less. Tastings are offered Friday from 5 to 7 p.m.

Corky Cellars
22511 Marine View Dr.
Des Moines
(206) 824-9462
www.corkycellars.com

Instead of opting for a theme-based tasting, Corky's goes for the unexpected during its Friday night tastings (4 to 6:30 p.m.), opting to introduce tasters to varieties that they've likely never heard of and would otherwise never try, like the casseta wines made from a grape that's only grown on 40 hectares in Italy, or selections from Uruguay. Saturday tastings (11 a.m. to 6 p.m.) focus on a single Northwest winery. The store also happens to be located near a meat shop and a flower shop, so it's the ideal place to shop for a guy who's planning a romantic evening or one who's trying to get out of the doghouse.

DeLaurenti Specialty Food and Wine
1435 1st Ave.
(206) 622-0141
www.delaurenti.com

The Catch: Tasting is $2 per person.

Italian wines may be the specialty at this Italian market on the edge of the Pike Place Market, but it sells wines from all over. DeLaurenti samples three to five wines each week, pairs them with cheese, and usually has a producer or a representative from a winery on hand to answer questions. Tastings are Saturday from 2 to 4 p.m. The store has a deep portfolio of Northwest wines, which sure beats binders full of women.

Esquin Wine & Spirits
2700 Fourth Ave. S
(206) 682-7374
www.esquin.com
Thursday 5 to 6:30 p.m., Saturday 2 to 5 p.m.

The store may have added spirits since the liquor laws changed, but still boasts the same helpful, knowledgeable staff willing to help even the least alcohol literate among us. The CB isn't saying he fits that description, mind you, but they helped him find a good replacement wine when he couldn't find his favorite bottle of Mogen David. We're just sayin'. Regular tastings are on Thursday from 5 to 6:30 p.m. and Saturday from 2 to 5 p.m. The first weekend of every month, the store does a sampling with wines featured in its regular mailer.

Fremont Mischief
132 N. Canal St.
(206) 547-0838
fremontmischief.com

It's hard to think up a more appropriate name for a distillery in the heart of the formerly Bohemian neighborhood that was once home to the artists and rabble rousers who deemed the area the Center of the Universe and who introduced Seattle to an annual Solstice Parade complete with naked bikers. The distiller samples vodka and whiskey Wednesday through Saturday from 11 a.m. to 6 p.m. and Sunday from 11 a.m. to 4 p.m.

Fremont Wine
3601 Fremont Ave. N
(206) 632-1110
www.fremontwine.net

The catch: Friday and Saturday tastings are $3 and Sunday tastings are free.

Don't you hate it when your favorite wine shop is offering a tasting of a wine you've been curious about, but it's when you can't make it? That rarely happens at Fremont Wine because the store only does tastings on weekends and it pours the same wines all three days (Friday and Saturday noon to 7 p.m., Sunday noon to 4 p.m.). All tastings are free. One last bit of good news for cheap bastards: Although the store focuses on small production wines, all of the wines in stock are under $25. There's even a special value section of wines bought out at closeout pricing ranging from $4 to $10. When they're gone, they're gone.

McCarthy & Schiering, Wine Merchants

Queen Anne
2401B Queen Anne Ave. N
(206) 282-8500

Ravenna
6500 Ravenna Ave. NE
(206) 524-9500
www.mccarthyandschiering.com

Although the two stores sample the same wines at the same time (Saturday 11 a.m. to 5 p.m.), their characters are decidedly different. The Ravenna shop is known for older specialty bottles, while Queen Anne's proximity to a meat shop and a number of restaurants prompts it to focus on rotating stocks of interesting selections for tonight's meal. The sampling includes one-ounce tastes of three to five wines along with maps or information about where the wines are made.

99 Bottles

35002 Pacific Hwy. S, Ste. A102
Federal Way
(253) 838-2558
www.99bottles.net

Sure, you have to pay $1 for the Wednesday afternoon beer tasting, but the good news is that it's an open-house tasting. So you can wander in any time between 4 and 7:45 p.m. and try two staff faves or new beers from the store's collection. You might even be able to take one down and pass it around—99 bottles indeed.

Northwest Wine Academy

South Seattle Community College
6000 16th Ave. SW
(206) 764-7942
nwwineacademy.southseattle.edu

Things are always less expensive when students do them, even wine. Students in the program produce between 1,500 and 2,000 cases a year (which vary depending on what grapes eastern Washington producers donate to the program) and hold two free blowout tastings each year coinciding with their release. The event is open to the public and even children can attend. The fall tasting is the weekend before Thanksgiving and the spring tasting is the first weekend in June. Can't wait that long? There's a tasting every Thursday and Friday from 1 to 4 p.m. that features one or two student wines and some wines produced by alumni. The program has also relocated to a building that's at the back of the north building, making it easier to find, bigger, and able to host more events. Personally, the CB will miss going to events in the old Wine and Welding Building.

Oola Distillery
1314 E. Union St.
(206) 709-7909
ooladistillery.com

What is it about doughnuts that prompts people in the business to want to make spirits? The former general manager of Mighty-O Donuts heads up this distillery, and the founder of another gourmet doughnut company started his own distillery and bar as well. Oola makes a vodka, a gin, a bourbon whiskey, and three infused vodkas—citrus, rosemary, and chili pepper–flavored—and all are available for tasting during a tour on Saturday at 3 p.m. by appointment. The appointment must be made at least 24 hours in advance. Be prepared to choose; you can only sample four of the beverages during your visit.

Pete's Wines Eastside
134 105th Ave. NE, Bellevue
(425) 454-1100

20617 Bothell-Everett Hwy., Stes. B and C, Bothell
(425) 949-5660
www.peteswineshop.com

And then there were two. The eastside sister store to an Eastlake neighborhood grocery known for its wine selection proved so successful that the company opened another in Bothell. The sister stores don't sell groceries, but they do have wine tastings (Saturday 3 to 6 p.m.). The Bellevue store can only serve wine in plastic cups. It also does occasional beer tastings on Saturday. Check website for details.

Pike and Western Wine Shop
Pike Place Market
1934 Pike Place
(206) 441-1307
www.pikeandwestern.com

When you're a wine shop smack dab in the middle of the Pike Place Market, you can draw an interesting crowd for a wine tasting. Pike and Western's weekly tastings (Friday 3 to 6 p.m.) attract folks who live in the neighborhood—yes, believe it or not, this is a neighborhood—and the tourist trade. So it's no surprise the focus is on inexpensive wines that are also good values.

Portalis Wine Shop and Wine Bar
5205 Ballard Ave. NW
(206) 783-2007
www.portaliswines.com

Portalis does two wine tastings on weekends because it sees two markedly different crowds. On Saturday from 3 to 5 p.m., they focus on buyers who see the shop as a destination and sample two more-expensive wines featuring the same winemaker, region, or grape. Sunday (11 a.m. to 4 p.m.) brings different shoppers because it's smack dab in the heart of the action that is the Ballard Farmers' Market, when people come from all over to buy local produce and crafts. So the store pours four reasonably priced wines centered on a theme, usually a regional winemaker. Then, many stay on at the informal 50-seat bar/restaurant and order a bite to eat. Portalis also occasionally offers a pricier presentation when winemakers from outside the US visit. The backroom tastings feature up to six higher-end wines. The events are publicized first to members of Portalis Frequent Wine Buyers Club, who usually snap up the tickets as soon as they are notified. If there's any space left, the tasting is publicized on the store's website. RSVP required. The special tastings are $8 to $10 for non-members and free for members.

Project V Distillers and Sausage Company
19495 144th Ave. NE, Ste. A130
Woodinville
(425) 398-1738
projectvdistillery.com

Sausage and vodka may sound like an odd combination, but when you think about it, it makes perfect sense. Project V gives the spent grain to Bucking Boar Farms, which feeds it to their pigs, which are turned into sausage. Project V does free tastings of its vodka from noon to 5 p.m. on weekends. Unfortunately, it can't do tastings of its sausage because it doesn't have cooking facilities. The distillery can sell it frozen, though.

The Shop Agora
346 15th Ave.
(206) 322-1103
www.theshopagora.com

Agora's tastings still have the informal air from its old days on Phinney Ridge, just in a new location. It opened a store on Capitol Hill and converted its old store into a wholesale warehouse. Its new digs are three times the size and include a wine bar where it offers some food and 30 wines by the glass. In addition to its Saturday tastings (2 to 6 p.m.), Agora also has tastings every other Thursday. One thing hasn't changed. It still has the largest Greek wine selection in the city.

Sidetrack Distillery
27010 78th Ave S
Kent
(206) 963-5079
www.sidetrackdistillery.com

When the state changed its liquor laws, the owners of a U-pick place in the Kent Valley went from being farmers to distillers of blueberries, strawberries, and raspberries. You can taste the fruit of their labors—fruit liqueurs, brandies, and the green walnut liqueur, nocino—on Saturday from 11 a.m. to 5 p.m. or by appointment. The distillery also does free tours on Saturday or by appointment, but they prefer an appointment for a tour even on Saturday.

Soft Tail Spirits
14356 Woodinville Redmond Rd.
Woodinville

12280 NE Woodinville Dr Ste C
Woodinville
(425) 770-1154
softtailspirits.com

Soft Tail may have two tasting rooms, but it prefers that people opt for the one on Woodinville Redmond Road. It makes five different grappas and a vodka from Washington state apples. The owner is quick to point out that it is not an apple-flavored vodka. Instead, the apple replaces the potato as the key ingredient. The distillery does free tastings on weekends. It also gives free hourly tours from 12 to 4 on Saturday and Sunday, but reservations are required.

Sound Spirits
1630 15th Ave. W
(206) 651-5166
drinksoundspirits.com

As it turns out, Sound Spirits was the first distillery to open in Seattle after Prohibition. It does tours and tastings of its gin and vodka by appointment and usually doesn't do either on Monday or Thursday.

Sun Liquor Distillery
512 E. Pike St.
(206) 720-1600
sunliquor.com

Sun Liquor is more of a bar than a tasting room, but if you happen to stop by during open hours and have your ID handy, they will give you a free taste of its Hedge Trimmer Gin—but they'd also prefer you buy something. Here's some cocktail party trivia to impress your friends: Sun Liquor founder Michael Klebeck also co-founded Top Pot Donuts with his brother Mark.

Twelfth & Olive Wine Company
1125 East Olive St.
(206) 329-2399
www.12thandolive.com

Considering that all of the staffers have degrees in wine-related fields, it's a bit of an understatement to say that the people who run the place are knowledgeable. They aren't snobs, though. Tastings (Friday 5 to 8 p.m., Saturday and Sunday 1 to 5 p.m.) draw a neighborhood crowd, have a casual feel, and are built around some sort of theme.

Vino Verite

208 Boylston Ave. E
(206) 324-0324
www.vinoverite.com

This shop is like the house on your block that always seems to have a big potluck going on with friends coming and going all the time. The only difference is that this living room offers Thursday night tastings from 5 to 8 p.m. of four or five wines and has an importer or distributor on hand to answer questions. Oh, and the fact that it sells good, inexpensive wine rather than just pouring it. The owner loves to find bargains for his customers.

West Seattle Cellars

6026 California Ave. SW
(206) 937-2868
www.wscellars.com

If *Cheers* had been set in a wine shop, it could have been filmed here. It's a friendly place where the owners seem to know everyone's name. It gets a little crowded during tastings as people chat with friends and compare notes. The regular tasting is on Thursday from 5:30 to 8 p.m. (or until 9 p.m. during Art Walk on the second Thursday of the month). One Saturday a month from 3 to 5 p.m., the store also hosts a tasting featuring a Washington winemaker.

Wine World

400 NE 45th St.
(206) 402-6086
www.wineworldspirits.com

If Wine World's fully packed calendar is any indication, the company believes that wine should be not only approachable but also a heck of a lot of fun. Recent events have included Yoga and Wine Tasting, a Five-Alarm Chili Cookoff, a *Game of Thrones* tasting, and a Super Bowl Junk Food Pairing. The superstore has tastings almost every day of the week from 6 to 8 p.m. Monday and Tuesday feature tastes of the wine of the day, with a try of beer or cider on Wednesday. Thursday focuses on offerings from local wineries, and Friday centers on a featured winery. Weekend events take place at the tasting bar and go from 2 to 5 p.m. and 5 to 7 p.m. Tastings are free except for Friday tastings, which often involve two wineries. The fee is waived for members of the store's Rewards Club, and employees often sign people up for the club at the time of the tasting. It's free and gets you 10 percent off purchases of six or more bottles of wine or beer. Wine World also has a free formal dog food tasting once a quarter for our furry friends and also puts out several bowls of gourmet kibble in front of the store for Spot and Fido to try on Saturday and Sunday.

Woodinville Whiskey Company
16110 Woodinville Redmond Rd. NE, Ste. 3
Woodinville
(425) 486-1199
www.woodinvillewhiskeyco.com

They make whiskey and they're in Woodinville. What more could be said? The distillery offers free tours and tastings of its whiskey from noon to 5 p.m. Wednesday through Sunday.

WOODINVILLE **WINERIES**

Tastings at wine shops aren't the only option for people who enjoy trying Northwest wines. Less than an hour away from downtown Seattle all the way out in Woodinville, there are more than 50 wineries, some with tasting rooms, others with regular tastings. Almost all charge for the chance to sample some of their most popular bottles. The catch is you can get the fee waived, but only if you end up buying something. To be free or not to be free, that is the question.

Here's a partial list of the wineries that offer such tastings:

- Baer Winery, 19501 144th Ave. NE, Ste. #F-100; (425) 483-7060; www.baerwinery.com. Open for tastings Saturday and Sunday from 1 to 5 p.m. Tasting fee of $5 is refundable with purchase.
- J. Bookwalter Tasting Studio, 14810 NE 145th St., Building B; (425) 488-1983; www.bookwalterwines.com. Friday and Saturday 11 a.m. to 8 p.m., Sunday through Thursday noon to 6 p.m. Tasting fee of $10 is refundable with purchase.
- Brian Carter Cellars, 14419 Woodinville Redmond Rd. NE; (425) 806-

9463; www.briancartercellars.com. Open noon to 5 p.m. daily. Tasting fee of $10 plus tax waived with purchase.

- Columbia Winery, 4030 NE 145th St.; (425) 482-7490; www.columbia winery.com. Open daily from 11 a.m. to 6 p.m, with a happy hour from 4 to 7 p.m. on Friday that has half-price flatbread pizzas and half-price wine by the glass. The $10 to $15 tasting fee is not refundable with purchase, but is refunded if you join the Wine Club. There's no cost to join the club, and you can get complimentary tastings for up to four people per visit no matter how many times you go; you will have to buy three bottles of wine each quarter. There will be a 20 percent discount on the retail price, but that price still ends up being around $288.

- Efeste Wine, 19730 144th Ave. NE; (425) 398-7200; www.efeste .com. Open Friday to Sunday noon to 5 p.m. Tasting fee of $10 waived with purchase.

- Facelli Winery, 16120 Woodinville Redmond Rd. NE, Ste. 1; (425) 488-1020; www.facelliwinery.com. Tastings on Saturday and Sunday from noon to 4 p.m. The $5 charge allows visitors to sample 4 of the winery's 18 wines. The tasting fee is applied to purchase.

- Guardian Cellars, 19501 144th Ave. NE, #E600; (206) 661-6733; www.guardiancellars.com. Tastings on Saturday and Sunday from 12:30 to 5 p.m. Tasting fee of $10 applied to wine purchase.

- Hollywood Hill Vineyards, 14350 160th Place NE; (425) 405-5779; www.hollywoodhillvineyards.com. Tastings on Saturday from noon to 5 p.m. Tasting fee of $10 is refundable.

- JM Cellars, 14404 137th Place NE; (425) 485-6508; www.jmcellars .com. Tastings Friday through Sunday from 11 a.m. to 4 p.m. Tasting fee of $10 is refunded with purchase of $30 or more.

- Matthews Estate, 16116 140th Place NE; (425) 487-9810; www.matthews estate.com. There's a tasting room at the winery as well as a smaller tasting room with a smaller selection at 19495 144th Ave. NE, Ste. A120. The winery tasting room is open daily from noon to 6 p.m., and the $10 fee is refundable with a wine purchase. The off-site room is open Saturday and Sunday from 12 to 5 p.m. Tastings are $10, refundable with purchase. Warehouse in the tasting district is open only from noon to 6 p.m. Saturday and Sunday; regular hours at the other location are noon to 6 p.m. daily.

- Northwest Totem Cellars, 15810 NE 136th Place, Redmond; (425) 877-7111; www.nwtotemcellars.com. Open one day a month (call or check website for hours). The tastings are $5, refundable with purchase.
- Page Cellars, 19495 144th Ave. NE, Ste. B235; (253) 232-9463; www .pagecellars.com. Open Saturday from noon to 4 p.m., Sunday 1 to 5 p.m. The $5 tasting fee is waived with purchase of any wine.
- Patterson Cellars/Washington Wine Co., Hollywood Hill Tasting Room, 14505 148th Ave. NE, Thursday through Monday, noon to 5 p.m.; Woodinville Winery and Tasting Room, 19501 144th Ave. NE, Ste. D-600, Saturday and Sunday, noon to 5 p.m.; (425) 483-8600; www.pattersoncellars.com. The $5 tasting fee is waived with wine purchase.
- Red Sky Winery, 19495 144th Ave. NE, Ste. B210; (425) 481-9864; www.redskywinery.com. Open Saturday noon to 5 p.m.; $5 tasting fee applied to purchase.
- Sparkman Cellars, Hollywood Hills Wine District Tasting Room, 14473 Woodinville Redmond Rd. NE, Thursday through Monday, 1 to 6 p.m.; Warehouse District Winery and Tasting Room, 19501 144th Ave. NE, Ste. E-400, Saturday and Sunday from 1 to 5 p.m.; (425) 398-1045; www.sparkmancellars.com. There's a $10 charge for five one-ounce tastings, but the fee is waived with any purchase.
- Stevens Winery, 18520 142nd Ave. NE; (425) 424-9463; www.ste-venswinery.com. Tastings on Saturday from noon to 4:30 p.m. The $10 fee is refunded with purchase.
- Woodhouse Family Cellars, 15500 Woodinville Redmond Rd. NE, Ste. C600; (425) 527-0608; www.woodhousewineestates.com. The winery pours four wines during daily tastings, noon to 5 p.m. The $5 fee is refunded with purchase.
- Woodinville Wine Cellars, 17721 132nd Ave. NE; (425) 481-8860; www.woodinvillewine.com. The tasting room is open 12 to 5 p.m. Saturday, March through December, Friday by appointment. Tasting fee is $5, refunded with purchase.

HAIR AND SPA SERVICES:
FREESTYLE

"If truth is beauty, how come no one has their hair done in a library?"
—Lily Tomlin

I admit it. I don't know hair because there's baldness on both sides of my family. Yes, that's right, even my mother was bald. Okay, I may be exaggerating there, but my maternal grandfather was as bald as a cue ball and my father had a rapidly receding hairline, so I never expected to have hair going into my 50s. Consequently, I've always been a Great Clips kind of guy. Now, I'm slapping myself for not realizing Seattle had so many places where I could get a great cut and save money. So what if I might not get to choose the style or that it could take a little longer? Most stylists who cut my hair do what they want anyway. Even if you're more particular, the area has options for people who want to save money on salon services. And if you really want to splurge, you could take the money you saved and spend it on an inexpensive massage or even spa services at clinics run by some local massage schools.

HAIR **SALONS**

Some of the best-known salons in town have training programs where you can go to get cuts and a variety of services from students. These aren't your typical trainees, though. When most people think trainee, they think of the young kid running the register at a burger place or a department store who takes three times as long to ring up your purchase. The trainees in these salons are fully licensed beauticians who know their stuff, but want to take their skills to the next level, so you won't risk falling asleep and waking up with a mullet or a crew cut. There are occasional drawbacks, though. If you agree to be a hair model, for example, you'll save money, but you might not have a say in the style you get and the cut may take a little longer. The training programs are still a good deal even if you aren't a model. You'll pay for the services you get, but it will be far less than the salon's regular prices. Even more importantly, when they're finished working their magic, they won't ask, "Would you like fries with that?"

Craigslist
seattle.craigslist.org/bts/

Is there any item or service you can't get through Craigslist? If the beauty section is any indication, apparently not. There always seem to be numerous students looking for hair models for free cuts at a variety of salons including Seven, The Loft, and Gary Manuel Aveda Institute. The student listings are usually quite specific about the type of model and type of hair they need to work with, and the hairstyle they need to practice. You have to act fast, though, because it's not unusual to see a posting requesting less than a day's notice. As with any Craigslist ad, the usual caveats apply. Be safe. Don't go if it doesn't feel right. And make sure everything's "legit."

Crux Academy at Habitude Fremont
513 N. 36th St.
(206) 633-1339
www.habitude.com

A newly minted graduate with a cosmetology license may be promising, but the folks at Habitude believe new stylists need a bit more polish and training before they're ready for the salon floor. That's why it takes new fresh-out-of-school hires and puts them through eight months of advanced training at Crux Academy. Cruxers perform many of the same services as Habitude's more senior stylists, but they do it for less. While a haircut at Habitude's regular salon starts at $35, Crux charges $20. Coloring is $60 at Habitude, $40 at Crux. Academy students also need live models to practice on as they learn new styles. Although they find most of their models via word-of-mouth, the company is open to considering new participants. The good news about being a Crux hair model is that your cut is free. The flip side is that you won't have a say in the cut you get and it will likely take longer than a typical cut.

Gene Juarez Academy
6007 244th St. SW
Mountlake Terrace
(206) 365-6900

2222 S. 314th St.
Federal Way
(253) 839-4338
www.genejuarezacademy.com

Gene Juarez may have closed its Advanced Training Academy, but its regular training academies live on with haircuts starting at $13.95 and scalp massage with conditioner for $12.95. The first appointment is at 8:15 a.m. Monday through Saturday and both academies accept walk-ins, but it's best to have an appointment on Fridays and Saturdays. The school offers discounts for students, seniors over 62, and members of the military. It's 20 percent off Monday through Thursday for all three groups.

Phase 3 by Gary Manuel Salon
2123A First Ave. (between Blanchard and Lenora Streets, next to Buffalo Deli)
(206) 728-9933

This small salon just a few doors down from Gary Manuel's main salon acts as a finishing school for the company. It allows interns to attain the proficiency Gary Manuel requires and more experienced employees to hone their skills. As a result, you can get a cut by a well-trained stylist for around $30 to $42 when a similar cut at GM's main salon would go for $50 to $170. Appointments are available, but the salon also takes walk-ins. Open Tuesday through Saturday 10 a.m. to 6 p.m.

Seven Academy
Westlake Center
400 Pine St.
(206) 903-1299
www.7salon.com/academy
Open by appointment only

The highly skilled and rewarding job of being a hair model isn't what it used to be. While supermodels get paid and occasionally get free clothes and hand models also get a decent amount of cash, hair models at Seven Academy have to pay for their cuts. Fortunately, they're not too expensive. Cuts are $15, color service is $20, and a combo is $35. We assume a combo is a mix of the two services and not a pizza with everything on it. To become eligible to be a Seven hair model (you must have more than seven hairs to do this), call the model hotline at (206) 903-1299 and an apprentice will get back to you. The cut takes longer, but it is cheaper. In case you were wondering, the most expensive service here is a color correction for $75.

BEAUTY & AESTHETICS SCHOOLS

Clover Park Technical College
4500 Steilacoom Blvd. SW
Lakewood
(253) 589-5800
www.cptc.edu

Driving to Tacoma to save on aesthetic treatments may seem like going to extremes, but then again, people travel across some states just to get mediocre deals at outlet malls. Given the programs that Clover Park offers, it's theoretically possible to get a day of beauty on the cheap. How cheap? A European facial is $28, facials in the cosmetology clinic start at $28, and salt scrubs are $32. Not only does the school have a student cosmetology clinic, a multi-vitamin power facial (which sounds like the cosmetic equivalent of a power wash) is $35, and eye treatments are $15. The aesthetics clinic also does mud wraps, salt scrubs, and body washes. The medical aesthetics clinic does chemical peels for $45 to $60, and a set of six microdermabrasion treatments for $280 (or $45 to $50 each). Clover Park also has student clinics for its barber and massage programs. Clover Park's facilities may not be as glamorous as a spa, but knowing how much money you're saving has a funny way of helping most folks to relax. Cosmetology appointments are available, but walk-ins are welcome.

PERSONAL CARE

Euro Institute of Skin Care
10904 SE Petrovitsky Rd.
Renton
(425) 255-8100, ext. 6
www.euroinstitute.com
By appointment only

Unlike most aesthetics programs involving students, the Euro Institute operates its spa six days a week all year long. Clients receive the same services they would at a spa only at much lower rates. Facials start at $48. Other treatments include microdermabrasion (starting at $70), waxing, salt scrubs, and peels.

Gary Manuel Aveda Institute
1514 10th Ave.
(206) 302-1044
www.gmaveda.com

Many people stumble on this salon without an appointment and get a cut without ever realizing that students are doing their hair. It provides all the services of its sister salon, Gary Manuel, but at much lower prices. Of course, what you save in money you may end up spending in time because the cuts can take longer. Cuts range from $16 to $22 and include a scalp massage, shampoo, and style.

Olympus Spa
8615 S. Tacoma Way
Lakewood
(253) 588-3355

3815 196th St. SW, Ste. 160
Lynnwood
(425) 697-3000
www.olympusspa.net

Women who go to Olympus know you don't have to spend much to have a spa day. In fact, $35 gets you a pass that allows you to spend as long as you want using the hydrotherapy pools, earth energy rooms, and sauna and steam rooms. Massages and other services are extra, but sometimes all you need is a place to get away and hide out from your spouse, the kids, the police, and anybody else who may be after you.

Seattle Vocational Institute
1500 Harvard Ave.
(206) 934-5477
sviweb.sccd.ctc.edu/p_cosmet.htm

SVI cosmetology students offer chemical services, haircuts, manicures, facials, and waxing Tuesday through Friday at deeply discounted rates. A facial is $15, waxing starts at $5, coloring is $30, and a simple shampoo and haircut is $9.50. In addition, a 90-minute facial costs $50. Walk-ins are encouraged for most services, but if you want a chemical-based treatment it's best to make an appointment to make sure a student with that area of expertise will be on hand. An hour-long facial costs $15. Walk-ins welcome. All services supervised by a licensed instructor.

MASSAGE **SCHOOLS**

Bellevue Massage School
15921 NE 8th St., Ste. C-106
Bellevue
(425) 641-3409
www.bellevuemassageschool.com

The availability of a massage at this student clinic varies depending on where the school is in the curriculum and how many people are in a given class. The best times to try are January through March and May through October. Students are observed as they give massages, but you'll never notice, and most of the assessment and instruction occurs after you leave. It's $33 for an hour massage ($28 for those over 55), but you'll need to allow 90 minutes for filling out paperwork and doing student feedback. At these prices, it's worth it. Call the school to set up an appointment.

Cortiva Institute
425 Pontius Ave. N, Ste. #100
(206) 204-3170
www.cortiva.com/locations/seattle/clinic

It's hard to go wrong with an hour massage for $35, but then again, the massages are being offered by students who need to gain experience. So, you're either paying to have a great experience or to be a guinea pig. Seniors can get an additional discount for weekday afternoon appointments. Allow an hour and 15 minutes for your visit so you'll have time for intake and a

post-massage assessment of the student. You can also book online at mtc
.cortiva.com.

Everest Student Clinic

2111 N. Northgate Way, Third Floor
(206) 526-7668
www.everest.edu

Talk about a bargain. Everest offers one-hour massages for $30, two-hour
massages for $60, and a selection of spa massages such as hot stone mas-
sages for $35. At that price, everybody can afford to get stone-d. Senior
massages are $25. There are also scrubs and wraps. To find out what spa
treatments are available, call the clinic.

Northwest Academy for the Healing Arts Health Center

2707 California Ave. SW, #201
(206) 932-5950
www.nw-academy.com

This school's clinic offers a standard massage that's a combination of a deep
tissue and Swedish massage. Appointments are usually available on Monday,
but only during certain times of the year. There are also occasional Fridays
and Saturdays as well. The best way to find out when appointments are
available is to go to the school's website. One-hour massages are $35.

Northwest School of Massage

13033 NE 70th Place, #4
Kirkland
(866) 713-1212
www.nwschoolofmassage.com

There's no receptionist here, so the school's students have to set up and
schedule their own appointments. All you need to do is call, leave a message,
and wait for a student to call you back, usually on the same day. Massages
cost $25 an hour, but you should budget an extra half-hour to fill out forms.

CHILDREN'S EVENTS
& ACTIVITIES:
FREE TO BE YOU AND ME

*"I take my children everywhere, but they
always find their way back home."*
—*Robert Orben*

Puget Sound abounds with stuff for the younger set. There are children's theater companies, children's museums, and even playgrounds that are enough to make many adults envious. And that doesn't even include the coffeehouses with play areas, gyms with child care, or the proliferation of baby-changing tables in men's bathrooms, which may be even more dangerous than nuclear proliferation. Now, if we only had enough preschools to go around.

DESTINATION **PLAYGROUNDS**

Crossroads Water Spray Play Area
Crossroads International Park
999 164th Ave. NE
Bellevue
(425) 452-4874

Although it's more watery playground than swimming area, you'll still hear kids shriek with delight as they play among a variety of animals that squirt, spout, or spit, but only in a good way. It's open year-round, but the water is turned on Memorial Day through Labor Day. For more information, call the community center at (425) 452-6914.

Gas Works Park
2101 N. Northlake Way
(206) 684-4075
www.seattle.gov/parks/park_detail.asp?id=293

This isn't your grandfather's playfield because . . . well . . . quite frankly, it used to be your grandfather's gas works, and no, I'm not talking about the restaurant where he used to eat beans. Instead, it's where coal was converted to gas until cheaper, imported natural gas made it too expensive to run. The land has since been converted into a park and the exhauster-compressor building has become a covered play area. There aren't a lot of traditional play structures on hand, but there are lots of cool machines to play on.

Gene Coulon Memorial Beach Park

1201 Lake Washington Blvd. N
Renton

Play structures, a waterslide, a beach, and free summer concerts are just a few of the things that keep this park and playground crowded throughout the summer months and it's a good thing. Otherwise, most people wouldn't be willing to make the trip down I-405 to get there.

Green Lake Park

7201 East Green Lake Dr. N
(206) 684-0780
www.seattle.gov/parks/park_detail.asp?id=307

This is a destination playground for everyone in the city, not just kids: powerwalkers who want to talk about their relationships, in-line skaters, bikers, joggers, and people who want to see and be seen. There are plenty of green areas for kids to run, a swimming pool, and activity rooms in the Greenlake Community Center as well as a playground that's always filled with children on the slides, swings, in the sandbox, and playing in the boat in the middle of the sandbox. During the summer, the wading pool here is one of the city's most popular spots for kids to cool off. Rather than waste time looking for a space in the small parking lot, it's best to look for street parking along Greenlake Drive.

The Junior League of Seattle Playground Magnuson Park

7400 Sand Point Way NE
(206) 684-4946
www.seattle.gov/parks/magnuson/

This playground is built on the site of a former naval air station's air control tower and features three climbing structures (including one for toddlers), a big sandbox, and a small track around the play area that's wide enough for kids to ride their bikes on. Another feature that makes it a favorite of small kids: its proximity to an off-leash dog park means that they get to see all types of dogs (on leashes) walking nearby on the way to a playground of their own.

Meridian Park
4649 Sunnyside Ave. N
(206) 684-4075
www.seattle.gov/parks/park_detail.asp?id=1104

Meridian is a destination playground that's hard to find. It's next to a major thoroughfare, but the rock wall and shrubbery surrounding it make it blend in with the scenery. Behind the walls, however, is the campus of a former Catholic school for wayward girls-turned-park that's a destination for kids and adults. The playground in what was once an orchard isn't huge, but the play structures are perfectly toddler-sized, including the monkey bars and wide slides surrounded by boulders. One of two sand areas in the park has a button kids can push to open a stream of water, creating a river on a wall next to the sand. When they tire of the play equipment, they can run along the open space, go through the children's garden, or have a picnic without ever realizing there's a busy road on the other side of the shrubs. Adults also like the park because it's home to Seattle Tilth, a non-profit organization that teaches people how to garden organically. Its classes aren't free, but it does hold a free harvest festival in September. You can also find the Wallingford Farmers Market here during the summer.

Powell Barnett Park
352 Martin Luther King Jr. Way
www.seattle.gov/parks/park_detail.asp?id=345

This is the thinking child's playground. Yes, there are slides and swings, but the play structures are more challenging than those found at typical playgrounds. The structures leading up to slides offer a variety of diversions for children to stop off and play along the way. There are no monkey bars in sight, but plenty of other climbing structures that allow kids to create their own adventures.

Saint Edward State Park
14445 Juanita Dr. NE
Kenmore
(425) 823-2992
www.parks.wa.gov/parks/?selectedpark=saint%20edward

This is the type of park that makes you wonder why they didn't have these kinds of playgrounds when you were a kid. Surely, it can't be because playground technology has advanced so much in the last 20 years. The play-ground is divided into two distinct areas. The Owl Forest is an enclosed play area where toddlers can run free along a boardwalk, playhouse (or fort), swing, or hop into a wooden airplane. The area for school children features a multi-level play structure with lots of nooks and crannies, slides for sliding, and multiple ways to get from here to there. The park itself can grow with you. Once kids feel they've outgrown playgrounds, there are plenty of hiking trails of varying lengths for the entire family to explore.

STORY TIMES

It used to be that the main time to read stories to kids was right before bed. And maybe right before nap. Possibly after school. And maybe on the toilet. But now, everybody's doing it all the time all day long. It's no wonder kids are confused. What with all this reading going on for no particular reason other than to keep them entertained, they might get to thinking they were the center of our world or something. And that would be—hold on, I'll be right back. I think I hear my kids calling.

Crossroads Mall
NE 8th Street and 156th Avenue NE
Bellevue
(425) 644-1111
www.crossroadsbellevue.com

Talk about story time central! This community shopping center has several story hours a day almost every day of the week. The options include family, Russian, Spanish, and Cantonese readings at the Crossroads branch of the King County Library and a story time at Barnes & Noble.

Frye Art Museum
Small Frye
704 Terry Ave.
(206) 622-9250
fryemuseum.org/program/small_frye/

What All the Noise Is About: Story Time

Libraries are supposed to be quiet places where one can go to do research, gather one's thoughts, write, read peacefully, and maybe even take a nice nap amid the hush. All those thoughts go out the door during story times, however, when the decibel level rises and the effectiveness of a well-timed "Shhhh!" is practically nil. If you're a parent with a child that needs to get your kid out of the house, it's the perfect time to go, but if you're just someone seeking solitude, you may want to delay your arrival or step out for coffee.

It's important to remember that reading times vary, so it makes the most sense to list the types of story times available at each branch, but not the specific times for each. The information was correct at press time, but it's best to call before you go.

Seattle Public Library System—www.spl.org

Ballard Library: Baby, toddler, and pajama story time
Beacon Hill: Baby, toddler, preschool, and family story time
Broadview: Baby, toddler, family
Capitol Hill: Preschool, toddler
Central Library: Baby, preschool, toddler, Spanish
Columbia City: Baby, preschool, toddler, Spanish
Delridge: Family, Vietnamese
Douglass-Truth: Baby, toddler, children, pajama
Greenlake: Baby, family
Greenwood: Baby, family, toddler, Spanish
High Point: Baby, family, toddler, Somali
International District: Mandarin Chinese
Lake City: Family, Spanish, Mandarin Chinese, pajama, ASL
Madrona: Children
Magnolia: Baby, toddler
Montlake: Children
New Holly: Family, Somali
Northeast: Preschool, toddler, pajamas, and puppets
Northgate: Family, pajama
Queen Anne: Family, pajama

Rainier Beach: Preschool, toddler
South Park: Spanish, bilingual preschool
Southwest: Baby, toddler, preschool
University: Baby, pajama
West Seattle: Family, toddler, preschool

King County Library System—www.kcls.org
If you need to go to a library and you're not inside Seattle city limits, then you're probably going to hit a library in the King County system.

Algona-Pacific: Toddler, preschool, family, Spanish
Auburn: Infant, toddler, preschool, Spanish
Bellevue: Mother Goose, young toddler, toddler, baby, preschool, family, Mandarin Chinese, Korean
Black Diamond: Family
Bothell: Preschool, toddler, infant, Chinese, Spanish, family, young toddler, Russian
Boulevard Park: Spanish, family
Burien Library: Preschool, infant, toddler, family, Spanish
Covington: Infant and young toddler, family, preschool, Spanish-English
Crossroads: Family, Russian, Spanish, Cantonese
Des Moines: Spanish, Raising Readers preschool, Raising Readers infant and young toddler, Raising Readers family
Issaquah: Preschool, Spanish, toddler, young toddler
Kent: Preschool, infant and toddler, family, Spanish
Kirkland: Toddler, preschool, young toddler, evening family, Spanish, French
Lake Forest Park: Toddler, preschool, family
Mercer Island: Infant, preschool, toddler, young toddler
Redmond: Baby, French, toddler, preschool, young toddler, Russian
Skyway: Toddler, preschool
Southcenter: Family
White Center: Family

Why don't more museums do programs like Small Frye? More importantly, why don't more museums have names that we can put into puns? Small Frye is a story time program that is held in the galleries of the museum from 11:15 to 11:45 a.m. on the first Friday of the month. The museum partners with the Seattle Public Library and Seattle's Children Theater for this interactive story time where actors create a parallel drama as the book is read to the crowd. During the event, the actors and young participants are confronted with a problem and the only way to resolve it is to go to the book. Along the way, kids learn new words and new sounds that help prepare them to read.

Half Price Books Lynnwood
Storybook Sundays
19500 Highway 99
(425) 776-8885
hpb.com/071.html

If the public library can have story hours for kids, why can't a discount book store? Half Price's Lynnwood store has Story Time Sundays on, you guessed it, Sunday at 3 p.m. Given kids' short little span of attention, the event lasts about half an hour at best.

Island Books
3014 78th Ave. SE
Mercer Island
206.232.6920
www.mercerislandbooks.com/evening-pj-story-time

It's not parents' night out, but Evening PJ Story Time might help lead to a nicer parents' night in. Held on the first Saturday of the month at 6:30 p.m., the event features storytellers from all over the region amusing pajamaed kids right before bedtime. Refreshments are served during the event. What are they thinking?

Mockingbird Books
7220 Woodlawn Ave. NE
(206) 518-5886
www.mockingbirdbooksgl.com

This children's bookstore has a story hour from 11 to 11:30 a.m. every day except Sunday. Because of its schedule, it doesn't set an age range on the readings and is open to whoever shows up, even if it means that the audience is made up of nursing moms. If your kids get a little antsy in the middle of a reading, they can always visit the train table, play with a puzzle, or spend time at the chalk table.

Pottery Barn Kids Book Club
University Village
4633 26th Ave. NE
(206) 527-5560
www.potterybarnkids.com/customer-service/store-events.html

Story hour or Pottery Barn gateway? You be the judge. Every Tuesday at 11 a.m., a staffer reads kids' books aloud for a half-hour. If you get there early enough, your child can pick one of the books, as long as it's short enough. Even if you're running late, they can still get a stampable passport. After getting five stamps, they (read: you) will get $10 off any purchase. Most Pottery Barn Kids also offer free decorating classes on some Saturdays, but times vary. Call your local store for details.

Santoro's Books
7405 Greenwood Ave. N
(206) 784-2113
www.santorosbooks.com

End your week with a 40-minute story time at a local independent bookseller. If you're late, don't stress. It's a little longer than the rest.

Third Place Books
Lake Forest Park Town Center
17171 Bothell Way NE
Lake Forest Park
(206) 366-3333
www.thirdplacebooks.com

Ravenna Third Place
6504 20th Ave. NE
Seattle
(206) 525-2347
www.ravennathirdplace.com

The big store does story time on Friday at 10 a.m., while its smaller sister in Ravenna does books for kids on Saturday at 11 a.m. with events that may include storytelling, reading from books, and music. Occasionally, they'll also have a children's author do a reading. The Ravenna reading is easy to find, but the Lake Forest Park gathering can be difficult to locate because it's tucked away in a small corner of a large (children's) section. Arrive early to find your way.

The Toy Place at Bellevue Art and Frame
13131 NE 20th St.
Bellevue
(800) 843-6348
www.thetoyplacetoys.com

This is one of those activities that should come with the warning, "Don't try this at home." Every Friday, the toy/art frame store hosts Paint Me a Story, where kids listen to a story while painting. It's geared for 2- to 6-year-olds and runs from 10 to 10:20 a.m. and again from 10:30 to 10:50 a.m. The event is free, but there's only space for 12 to 15 kids.

Tugboat Story Hour
Northwest Seaport
Historic Ships Wharf
860 Terry Ave. N
(206) 447-9800
www.nwseaport.org

Tugboat Story Hour has the coolest location for a reading: aboard the historic tugboat, *Arthur Foss*. In keeping with the theme, all of the stories are maritime-centric, focusing on its audience's favorite things. Namely, boats, sea-bound adventure, and people their own age. Second and fourth Thursday of the month at 11 a.m.

University Book Store
4326 University Way NE, Seattle; (206) 634-3400
990 102nd Ave. NE, Bellevue; (425) 462-4500
Mill Creek Town Center, 15311 Main St., Mill Creek; (425) 385-3530
Renton Landing, 800 N. 10th Place, Renton; (425) 988-2812
www.bookstore.washington.edu

It never hurts to introduce kids to this store early because they may end up buying books here if they attend the UW or one of its branches. All four stores have story hours. The main branch store in Seattle has readings at 11 a.m. on Tuesday and Saturday and the Bellevue and Renton Landing stores do their story times at 11 a.m. Thursday. The Mill Creek serves up its kids' event on Wednesday at 11 a.m. with a side of cookies or doughnuts. After all, there's nothing like sending kids out into the world all sugared up. There's also coloring before the event.

CHEAP, **BUT** NOT **FREE**

Toddler Tales and Trails
Seward Park
5902 Lake Washington Blvd. S
(206) 652-2444

As with story time at the Miller Library (see below), there's more to this story time than just reading. Once the reading is finished, participants head outside for a themed walk. As a rule, the walks are easy and often involve getting dirty, whether it be climbing trees or playing in the mud. Unlike the Miller Library, there's a small charge. While it's free for toddlers up to age 4, it costs $2 for kids 5 to 14 and $4 for adults. The readings are from 10 to 11 a.m. on the second and fourth Wednesday of the month and 11 a.m. every other Saturday.

ARTS, **CRAFTS** & **PERFORMANCE**

Bellevue Arts Museum
510 Bellevue Way NE
Bellevue
(425) 519-0770
www.bellevuearts.org

The Catch: $2 materials fee

Kids can get crafty every Saturday during a weekly event appropriately called Get Crafty Saturday, which runs from 1 to 3 p.m. Every two weeks, there's a new activity relating to a current exhibit. Recent events have included making pinhole cameras, piggy banks, and even bowls with air-dry clay. Participation costs $2 for materials or is free with a museum admission. Students can also visit free on the Student Wednesday, the second Wednesday of the month from 1 to 5 p.m.

Home Depot
11616 Aurora Ave. N
(206) 361-9600
www.homedepot.com
Consult the website for additional information.

Maybe the workshops offered on the first Saturday of every month will allow children to succeed where we've failed. I have no doubt that the classes that teach them how to build things like rain gauges and racecars will make them feel more comfortable around tools at an earlier age. What I want to know is will it help them learn the secret to finding where all the employees are hiding whenever you have a question? Classes go from 9 a.m. to noon, there are no materials fees, and kids get to keep what they build and they even get a child-sized orange apron, which should come in handy when they play hide-and-seek.

Lakeshore Learning Center
11027 NE 4th St.
Bellevue
(425) 462-8076
www.lakeshorelearning.com

Big, Watery Fun

No matter how old you are, it seems like you're never too old to enjoy watery fun. Think about it: Every child's love of water goes back to happy times in the tub and then to wading pools and family trips to the beach. And if you think you outgrow it, you may not have been paying attention. As you get older, you graduate to other types of activities including swimming, snorkeling, scuba diving, kayaking, canoeing, water skiing, and jet skiing. Heck, it could even be said that snow skiing involves water. It's hard, flaky, and frozen water, but it's water no less. Here are some places where that love affair begins.

On those rare summer days when the weather gets really hot, it seems like there's no more-popular place for toddlers than one of the many wading pools found in parks throughout the city. Seattle Parks and Recreation operates 25 in all (see Appendix C for locations), and most are open seven days a week from late June to early September. For more details on when the nearest wading pool will open and its operating hours, call the wading pool hotline at (206) 684-7796.

While the area's best water spray park could well be Bellevue's Water Spray Play Area (see the Destination Playgrounds listing earlier in this chapter), Seattle is no slouch, either. Ballard Commons Park (5701 22nd Ave. NW) has a variety of water squirters including fixed sprayers and ones that pop up. At the same time, the Dr. Blanche Lavizzo Water Play Area at Pratt Park (1800 S. Main St.) has water cannons and animal sculptures that squirt.

And if you've ever needed proof that you're never too old to enjoy the water, you need look no further than the International Fountain at the Seattle Center. Located in the middle of a vast expanse of lawn at the center, the water feature is a draw for kids and adults alike. The sides of the fountain gently slope toward a silver dome that shoots water high into the air, often in time to music piped in from speakers on the fountain's sides. If the delighted screams of children are any indication, the seemingly random order of sprays from a combination of micro-shooters and super-shooters are a big hit. The same is true with adults who are too old for wading pools but need relief from the heat just the same.

Lakeshore is a throwback to your school days because it has every toy, game, or bulletin board illustration your teacher ever used. Now you can get them for your kids. And if you show up between 1 and 3 p.m. every Saturday, they can do a free craft project while you shop for them . . . or yourself.

Lowe's
Build and Grow Clinic
12525 Aurora Ave. N, Seattle
(206) 366-0365
www.lowes.com
Consult the website for additional information.

Even the non-DIYers among us can inspire their little ones to be handy by taking them to a Lowe's class with a building project. Provided that they don't hate you forever and need counseling for the rest of their lives because you made them get up so early on a Saturday. Each class tackles a different project, such as a tabletop basketball game or a toy that's a car on one side and a robot on the other. Attendees keep their finished projects and also get to keep an apron, safety glasses, and a patch. The classes are free and typically start at 10 a.m. at least one Saturday each month.

Miller Library
Center for Urban Horticulture
3501 NE 41st St.
(206) 543-0415
www.millerlibrary.org

Are your kids tired of story times where they just sit around and listen to someone read a book? The Saturday morning gatherings at the Center for Urban Horticulture's Miller Library include a craft activity that celebrates plants and nature. Children generally color or do a craft project based around a theme such as "growing kindness" or "hooray for mud." The events are free and held at 10:30 a.m. on the first Saturday of the month except July and August.

Pratt Fine Arts Center
1902 S. Main St.
(206) 328-2200
www.pratt.org

Instead of offering drop-in art or craft classes, the Pratt works with children on a longer timeframe, producing more ambitious projects including painting, collage, and silk screening. Classes are divided by age group—kindergarten; second grade; third through fifth; and sixth through eighth—and last for eight weeks. There is a suggested $15 donation, but it's not required. Move quick if you want to get your budding artist into a class, though. There's only space for 25 students and registration is open as soon as the quarterly course catalog is published.

Seattle Asian Art Museum
Volunteer Park
1400 E. Prospect St.
(206) 654-3100
www.seattleartmuseum.org

As part of its Free First Saturday event, SAAM offers art projects for children based around a current exhibition. Parents and singles can belly up to the art table, too, and create their own masterpiece from 11 a.m. to 2 p.m. The museum also shows a family-friendly movie at 1:30 p.m.

Village Play Days
University Village
2660 NE 49th St. (25th Avenue NE and NE 45th Street)
(206) 523-0622
www.uvillage.com

It's hard to know where to put this weekly Tuesday morning activity because there's so much overlap. One week there could be craft making at Kids Club and the week after that it could be yoga for children at Lululemon Athletica. The only thing that's sure is that the event goes from 10 to 11 a.m. For more details about each week's event, check the website. Many participating merchants also offer discounts each play day.

Wing Luke Museum of the Asian Pacific American Experience
719 King St.
(206) 623-5124
www.wingluke.org

The museum's name recently changed, but one of its most popular events hasn't. Family Fun Day is still the third Saturday of the month and kids can still take on craft projects that allow them to interact with the artists who created the activity. The projects are things that kids can do quickly and then spend the rest of their time adding details.

FUN **WITH** SCIENCE

Discovery Park
3801 Discovery Park Blvd.
(206) 386-4236
www.seattle.gov/parks/environment/discovery.htm

This 534-acre recreational area is one of the city's largest parks and it has lots for kids to do. There's a small children's play area, but what may interest them more is the Discovery Room in the Environmental Learning Center. The center uses interactive exhibits and a playroom where they can do all the things kids love doing, including playing and coloring while learning more about the nature surrounding them. There are also books covering bird-watching, botany, and roaming trails. Families with children seven or under can get a pass that allows them to drive down and park near the beach. There are only eight passes available, however. Because the park is located on Magnolia Bluff, it has amazing views of area mountains and Puget Sound.

THE **GAMES** PEOPLE **PLAY**

Blue Highway Games
2203 Queen Anne Ave. N
(206) 282-0540
www.bluehighwaygames.com

Does being happy whiling away hours playing board games with close friends on a Saturday night make me a nerd? If not, I'm sure something else does. I'm a writer after all. Although I like doing it on weekends, you can stop in any time they're open and try out any of the games in the store's game library. Now that it serves beer and cider, it's an even better way to waste an evening.

Crossroads Mall
Game Lane
15600 NE 8th Ave.
Bellevue

You can play games at almost any table in the dining area at Crossroads, but the Game Lane outside Uncle's Games has five tables with boards on them under glass. The selection is switched from time to time, but at last check, it included Monotony . . . er . . . Monopoly, Parcheesi, and Settlers. You can get the game pieces from Uncle's and play to your heart's content. The mall also has a large chessboard where people hang out and wait to play near a branch of the King County Library.

Uncle's Games
Crossroads Mall
15600 NE 8th Ave.
Bellevue
(425) 746-1539
www.unclesgames.com

He's not really related, but his store wants to bring your family together for Family Game Night every Saturday from 6 p.m. to midnight and Family Board Games from 11 a.m. to 6 p.m. Sunday. There's also Magic: The Gathering game night from 6 to 10 p.m. Fridays. Check the calendar on the website for other events. Also worth mentioning, demo games are 15 percent off.

FAMILY **FILM**

Regal Family Film Festival
Thornton Place Stadium 14 & IMAX; 316 NE Thornton Place, Seattle; (206) 517-9943
Crossroads Stadium 8; 1200 156th Ave. NE, Bellevue; (425) 562-6596
Alderwood Stadium 7; 3501 184th St. SW, Lynnwood; (425) 672-2077
www.regmovies.com (select "Browse Movies")

Remember those movies our parents used to drop us off at when we were kids so they could get a few hours of peace and we could run wild? Regal has brought them back. Participating theaters show one G-rated and one PG-rated movie starting at 10 a.m. on Tuesday and Wednesday, June through August, and there are no restrictions on age. Seats are limited and available on a first-come, first-served basis. I wonder if a corporate-owned theater chain has any better luck controlling the little devils than the ushers at the mom-and-pop theaters we used to go to. Check before you go. Not all Regal Theaters participate every year.

ODDS **&** ENDS

Outdoor Opportunities
Camp Long, (206) 684-0797
Discovery Park, (206) 390-1018

Outdoor Opportunities is yet another program that makes me wish I were a kid. Nicknamed O2, its goal is to introduce teenagers from a variety of backgrounds to such issues as environmental awareness and urban conservation. Participants aged 15 to 19 go on two overnight trips, complete service projects, and attend weekly workshops. The trips include a variety of activities ranging from snowboarding and snowshoeing to sailing and kayaking. Best of all, it's all free.

KIDS **EAT** FREE

Everyone knows that some restaurants offer free meals for kids, but I wonder if anyone has ever asked, "Is this a good thing?" I understand that it helps bring more people into restaurants while allowing beleaguered parents a chance to save a little money on a night out, but do we really want to inflict our kids on others, no matter how well mannered our offspring may be? Still, there are times when we have no choice in the matter and really must clean them up and take them out. So, it's nice to know that these places can help improve our bottom line—if we could only keep our kids' bottoms in their chairs. Just remember to read all the fine print before ordering. Some places allow only one kid's dish per adult entree purchased, and most require the free meal to come from the kids' menu, which can often be a junk food junkie's delight.

Angelina's West Seattle Restaurant

2311 California Ave. SW
(206) 932-4550
angelinaswestseattle.com

The Mamas and the Papas may not have liked Mondays, but parents of children 12 and under have reason to like it here. The pre-teen set eats free with the order of an adult entree every Monday.

Beach House Bar & Grill

6023 Lake Washington Blvd.
Kirkland
(425) 968-5587
www.beachhousekirkland.com

Kids 11 and under eat free on Sunday at this casual waterfront restaurant.

Blue Star Café & Pub

4512 Stone Way N
(206) 548-0345
www.bluestarcafeandpub.com

Juniors 12 and under eat free 5 to 7 p.m. Saturday nights. Up to two children can eat with each adult entree, and if they get bored waiting, they can go to the world-famous novelty shop, Archie McPhee's, right next door. Just one word of warning: When we called to double-check this deal, some waitresses weren't aware of it.

Bryant Corner Café

3118 NE 65th St.
(206) 525-1034

This much-loved neighborhood cafe offers free kids' meals for children under 10 all day Monday. Kids order from the kids' menu and it's valid for one child per adult. It also offers many other specials including half-price cookies on Tuesday, 16-ounce lattes for $2 on Wednesday, half-price pastries on Thursdays, and a monster loaf of homemade wheat bread for $1.90 on Fridays.

Celtic Bayou Irish Pub & Cajun Cafe

7281 W. Lake Sammamish Pkwy. NE
Redmond
(425) 869-5933
www.celticbayou.com

The combination of Irish and Cajun may sound like a train wreck in the making, but they must be doing something right because this place has been open for years. Kids 10 and under eat free all day on Saturday and Sunday. One free kid's meal with the purchase of an adult meal.

Eat's Market Café

2600 SW Barton St.
(206) 933-1200
www.eatsmarket.com

Children eat free from 4 to 9 p.m. Wednesday. One free kid's meal with each adult meal purchased. Dine in only.

Ikea

601 SW 41st St.
Renton
(888) 888-4532

Good news! Not only can kids get a free combo meal at the cafe on Tuesday from 11 a.m. to close, but you don't have to build it yourself. Actually, the cafe frequently has good deals for adults as well. Add to that the opportunity to shop in peace while your children play in the ball room, and you've got yourself the makings of a great day. Some assembly required.

International House of Pancakes
1002 Aurora Ave. N
(206) 517-4467

On Thursday, children 12 and under eat free with one child's meal free per every paying adult at IHOP's Seattle location.

Michoacan Mexican Restaurante
8311 15th Ave. NW
(206) 789-6933

On Tuesday from 4 to 7 p.m., kids can get a free meal from the kids' menu with purchase of adult entree. Limit two kids per table.

Ohana
2207 First Ave.
(206) 956-9329
ohanabelltown.com

On Sunday, small fry aged 7 and under eat free from 11:30 a.m. to 6:30 p.m. with purchase of qualifying entree or sushi.

Pallino Pastaria
University Village, 2626 NE 46th St., Seattle; (206) 522-8617
East Lake Sammamish Shopping Center, 6150 E Lake Sammamish Parkway SE, Issaquah; (425) 394-1090
Redmond Town Center, 7545 166th Ave. NE, Space D110, Redmond; (425) 861-6900
17848 Garden Way NE, Ste. 102, Woodinville; (425) 488-7900
www.pallino.com
Consult the website for additional locations.

Children 12 and under eat free all day Sunday and Wednesday when an adult purchases a full-price entree. Kids order from the children's menu. It's not the best Italian food in the world, but at least it's fast.

The Ram

Northgate Mall, 401 NE Northgate Way, Ste. 1102, Seattle; (206) 364-8000
University Village, 2650 University Village, Seattle; (206) 525-3565
512 Ramsay Way, Ste. 4-103, Kent; (253) 520-3881
www.theram.com

It may not be free, but at $1 for a meal from the kids' menu on Monday nights, it's close enough.

Rikki Rikki

442 Parkplace
Kirkland
(425) 828-0707
www.rikkirikki.com

Children 10 and under eat free 4 p.m. to close on Tuesday at this eastside Japanese restaurant. One child meal per adult entree.

Romio's Pizza and Pasta

11422 NE 124th St., Kirkland; (425) 820-3300
3615 Factoria Blvd. SE, Bellevue; (425) 747-3000

Children under 10 eat free from 4 to 9 p.m. on Monday and Tuesday. Dine in only.

Sand Point Grill

5412 Sand Point Way NE
(206) 729-1303
www.sandpointgrillseattle.com

Yes, the deal is good only from 5 to 6:30 p.m., but it's good Sunday, Monday, and Tuesday for kids 12 and under. All child meals come with veggies and fresh fruit, which parents love. Kids, not so much.

Serendipity Café

3222 W. McGraw St.
(206) 282-9866
serendipitycafeandlounge.com

Purchase one adult entree on Tuesday night and get a free meal from the kids' menu.

Wedgwood Ale House

8515 35th Ave. NE
(206) 527-2676
wedgwoodalehouse.com

One child eats free per party on Tuesday nights, regardless of the number of adult entrees purchased.

Whistle Stop Ale House

809 S. 4th St.
Renton
(425) 277-3039
www.whistlestopalehouse.com

One child eats free from 4 p.m. to close on Monday with the purchase of one adult meal. Dine in only.

Wing Dome

7818 Greenwood Ave. N, Seattle; (206) 706-4036
21008 108th Ave. SE, Kent; (253) 854-9464
232 Central Way, Kirkland; (425) 822-9464
www.thewingdome.com

The cheap bastard doesn't know whether to be offended or amused that the Wing Dome has a kids-eat-free special on the night the company refers to as "Dad's Night to Cook." Regardless, one child gets a free meal from the kids' menu with the purchase of each adult meal.

INSURANCE

Washington Apple Health for Kids

(877) 543-7669
www.dshs.wa.gov/onlinecso/childrens_medical.shtml

The Catch: Eligibility is based on income.

This program could well address the concerns of parents of the state's thousands of uninsured children—if only they knew about it. The needs-based program covers major medical and certain preventive health care visits at an extremely affordable price for kids through age 18. The only catch is that eligibility is based on income. The program can also help prospective clients connect with other services including food banks and federally funded programs such as food stamps.

LITERATURE, LIBRARIES & OTHER LIFE LESSONS:
FREE ASSOCIATION

"We're going to have the best-educated
American people in the world."
—Former Vice-President Dan Quayle

It doesn't snow much in Seattle, but winters are unfailingly gray and rainy. We're not talking about Midwest-style gullywashers or the monsoons of Southeast Asia. Instead, it's the slow, misty drizzle that is the stuff of film noir. While lesser folk might be inclined to curl up with a good book and go into hibernation, Seattleites are made of sterner stuff. Once the weather turns gray, we jauntily pull out seasonal affective disorder treatment lamps until we've recharged ourselves enough to trudge in the rain, go out and try to be social, or curl up with a good book at a cafe, coffeehouse, or bookstore. We know we have to do these things during the dreary months because when the weather turns nice we won't want to be stuck indoors. And who knows? If we find something we like now, we may do it during the summer for a change of pace. Here are some of the free things with which we busy ourselves to prevent the onset of cabin fever during winter.

READINGS & OTHER **LITERARY** EVENTS

Barnes & Noble

Pacific Place, 600 Pine St., Seattle; (206) 264-0156
Northgate Mall, 401 NE Northgate Way, Seattle; (206) 417-2967
South Center, 300 Andover Park W, Tukwila; (206) 575-3965
Westwood Village, 2600 SW Barton St., Seattle; (206) 932-0328
626 106th Ave. NE, Bellevue; (425) 451-8463
Crossroads, 15600 NE 8th St., Bellevue; (425) 644-1650
Pickering Place, 1530 11th Ave. NW, Issaquah; (425) 557-8808
www.barnesandnoble.com

In some places, B&N may be the only game in town for people who want to attend an author reading. Not so in Seattle, where two independent booksellers hold a total of 700 author events every year. And that doesn't include the smaller fish in the market. Still, it never hurts to put in the effort. After all, most B&Ns are at shopping centers, so people can attend a reading and do their shopping. The same can't be said for most independent booksellers.

Cheap Beer and Prose

Richard Hugo House
1634 11th Ave.
(206) 322-7030
www.hugohouse.org

With a name like this, what more can you say? A spinoff of the Hugo House's Cheap Wine and Poetry, the program features four writers doing long readings from their own works, and Pabst Blue Ribbon for a buck. After they're done, there's time for about 10 open mic readers to emote for five minutes each. The curator says the event is "not quite a monthly thing. [It's] kind of haphazard. We like to keep people on their toes." It usually occurs on an every-other-month basis, alternating with Cheap Wine and Poetry during non-summer months. It always starts at 7 p.m., but if you want a seat, arrive early because it attracts between 100 and 200 people and it's in a small cabaret space. Admission is free, the crowd is lively, and the beer is . . . cheap. Check the website to find out when the next one will be.

Cheap Wine and Poetry

Richard Hugo House
1634 11th Ave.
(206) 322-7030
www.hugohouse.org

The people who find the idea of an evening of wine and poetry hopelessly pretentious have never been to this event. For starters, it's $1 for a glass of Charles Shaw's finest, also known as Two Buck Chuck, and the crowd can get rather raucous, responding to readers and even joining them on stage if the situation calls for it. The most infamous performances have included a lip-synching dog and a chance for audience members to play rock-paper-scissors with someone dressed like Jesus. It alternates with Cheap Beer and Prose on an every-other-month basis and starts at 7 p.m. Admission is free and the turnout is always big. Check the website or contact Hugo House for dates and additional details.

Eagle Harbor Book Company

157 Winslow Way E
Bainbridge Island
(206) 842-5332
www.eagleharborbooks.com

This small but mighty community bookstore in downtown Winslow, a half-hour ferry ride from Seattle, brings in top-notch authors you'd typically expect to see at larger venues, including such names as Christopher Paolini, Erin Hunter, and Timothy Egan. It also hosts several book groups.

Elliott Bay Book Company
1521 10th Ave.
(206) 624-6600
www.elliottbaybook.com

I may not get out as much as I used to when I was a single, poor, starving free-lance writer, but if I did, the author readings at the Elliott Bay Book Company would still be a staple of my entertainment budget. It does about 400 readings a year, most of them free, occasionally as many as three in one day.

Most evening readings start at 7 p.m., unless there are two scheduled the same evening. Then, the first usually starts at 5. Sunday readings typically deal with more serious topics like social justice, slow food, or even progressive Christianity. In addition, Elliott Bay has featured staged play readings featuring the Seattle Playwrights Collective or ReAct Theater one Sunday a month. The store also does readings off-site in partnership with other organizations ranging from Town Hall to Seattle First Baptist Church. Check the website for the jam-packed calendar of events to find out what's going on tonight. Don't be surprised if you see authors such as Caroline Kennedy, Gary Wills, Isabel Allende, and Sherman Alexie. Most on-site events are free, but get advance tickets and arrive early. Some off-site events do have admission fees.

Island Books
3014 78th Ave. SE
Mercer Island
(206) 232-6920
www.mercerislandbooks.com

The only bookshop on Mercer Island serves its clientele with a mix of book groups and occasional readings. The staff is friendly and knowledgeable. They do sell online, but they're just as happy to have you stop in because the staff would really rather you come in to spend some time, buy, and maybe even chew the fat. What's your rush? It is an island, isn't it? Okay, maybe not that kind of island, but still . . .

Meet the Author
King County Library System
Various branches
www.kcls.org

Most of us think about libraries when we want to read a particular book that we can't find at our local bookstore, aren't sure we want to spend the money on, or just don't want to keep, but have we ever thought of such places as a good venue for author readings? Probably not, considering that most authors do readings to sell their books, not lend them out. That's too bad because KCLS does a monthly Northwest Author Spotlight event at the Bellevue Library and holds many author readings each month at branches throughout the system. The author's books are usually on sale at the events. So you won't have to worry about having the author sign a library book.

Open Books: A Poem Emporium
2414 N. 45th St.
(206) 633-0811
www.openpoetrybooks.com

One of only two all-poetry bookstores in the country, Open Books has several readings a month by poets from near and far. Weeknight readings start at 7:30 p.m., weekend readings around 3 p.m. The readings last about 40 to 60 minutes and all feature a published poet publicizing a book, not amateurs who are suffering for their art and making us suffer along with them.

Queen Anne Book Company
1811 Queen Anne Ave. N
(206) 283-2427
www.qabookco.com

Although the owners of the newly opened Queen Anne Book Company said things were still up in the air at press time, the small independent bookseller planned to have at least one or two author readings a month. It had already begun holding a monthly meeting of its bookclub, QABC Reads.

Seattle Public Library
Various locations
www.spl.org

SPL holds many author events and lectures for adults every month, ranging from book groups to author readings. All author readings are free and there's a pretty good chance that you'll be able to get an author to autograph a book, but only if you buy it somewhere else. The library prohibits sales of merchandise at any events that occur on-site. For more information about lectures and readings, go to the website at www.spl.org. Seattle Library cardholders can also access a wide range of magazines including *Consumer Reports* through the databases on the library's website.

Stage Fright
Richard Hugo House
1634 11th Ave.
(206) 322-7030
www.hugohouse.org

The oldest youth open mic night in Seattle is a chance for 13- through 19-year-olds to gather and share prose, whether it be fiction, poetry, or even a song they just wrote. There are anywhere from 5 to 15 readers a night, depending on the month. The best part is that it's free and snacks are provided. Stage Fright season runs from September through June and the frequency varies, but often is held at 7 p.m. on a Wednesday night every other month. The Hugo House also hosts a drop-in writing circle every Wednesday night from 6 to 7 p.m., and many of the writers stay for the show.

Third Place Books
17171 Bothell Way NE
Lake Forest Park
(206) 366-3333

6504 20th Ave. NE
Seattle
(206) 525-2347
www.thirdplacebooks.com

Third Place Books' main store in Lake Forest Park is so big it has three possible locations to choose from for its readings—the children's department for the younger set; a small in-store area near travel books and mysteries with room for 50 (The Den); and Third Place Commons, an indoor area next to the store with the capacity to seat several hundred. All readings here are free and start at 7 p.m., but participation in the signings may require

Going to Your Special Place

When is a bookstore more than just a bookstore? When it's Third Place Books.

Shopping center developer Ron Sher developed the 30,000-square-foot space with a plan to make it as much a gathering space as a retail place. He based his ideas on the work of sociologist Ray Oldenburg, who suggested that every person has three important places where they spend most of their lives. Home is the first place, and work is the second. The third is a friendly place where members of the community come together in their off hours to be social and exchange ideas. The concept not only proved successful here and at Third Place Books in Ravenna, but also at Crossroads in Bellevue where his ideas helped save a mall that was on the brink of disaster. The city surrounding the bookstore, Lake Forest Park, and much of Seattle have happily embraced Sher's brainchild, attending the more than 1,000 events held here every year, stopping in for a bite, taking in author readings by their favorite authors, attending musical performances, holding meetings, hanging out with friends, and, yes, even buying books.

purchase of a book at the store for events involving highly popular authors. The Ravenna store is smaller and has a smaller event space where readings are typically scheduled for Tuesday and Wednesday. There the focus is on local authors. Readings start at 7 p.m. If you attend a reading by a major author and buy a book, you'll get a ticket that will allow you to sit and wait for your group to be called rather than standing in line with the rest of us cheap bastards.

Thrilling Tales: Story Time for Adults
Seattle Central Library
Microsoft Auditorium
1000 4th Ave.
(206) 386-4636
www.spl.org

Finally, a story time for adults. Every first and third Monday of the month at 12:05 p.m., the Central Library hosts a story hour with slightly more sophisticated fare. And since it ends at 12:50, you still have enough time to return to the office. The staffer who does the readings has an acting background and brings the stories to life. As with many library programs, timing is subject to change. Can't make it to a reading? You can always go to the podcast page (www.spl.org/library-collection/podcasts) and look for Thrilling Tales. Just a warning, the Thrilling Tales podcasts aren't all that easy to find.

University Book Store
4326 University Way NE, Seattle; (206) 634-3400
990 102nd Ave. NE, Bellevue; (425) 462-4500.
Mill Creek Town Center, 15311 Main St., Mill Creek; (425) 385-3530
800 N. 10th Place, Renton; (425) 988-2812
www.bookstore.washington.edu

Unlike most Seattle booksellers, the University Book Store's main branch never has to worry about running out of space for readings. If turnout is a concern, the store can always use one of the auditoriums at the University of Washington nearby, which it has done frequently. The company hosts over 500 readings a year split among its stores. Although all three host events covering a wide range of genres, the Seattle store is known for doing science fiction and fantasy readings well, while the Bellevue location has built a following for hosting authors of popular thrillers and mysteries such as Stewart Woods and Phillip Margolin. Literary fiction events are also popular at the eastside store. Most in-store events are free and begin between 7 and 7:30 p.m. on a weeknight. The chain tries to avoid scheduling weekend readings because turnout tends to be lighter than during the week. The store also co-sponsors a series of science lectures held at Town Hall, but those events usually cost around $5.

RIDICULOUSLY **CHEAP** SPOKEN **WORD**

Seattle has always been a quirky kind of place, but that brand of silliness doesn't always come free. Sometimes, you have to shell out a few bucks to get in the door, but if you've got an odd sense of humor, you won't regret the investment.

Ignite Seattle
King Cat Theatre
2130 6th Ave.
www.igniteseattle.com

An event that only a geek could love. Ignite's tagline is "Enlighten us, but make it quick." Ignite participants have only five minutes and a 20-slide PowerPoint presentation to enlighten, inform, amuse, or baffle their audience. And there's another catch: the slides automatically rotate after 15 seconds. The quarterly event costs just $5. Of course, you could save the money by waiting until the presentations are posted on the Internet, but you won't get to experience the roar of the greasepaint and the smell of the crowd . . . or something like that.

Seattle Poetry Slam
The Re-bar
1114 Powell St.
www.seattlepoetryslam.org

If you're a poetry fan who digs watching poets compete, the Re-bar is the place to be on Tuesday nights. Open mic starts at 8:30 p.m., featured poet at 9 p.m., Slam starts at 10 p.m. Cover is $5. It all builds up to a Grand Slam in the spring where poets compete for the right to represent the city at the National Poetry Slam and appear on ESPN 4. Okay, I made that last part up.

Town Hall
1119 8th Ave.
(206) 652-4255
townhallseattle.org

Founded in 2000 as a home for itinerant arts organizations, Town Hall has evolved into a cultural center that reflects Seattle's cultural interests. It's like New York City's 92nd Street Y, only cheaper with most of its science lectures, arts and cultural events, and concerts costing $5 or less. While a recent speech by author Calvin Trillin was $18 at the 92nd Street Y, Town Hall tickets for an event with Trillin were $5. It also offers a Saturday morning family concert series where tickets are $5 for adults and nothing for kids.

Brainy Competitions

Pub trivia isn't just a cheap way to pass a night; it may also be a way to turn a tidy profit if you and your team are at the top of your game on the right night. Although the setup varies from bar to bar, teams usually pay a nominal amount to play, a quizmaster asks several rounds of questions, and the team with the most correct answers at the end of the evening wins the kitty or some other prize. There are far too many pub trivia quizzes in the area to list them all, but here's a quick sampling of what's available by day, how much it costs, maximum team size, and possible prizes. (There are also a number of free pub trivia nights in the area as well, but most don't offer cash prizes.)

Wedgwood Ale House, 8315 35th Ave. NE, Seattle; (206) 527-2676; Sunday, 9 p.m.; no limit on team size. Winning team gets free pitcher; second- and third-place teams get random prizes.

Celtic Bayou, 7281 W. Lake Sammamish Pkwy., Redmond; (425) 869-5933; Monday, 8 p.m.; $2 per person, up to eight players per team. Winning team gets half the pot, second place gets 30 percent, and third place gets 20 percent. Everybody who plays gets a prize, although it might be a kitschy one. The biggest loser gets a free pitcher.

FREE **CLASSES** WITH **CLASS**

There are times when a book just isn't good enough. We want to know more, gosh darn it, but we don't want to pay for it. Either that, or we're just looking for an excuse to get out of our houses and hang out with other people so that we won't go stir crazy during those short days when the sun refuses to show its face and daylight lasts from about 9 a.m. to, oh, let's say about 3 p.m.—if we're lucky.

Finn MacCool's, 4217 University Way NE, Seattle; (206) 675-0885. Free trivia starts at 9 p.m. on Tuesday with the winning team getting $25 taken off its tab.

Ballard Loft, 5105 Ballard Ave. NW, Seattle; (206) 420-2737. Offers free trivia at 8 p.m. Tuesday. Winner gets free gift certificate.

Cooper's Alehouse, 8065 Lake City Way NE, Seattle; (206) 522-2923; Tuesday, 8:45 p.m.; $1 per player, no team size limit. Top placing teams divide pot; other top finishers get prizes.

Big Time Brewery, 4133 University Way NE, Seattle; (206) 545-4509; Wednesday, 7 p.m.; $3 per person, up to six people a team. Prizes are cash and gift certificates.

Georgetown Liquor Company, 5501 Airport Way S, Seattle; (206) 763-6764; Thursday, 8:30 p.m. Free to play for cash prizes. Up to six people per team. Three bonus pints offered during the competition.

College Inn Pub, 4006 University Way NE, Seattle; (206) 634-2307; first Thursday of the month, 8 p.m.; $5 per team, up to six players per team. Hosted by the Burke Museum of Natural History, prizes are drink vouchers and museum passes. The host has also been known to bring in bonus prizes.

The Monkey Pub, 5305 Roosevelt Way NE, Seattle; (206) 523-6457; Friday, 8 p.m.; $3 per player, up to six per team. First-place team gets entire pot.

In a Class by Itself

Seattle Free School
Locations vary
(253) 642-6365
www.seattlefreeschool.org

Asking how much a class costs at Seattle Free School is like visiting a dollar store and asking how much everything is. There are no hidden fees or attempts to upsell, just free classes on whatever the unpaid instructors feel passionate enough about to teach. Of course, that also means that there's no regular class schedule. Instead, the sessions are announced on the website,

Giving the L-I-B-R-A-R-Y some R-E-S-P-E-C-T

If you needed proof that Seattle area residents value the offerings of their local libraries, you need look no further than famed novelty wholesaler and retailer to the masses, Archie McPhee. The same Seattle-based company that brought you the Moses, Jesus, and Freud action figure dolls also created a Librarian action figure and based it on much-loved local librarian Nancy Pearl. If Pearl's name sounds familiar, it probably should. She's the author of Book Lust, More Book Lust, and Book Crush for kids. All of the books list recommended reads based on everything from age and personality to occasion and mood.

Although she's no longer with the Seattle Public Library, there's no question that Pearl is a librarian with class. But she's not the only class at many local libraries. In fact, most offer a wide array of classes for every age and interest.

The Seattle metro area has two main library systems: the Seattle Public Library (www.spl.org) and the Bellevue-based King County Library System (www.kcls.org). Here's a quick look at some of the subject areas their classes cover:

Anime	Health insurance benefits
Art and technology	Homework
Arts and crafts	Internet instruction
Book groups	Job searches
Budgeting	Library catalogues
Business	Music
Citizenship	Mythology
Computer skills	Nutrition
Cooking	Online marketing
Crafts with duct tape	Resume basics
Dance	SAT prep
Disaster preparedness	Science
English\second language	Singers
Finance	Taxes
Foreign languages	Theater
Gardening	Writing
Genealogy	

Facebook, and Twitter. Over the last year, the offerings have included crafts and instruction on how to make your own cheese. Locations also vary, but many classes have been held at the Seattle Public Library Central Library, the Cascade People's Center, and Street Bean Espresso.

Arts

Teen Art Studios
Gage Academy of Art
1501 10th Ave. E

The Treehouse Building
2100 24th Ave. S
(206) 323-4243
www.gageacademy.org/TAS

Gage's free Friday night art studio for 13- to 18-year-olds has proven so popular there's now one in the south end on Saturday. Both include all the art supplies teens need to express themselves and free snacks as well. The popular drop-in event goes from 6:30 to 9:30 p.m. on Friday at the Gage Academy and on Saturday in the south end, and centers on a different theme or medium every month, ranging from figure drawing and printmaking to anything else they can dream up. Gage also has two free art lectures for adults every 11 weeks. One is called Art Talks and features an interview with a working artist. The other, Artist Tool Kit, covers the practical side of being a professional artist, including how to promote your art and make a living being an artist. Professional artists teach both programs.

Fitness

Lululemon Athletica
www.lululemon.com
Pacific Place, 600 Pine St., Ste. 210, Seattle; (206) 682-1286
University Village, 2643 NE University Village St., Seattle; (206) 524-6025
Bellevue Square, 575 Bellevue Way NE, Bellevue; (425) 462-5530

One of the best ways to keep people from seeing through your Lululemon yoga pants is to keep moving. And the best way to do that could well be to take one of the free weekly fitness classes offered at all three area locations. The Pacific Place store has free yoga on Sunday from 9:30 to 10:30 a.m. and a Wednesday afternoon run club that meets at 5:30 p.m. At University Village, there's a Sunday morning run at 8:30 a.m. followed by a yoga class at 9:30. The Bellevue store offers either yoga or a fitness class every Sunday at 9 a.m. For more details, see each store's community calendar.

Food and Beverage

Caffe Vita Public Brewing School
1005 E. Pike
(206) 709-4440
www.caffevita.com

We all know the best way to save money on coffee is to make it at home; the problem is most of us don't know how to make really good coffee. Fortunately, Caffe Vita has a class that could help us cut out those daily trips to our local coffeehouse. The two-hour gathering covers different brewing methods and discusses the importance of manual brewing versus the automatic coffee machine approach. Although dates vary, the class is typically held from 10 a.m. to noon on the third Saturday of the month.

Redmond Whole Foods
17991 Redmond Way
Redmond
(425) 881-2600
www.wholefoodsmarket.com/stores/redmond

As a rule, Whole Foods is so expensive that even its classes are spendy, but two classes offered by the Redmond store are free. Healthy Eating on a Budget is essentially a store tour that teaches Whole Foodies how to score deals and make easy meals. The store also offers a special diet store tour. Times and dates vary from month to month, so it's best to call the store or check its website.

Sur La Table
90 Central Way, Kirkland; (425) 827-1311
84 Pine St., Seattle; (206) 448-2244
The Bravern, 11111 NE 8th St., Bellevue; (425) 450-4010
www.surlatable.com

Many of the national gourmet kitchen shop's stores offer a variety of product demos on Saturday at 11 a.m. Recent examples include a knife skills class, doughnut making, and Sous Vide cooking. The Pike Place location does product demonstrations on weekends, but doesn't follow the same schedule. The Kirkland store also holds a variety of cooking classes each month with prices ranging from $39 to $150.

Williams-Sonoma

University Village, 2530 NE University Village, Seattle; (206) 523-3733
Pacific Place, 600 Pine St., Seattle; (206) 624-1422
Bellevue Square, 212 Bellevue Square, Bellevue; (425) 454-7007
Alderwood Mall, 3000 184th St. SW, Lynnwood; (425) 778-8053
www.williams-sonoma.com

The purveyor of pricey pots, pans, and other kitchen paraphernalia offers complimentary cooking technique classes several Sundays a month. Times vary by location, but classes generally start between 10 a.m. and noon. They're free, but you should call and sign up. Not too surprisingly, the Bellevue Square store has found a way to cash in on the interest in cooking classes and is now offering additional classes . . . for a price.

Languages

Mango Languages
Seattle Public Library
(206) 386-INFO
www.spl.org

Sometimes you don't even need to leave your house to take a free class. Mango Languages is a good example. Anyone with a valid Seattle Public Library card can login to SPL's website, find mangolanguages on its list of databases, sign up, and begin learning French, Portuguese, Russian, Italian, Japanese, or a variety of other languages for free. Before you know it, it really could be Greek to you. The library also offers other online language courses including Live Mocha, Muzzi, and Transparent Language. Hey, the CB doesn't make them up, he just reports them.

Rick Steves Europe Through the Back Door
Rick Steves Travel Center
130 4th Ave. N

Learning from a MOOC

What's that you say? What can you possibly learn from someone foolish enough to be called a mook?

Not that kind of mook. Instead, we're talking about Massive Open Online Courses (MOOC), which are essentially courses from major universities around the country that you can take online for free. Some even come with certificates upon completion. At press time, the University of Washington offered 14 MOOCs including such classes as Introduction to Data Science, Computer Networks, and Introduction to Public Speaking. Since the courses are offered online, there's no need to stick with the UW. You could take The Future of Humankind from Rutgers, An Introduction to the US Food System: Perspectives from Public Health from Johns Hopkins University in Maryland, and A History of the World Since 1300 from Princeton University, to name a few.

For more details about participating universities and what courses are available, visit www.coursera.org.

Edmonds
(425) 771-8303
www.ricksteves.com/about/travelcenter.htm

With classes lasting only 60 to 90 minutes, you're not going to leave the language classes here with the fluency of a native speaker, but the crash courses should provide you with enough knowledge to cover the basics, including getting to your hotel, ordering food, and asking where the bathroom is. Classes are held Thursday and Saturday and languages include Czech, Italian, German, French, and Turkish. Classes are free, but reservations are required.

Travel and Other Adventures

REI
Seattle Flagship Store, 222 Yale Ave. N, Seattle; (206) 223-1944
www.rei.com/stores/11
Redmond Town Center, 7500 166th Ave. NE, Redmond; (425) 882-1158
www.rei.com/stores/20

735 NW Gilman Blvd., Issaquah; (425) 313-1660
www.rei.com/stores/116
240 Andover Park W, Tukwila; (206) 248-1938
www.rei.com/stores/78
Alderwood Mall, 3000 184th St. SW, Ste. 952, Lynnwood; (425) 640-6200
www.rei.com/stores/35

You could just go into an REI store, get outfitted, and consider yourself done, but wouldn't it be helpful to learn how to use the stuff? Or be inspired to do more? Every location in the region offers free classes covering a wide range of topics of interest to people not because they want to adopt the protective colorings of a Northwesterner and just fit in, but because they want to learn more about their favorite active pastimes. Recent offerings have included such topics as how to use your GPS unit, snowshoeing, and preparing for climbing Mount Rainier. Many classes are free, but space is limited so advanced registration is suggested. For more details on classes, go to each store's website.

Rick Steves Europe Through the Back Door
Rick Steves Travel Center
130 4th Ave. N
Edmonds
(425) 771-8303
www.ricksteves.com/about/travelcenter.htm

Even though Steves made his name on his Europe Through the Back Door books and guided trips, it's still okay to use the front door. Once you're there, you can even sit in on one of the free classes, as long as you pre-registered. The sessions cover some things you'd expect, like digital photography and how to pack light, as well as others you might not, such as volunteer travel. Most classes are held at the Travel Center, but others are offered at Edmonds Theater and the Edmonds Center for the Arts.

The Savvy Traveler
112 5th Ave. S
Edmonds
(425) 744-6076
www.savvytraveleredmonds.com

Less than a mile from Rick Steves' off-the-beaten-path travel empire is a smaller, less well-known travel store that also offers free seminars and classes. While the schedule tends to be destination-oriented, it also offers classes on packing, volunteer travel, and the like. Instead of providing quick and dirty lessons, Savvy Traveler offers longer, more detailed classes. Where Steves' language courses are one-dayers, a recent Italian class at Savvy Traveler had four two-hour sessions. Five-week language classes are $85.

Odds & Ends

Babeland
707 E. Pike St.
(206) 328-2914
www.babeland.com/community/stores/seattle
babelandseattle.eventbrite.com

You might not think of a sex shop as a good place to take a class, but Babeland isn't your typical adult store. In addition to the standard mix of vibrators and other . . . um . . . marital aids, the Capitol Hill company also offers a variety of classes—many are free, and others cost up to $35. Recent offerings include flirting tips, a lesson on sexual positions, and an Earth Day Kinky Crafts class that taught how to make your own flogger out of recycled bicycle tubes. Most free classes typically last 20 to 30 minutes and serve as introductions to a particular topic while pay classes go one to two hours and go into greater detail. The store also has a free Kinky Crafts class where you can make a sex toy on the cheap (there may be a small fee for materials). There are many other ways to save as well. Register for a class a week or more in advance and you can save $5. If you would like to attend a pay class, but can't afford it, you may be able to negotiate a rate on a sliding scale. When you attend a paid class, everything in the store is 20 percent off. Everything is 10 percent off when you attend a free class. Students get 25 percent off workshops and 10 percent off items in the store when there's no class. Military members get 10 percent discount. As if all that weren't enough, the store also has two major sales a year: one around New Year's, the other about the third week in July. What, no senior discount?

Sew Up Seattle
Locations vary
(206) 652-2327
www.sewupseattle.blogspot.com

This organization teaches classes on how to sew and turn recycled fabric scraps into all sorts of cool new things. The classes are held from 11 a.m. to 1 p.m. on the fourth Saturday of the month. The classes are free, but signing up in advance is a good idea as space is limited. Recent classes have covered mending and remaking, buttons and buttonholes, and bags for the beach. Check the website for details.

UW Graduate School Public Lecture Series
Kane Hall, Room 130
University of Washington Campus
(206) 543-0540
www.grad.washington.edu/lectures

The UW graduate school hosts a monthly series of lectures by an eclectic mix of scholars on a wide range of topics every year. In 2012, the speakers included author Amy Tan and performer Laurie Anderson. Although the lectures are open to the public, the best way to make sure you'll have a seat is to register in advance by calling the UW Alumni Office at the above number. The series runs from October through April. The UW offers a range of other free lectures throughout the year including an engineering lecture series and a psychology lecture series.

Meditation

Sahaja Meditation
Crossroads Mall Community Room
NE 8th Street and 156th Avenue NE
Bellevue
(425) 753-0634
www.sahajameditation.com

Meditation in a mall. On the eastside no less. Who'd have thunk it? The method is said to be very easy and the curious are invited in to drop in and experience internal peace at 7 p.m. every Thursday. And if that doesn't work, you can always cut out early and contemplate bargains. If Bellevue is too far, the New Meditation Center in Seattle's Northgate neighborhood also offers free meditation 7 p.m. every Thursday and a variety of other free classes at 12317 15th Ave. NE, Ste. #104. For more information, call (206) 486-6526.

Vidyana Foundation

Talaris Conference Center
4000 NE 41st St.
(206) 949-7933
www.thewayofseeing.com

It may be nice to achieve the relaxed state meditation can bring you and gain useful tools for helping cope with aspects of our everyday lives, but the organizers aren't as relaxed about your arrival time. The organization's website suggests arriving early because the doors are locked at 6:30. Does that mean you can zone out any time you'd like, but you can never leave? Classes at 6:30 every Monday night.

HEALTH & MEDICINE:
LIVE FREE OR DIE

"We Americans live in a nation where the medical-care system is second to none in the world, unless you count maybe 25 or 30 little scuzzball countries like Scotland that we could vaporize in seconds if we felt like it."
—*Dave Barry*

Even if you have health insurance, the price of health care seems to keep going higher and higher. While the best way to save money on medicine and other care is to not get sick or, at least, keep from getting kicked off your insurance company rolls simply because you actually needed to use your insurance, there are times when you just can't avoid spending money. Even if you're a guy and you insist that the huge gash in your chest is "only a flesh wound." That's when some of these organizations come in handy. You might not be able to do anything about the high cost of insurance, but some of the options below might help lighten the impact on your wallet or purse.

Seattle-King County Public Health

(206) 296-0100

www.kingcounty.gov/healthservices/health.aspx

The go-to place for advice on all sorts of medical issues and concerns. The department runs 10 public health centers, a variety of clinics (including dental, family planning, HIV/STD, and Teen Health), smoking cessation, and substance abuse programs, to name just a few. In fact, the department is also responsible for restaurant inspections and environmental health. If its medical personnel can't treat you, they will be able to point you in the right direction for affordable options. It also has a family health hotline (206-322-2588) that may be able to help you find affordable treatment options, inexpensive insurance, and other assistance.

TESTING, **TESTING** . . . IS **THIS** THING **WORKING?**—CLINICAL **STUDIES**

With so many medical research facilities located here, there's no shortage of opportunities for you to become a human guinea pig. Of course, not everyone who signs up for a particular clinical study is sick. Some do it just because they want to advance medical science and others do it for pay (or the free health care that's involved). If you're one of the people looking for a miracle cure, though, it's important to remember that there's always a control group that's given a placebo, so there's no guarantee the medicine you're trying will help. Of course, the hope is that it won't hurt, either.

Participating in such trials isn't for everyone. They can be time-consuming, call for changes in lifestyle, or even be potentially risky because not all of the side effects of the drug are known at the start, but here's where to look if you're willing to become an explorer on the frontiers of medicine:

AIDS Clinical Trial Information Service: (800) 874-2572; www.aidsinfo .nih.gov

CenterWatch (listing by category): www.centerwatch.com

Clinical Trials Search: www.clinicaltrialssearch.org

National Cancer Institute: www.cancer.gov/clinicaltrials

National Library of Medicine: www.clinicaltrials.gov

Area medical centers looking for volunteers:

Evergreen Hospital Medical Center: www.evergreenhospital.org/landing .cfm?id=340

Fred Hutchinson Cancer Research Center: www.fhcrc.org/patient/treat-ment/trials/index.php

Group Health Cooperative Center for Health Studies: www.grou-phealthresearch.org/participate/joinastudy.html

Seattle Cancer Care Alliance: www.seattlecca.org/clinical-trials/clinical-trials.cfm

Seattle Children's Hospital: www.seattlechildrens.org/research

Swedish Medical Center: www.swedish.org/Classes-and-Resources/ Research-Studies/Cancer-Research#axzz2QjGX8U68

University of Washington Warren G. Magnuson Health Sciences Center: www.medical.washington.edu/studies/

VA Puget Sound Health Care System: www.pugetsound.va.gov/services/ research.asp

Valley Medical Center: www.valleymed.org/Multimedia/research-CISCRP-flv/?terms=CLINICAL%20TRIAL

FREE **CONDOMS**

Gay City Health Project
517 E. Pike St.
(206) 860-6969
www.gaycity.org

This health organization for gay, bisexual, and transgendered inviduals who have sex with men is one of the top HIV- and STD-testing organizations in the area. It forwards the cause of a healthy lifestyle among gay and bisexual men by building self-esteem and creating a supportive community.

Lambert House
1818 15th Ave. (between E. Howell and E. Denny Way)
(206) 322-2515
www.lamberthouse.org

A drop-in center for gay, lesbian, bisexual, and transgendered youth, Lambert House keeps its supply of free condoms in a basket near a resource center filled with pamphlets on a variety of health topics of concern to its target population. The center is designed to be a safe hangout for people 22 years old and younger and provides counseling and support groups as well as a variety of activities and events.

Lifelong AIDS Alliance
1002 E. Seneca
(206) 328-8979
llaa.org

Rather than wait for people to visit their offices and grab free condoms, Lifelong AIDS Alliance takes them to where the need is greatest: the places where people hook up. The condoms are part of a free safer-sex packet featuring lubricants and education cards that can be found at gay bars throughout town.

Planned Parenthood
5020 Roosevelt Way NE, Unit 1, Seattle
2001 E. Madison St., Seattle
9641 28th Ave. SW, Seattle

2111 N. Northgate Way, Ste. 218, Seattle
1229 Madison St., Ste. 2040
1420 156th NE #C, Bellevue
1105 S. 348th St., Federal Way
75 NW Dogwood St., Ste. B, Issaquah
6610 NE 181st, #2, Kenmore
10056 SE 240th, #A, Kent
19505 76th Ave. W, Lynnwood
(800) 769-0045
www.plannedparenthood.org

Condoms are easy to come by at the nationally known, reproductive health organization. They're often sitting in a fishbowl or some other container in the reception area of most of its clinics.

ALTERNATIVE **CARE**

Bastyr Center for Natural Health Care
3670 Stone Way N (38th and Stone)
(206) 834-4100
www.bastyrcenter.org

Bastyr University may be out in Kenmore, but the teaching clinic for its naturopathic medicine, acupuncture, and nutrition programs is more conveniently located in Wallingford. The first visit usually takes 90 minutes with two students taking patient history and doing an exam, and then consulting with a supervising, more experienced naturopath to reach a diagnosis and a treatment plan. Follow-up visits for treatment typically take an hour. Remember that this is alternative medicine. On the plus side, that means longer consult times with the people treating you rather than the drive-by gawkings associated with Western medicine. On the negative side, alternative medicine can seem strange to people used to another medical model. The good news is that, unlike many Western medical treatments, when naturopathic and acupuncture treatments don't work, they usually don't make things worse. Seniors pay a flat $20 fee for treatments while low-income patient fees are available on a sliding scale based on income. Acupuncture visits for seniors are $15. Bastyr also offers psychological counseling for $20 per session for seniors and the uninsured, and nutrition counseling for $25 for seniors and the uninsured.

Pharmaca

15480 Redmond Way, Redmond; (425) 882-1475
4130 E. Madison, Seattle; (206) 324-0701
1815 N. 45th St., Seattle; (206) 547-1208
4707 California Ave. SW, Seattle; (206) 932-4225
www.pharmaca.com

Pharmaca hopes that if you take one part pharmacy and add one part holistic medicine, you won't have to call them in the morning. In addition to offering traditional pharmacy services, it also sells holistic remedies and provides information about alternative treatments. It also occasionally gives out samples of products and does free health events throughout the year. Local events have included a spa day with mini-facials and mini-makeovers (with a small registration fee), a fitness event with free 10-minute chair massages and food samples, a session on the benefits of chocolate, and an aura-reading workshop.

Seattle Institute of Oriental Medicine

916 NE 65th St.
(206) 517-4541
siom.edu

When my friends found out I once went to an acupuncture teaching clinic, they asked if the needles were painful. Of course not, I told them. You barely feel the needles. It's the sledgehammers they use to pound them in that hurt. I'M JOKING! The needles are small, there are no sledgehammers, and all of the practitioners here are second- or third-year students working under the supervision of a licensed acupuncturist. Community clinics cost $20 and require an appointment. Community clinic patients sit in lounge chairs in a large room with as many as five other patients while they are treated. More private treatments start at around $35. SIOM also offers massage clinics for Chinese medical massage, tuina, and Japanese shiatsu. Each massage lasts an hour and costs $25. Appointment required. Check website for community clinic hours.

FITNESS & FUN:
FREE KICKS

*"You can't leave footprints in the sands of time
if you're sitting on your butt. And who wants
to leave buttprints in the sands of time?"*
—*Bob Moawad*

Seattleites are an interesting lot. Not only are many seemingly less materialistic than folks in other cities across the country, but many so value quality of life that stories abound of folks taking pay cuts to move here just so they could live in a place with so many outdoor recreational possibilities. Kayaking. Hiking. Biking. Skiing. Boating. Sailing. Running. Jumping. Sitting here writing this in the middle of winter, it hurts just to think about it. Still, it's not unusual for corporate offices to empty out on the day the ski slopes open in winter and on the first sunny spring day. Those days are so eagerly anticipated that some spend top dollar to get the latest, most expensive equipment just to be prepared, no matter what the sport. So much for a lack of materialism. The bad news is that spending so much on equipment doesn't leave a lot to spend on actually leaving town, so they have no choice but to look for low-priced activities. The good news is that there are plenty of them that aren't far away.

PARK **IT** HERE: **NEARBY** GETAWAYS **THAT** WILL **KEEP** YOU **BUSY** ALL **DAY**

Green Lake/Woodlawn Park Zoo
7201 Green Lake Dr. N
(206) 684-4075
www.cityofseattle.net/parks/park_detail.asp?id=307

It's hard to tell where one park ends and the other begins. In any case, the opportunities seem endless. There's a 2.8-mile path around the lake popular with walkers, bikers, skaters, and those who just want to people-watch while they walk; two small beaches with lifeguards in summer; boat rentals; kayaking; a nine-hole pitch 'n' putt golf course; a community center with an indoor swimming pool and weight room; outdoor tennis courts; baseball fields; a basketball court; a playground; and a wading pool. And that doesn't even include the picnic areas, lawn bowling courts, and the Woodland Park Zoo (the zoo has an admission fee) all located across Aurora Avenue North from the lake. It's also a popular venue for theater in the park performances by Greenstage during the summer and indoor performances by the Seattle Public Theater at the Green Lake Bathhouse.

Marymoor Park

6046 W. Lake Sammamish Parkway NE
Redmond
(206) 205-3661
www.kingcounty.gov/recreation/parks/inventory/marymoor.aspx

At 640 acres, Marymoor is one of King County's largest and most popular urban parks. Located near the end of Highway 520, the park has plenty of ways to while away the day. There are three playgrounds, a velodrome (bicycle race course), a climbing rock, and playing fields for sports such as soccer, lacrosse, rugby, baseball, and cricket, as well as an off-leash dog area and a bird loop trail. In the summer, you can also catch a free outdoor movie, shell out the big money for a concert, or just keep walking. The park has a connector trail that links the 27-mile Burke Gilman Trail with the 11-mile East Lake Sammamish River Trail. If you have a need for a bit more speed, you can even take advantage of a program originally funded by a donation from the Dasani Corp. and ride a Trek Classic Cruiser along the route for free. Once you're through with all that walking or riding, you can take your tired feet to the reflexology path before heading home.

Warren G. Magnuson Park

7400 Sand Point Way NE
(206) 684-4946
www.cityofseattle.net/parks/magnuson/

Magnuson Park is probably the result the federal government had in mind when it created a base closure commission. The 320-acre Sand Point Naval Air Station has become Seattle's second-largest park and it has plenty to rec-ommend it. Located on the shore of Lake Washington, it's a popular place for boat launching, wind surfing, picnicking, and hanging out on a beach. It's also a popular walking spot with lots of trails throughout the park including the Burke-Gilman Trail, which runs along Magnuson's edge. The park has a number of sports fields and was slated to add an indoor tennis center with 10 indoor courts. It's also a hit with the younger set because of its large playground, off-leash dog area, kite flying, and motorized airplane flying area. In addition, it's also home to a wide range of community organizations including the Cascade Bicycle Club, EarthCorps, and the outdoor recreation group, the Mountaineers.

RECREATION **CENTERS** & **POOLS**

One of the joys of living in a large metro area is that there are plenty of recreational options nearby and a little farther away. If you like the local mix, you can go to your neighborhood recreation center and partake. If not, you can go to another locality's recreation program and mooch off them. It is getting harder to do it for free, though. While Seattle doesn't ask for proof of residency, Bellevue charges non-residents more to take classes or swim in the community pool, for example. Even so, most parks and recreation department programs are far cheaper than similar offerings you might find at private sector alternatives such as fitness clubs. While gyms require memberships, locals can do a drop-in workout at a Seattle Community Center with a fitness room for $2, even less if they get a punch card. Even better, that same $2 could also give a parent a bit of relief when they've got a kid stuck inside on a rainy day. Many community centers operate drop-in indoor play programs or toddler gyms. In fact, most local recreation centers do a great job with programming for kids and seniors.

Seattle Parks and Recreation
(206) 684-4075
www.seattle.gov/parks

The city of Seattle has 26 community centers with 10 pools, 16 wading pools, and 6 weight rooms (see Appendix C for locations). Currently, non-residents are subject to the same fee schedule for the use of pools and weight rooms as residents. Youth and seniors pay $3.75 per pool visit while adults 18 to 64 pay $5.25. You can save a little by buying a multi-use pass, however. A 10-visit swim card is $33.50 for youth and seniors, $47 for adults. A month-long personal fitness fast pass is $45 for seniors, $60 for adults. Drop-in use of weight rooms is $2 per visit but multi-use passes are available. The city also runs four municipal golf courses.

King County Parks and Recreation
(206) 296-0100
www.kingcounty.gov/recreation/parks.aspx

As the department's website is quick to point out, the county has "200 parks, 175 miles of trail, 26,000 acres of open space." It operates three community centers, one outdoor pool, and one indoor pool, the Weyerhauser King County Aquatic Center, which was built for the 1990 Goodwill Games. Fees range from $3.25 per person for a family swim in the recreation pool and $5 per adult in the competition pool, to $6.25 for an adult to take a water exercise class. A 10-visit card for fitness class is available at a reduced rate. Adult and senior lap swim is $5. There is also a discounted pool pass that is worth purchasing if you swim at least three times a week and are willing to commit to a three-month pass or a full-year pass.

Bellevue Parks and Community Services
Bellevue
(425) 452-6885
www.ci.bellevue.wa.us/parks-community-services.htm

Bellevue has five community centers and an indoor aquatics center with two pools. Swim fees range from $5.50 for youth open swim to $6.50 for adults. A membership card offering 12 swims for the price of 10 and discounted three-month passes are also available. If you're an early bird, you can swim before 10 a.m. on weekdays for $4. The South Bellevue Community Center has a 2,500-square-foot fitness center including free weights, treadmills, weight machines, and elliptical trainers. Fees range from $5.50 for drop-in ($7 for non-residents) and a three-month pass for $100 ($120 non-residents) to an annual pass for an individual at $315 ($378 non-resident) and a pass for a family with two adults and children for $564 ($684 non-residents).

City of Redmond Parks and Recreation Department
Redmond
(425) 556-2900
www.redmond.gov

The city has one community center and pool, but the community center doesn't offer recreational opportunities and the city doesn't operate the pool. General admission for lap, public, and family swims for folks aged 4 and up is $4.40 for residents, $5.50 for non-residents. Discount 10-swim passes cards are also available. The city also operates a variety of walking trails. All activities at Redmond Parks are offered on a two-tier fee system with residents and non-residents paying different rates. Non-residents even have a different registration date for programs.

Kirkland Parks and Community Services
(425) 587-3000

www.ci.kirkland.wa.us/depart/parks.htm

Kirkland operates two community centers and has a range of fitness classes. The North Kirkland Community Center focuses on programming for children while Peter Kirk Community Center offers classes for adults and seniors. The city also operates a heated outdoor pool, which is open June through September. Single admission is $4 for all ages, a 10-visit pass is $35, and a season pass for an individual is $90. Household passes are $260.

FREE CHI: FREE YOGA & OTHER STUFF

Discover Yoga
15744 Redmond Way

Redmond

(425) 861-1318

www.discoveryoga.com

There's plenty of need for grounding and relaxation here in the land of Microsoft, what with the long hours and even longer commutes. Fortunately, there's a place where people can try something new for not a lot of money, even if they have plenty of it. Discover holds a free class the first Friday of the month from 6 to 7:30 p.m. and also offers the first class for any new student for free.

Samadhi Yoga
1205 E. Pike St.

(206) 329-4070

www.samadhi-yoga.com

This Capitol Hill yoga studio offers a free yoga class to the community on Sunday from 2:30 to 3:45 p.m. According to Samadhi's website, most classes feature "breath work, chanting, seated meditation, and inspirational words and music."

The Samarya Center

1806 E. Yesler Way
(206) 568-8335
www.samaryacenter.org

Samaraya offers one or two free community classes per quarter as well as some of the cheapest classes in town at $11. Class size is limited to 25 people. Check the website calendar for dates of free community classes.

Tai Chi

Third Place Books
17171 Bothell Way NE
Lake Forest Park
(206) 366-3333
www.thirdplacebooks.com

This is yet another one of those times when Third Place proves it really is trying to be all things to all people. The weekly Tai Chi drop-in gathering runs from 8:45 to 9:45 a.m. on Saturday and is open to all, regardless of age, experience, or ability.

SPORTING **EVENTS**

Things aren't the way they were in our grandparents' day. You know, when you could take in an entire Major League baseball game by looking through a hole in a wooden fence . . . as long as the local constabulary didn't happen along, catch you in the act, and chase you off. At today's superstadiums, there aren't any wooden fences with knotholes in them and it seems like there's nothing free, but there are a few places you can go to see action for nothing or next to nothing. Who knows? A team you knew nothing about could suddenly become your favorite. It worked for beach volleyball in the London Summer Olympics, didn't it?

Everett Aquasox
3802 Broadway
Everett
(425) 258-3673
aquasox.com

If Seattle Mariners games at Safeco Field are getting too spendy, you can go see some of the team's future stars today just an hour north at Everett Memorial Stadium, the home of the M's Short Season A Classification farm team, the Everett Aquasox. At $7, the price of being a bleacher bum is a little higher than it used to be, but there's a family-friendly feel here you won't find at Safeco. Kids run around free chasing after foul balls and there are more chances for children to run the bases after a game here than there are in Seattle. In 2013, the club also had a lottery ticket promotion where fans who had a non-winning lottery ticket could get a $7 general admission seat for $2. The team also has a variety of additional money-saving offers each season including Boeing Employee Credit Union Night when box seats are $5 and Two-For-Tuesdays when a coupon from Carls Jr. gets you two box seats for the price of one. For more details, see the "Tickets & Promotions" tab on the website.

Seattle Mariners
Safeco Field
1250 First Ave. S
(206) 346-4000
mariners.com

There are many reasons to catch a Major League baseball game at Safeco Field and the team is just one of them. There's the beauty of the stadium, the pretty sunsets you can see over Elliott Bay from the right seats, and the sounds of the trains as they pass by. I mention all these things on the off chance that you happen to have this book with you when you're at an M's game and they're in the middle of their summer swoon. Just so you can't say I didn't warn you. At $7, the cheapest seats in the house are still less than what you'd pay for a movie and there are also a variety of specials that push down the cost of $20 Reserved View Level seats to prices nearing budget friendly. On Monday and Tuesday, Boeing Employee Credit Union Family Nights, select View Level seats are $10 off. On days when there are senior specials, usually Sundays, select View Level seats are $5 off and select Main

Level seats are $10 off for people over 60 with ID (limit one per senior). The same is true of military nights (limit four per military member). The seats can go down to $8 on college nights or when there's a group of 40 or more buying a block of tickets. In 2013, college students could make the deal even better by showing up for Happy Hour in the Pen two-and-a-half hours before the game when there are great deals on beer, pizza, and soda. The Mariners have also instituted dynamic pricing, allowing the organization to change prices as games approach. An M's spokesperson said that means bleacher seats for the game you want to see might be $5 now, but $15 if you wait until next week to buy. That's the bad news. The good news is that it allows the M's to offer "dynamic deals," possibly based on lower than expected sales for a particular game. The best way to find out about those deals is to follow the Mariners on Twitter or Facebook, sign up for Mariners Mail on the website, or check the website at mariners.com/tickets.

Seattle Pacific University
Brougham Pavilion
3414 3rd Ave. West
(206) 281-2000
www.spufalcons.com

There's no such thing as a free game at SPU, but most games featuring the school's NCAA Division II teams, the Falcons, are ridiculously cheap, especially for students, youth, or seniors—they pay $3. Adult general admission to all events is $6 or $8 if you want to feel like a big spender. Soccer matches are played at Interbay Stadium on 17th Avenue West and Dravus Street.

Seattle Thunderbirds
ShoWare Center
625 W. James St.
Kent
(253) 856-6999
www.seattlethunderbirds.com

Regular season tickets for the Western Hockey League team's games range from $16 to $40, but it's possible to see training camp practices and scrimmages free at the ShoWare Center. Although practices are usually held on the Thursday or Friday before Labor Day, the best way to make sure you have the right day is to check the website or get the latest updates by subscribing to the club's e-news or following the club on Facebook or Twitter.

Seattle University

Logan Field
14th and Cherry
(206) 296-6000
www.goseattleu.com

The NCAA Division I school's team, the Redhawks, participates in 14 sports including basketball, baseball, cross country, and golf. The only sport that's free to see is softball.

Tacoma Rainiers

Cheney Stadium
2502 S. Tyler St.
Tacoma
(253) 752-7707
tacoma.rainiers.milb.com/index.jsp?sid=t529

Looking for a higher class of farm team than Everett? Hit the City of Destiny for a game by the Mariners' AAA farm team where players are just a step away from going to The Show (that's the major leagues, for folks who don't speak baseball). You can get tickets on the grass berm starting at $7 and reserved seats for $13 ($12 for kids and members of the military). The Rainiers aren't cheaper than the Aquasox, but the caliber of play is definitely higher given the AAA designation.

University of Washington

Locations vary

Free tickets for UW Huskies' sports are few and far between. There are men's and women's tennis at the Nordstrom Athletic Center, rowing on the Montlake Cut, and indoor and outdoor track and field meets. Cross country has the Sun Dodger Invitational on a Saturday at a local park. You can also see free golf in the fall if you don't mind traveling to Gold Mountain in Bremerton or Washington National in Auburn to see the men play or Sahalie Country Club to see the women play. Volleyball is a bargain, though, with single game adult general admission at $6 (youth for $4), a family plan with four tickets for one game selling for $15, or season tickets for $50 per person.

GROUP **BIKE** RIDES **&** RUNS

Why let a silly thing like rain get in the way of a good time? Although some Seattle motorists seem to forget how to drive in the wet once the first rainfall of the season comes, those of fleeter foot and wheel seem to do just fine, thank you, as is evidenced by the number of groups that ride and run even in the ugly months.

The Balanced Athlete
The Landing
800 N. 10th Place, Ste. F
Renton
(425) 282-4556
www.thebalancedathlete.com

The store has free group runs Tuesday and Thursday evenings at 6 p.m and on Sunday at 8 a.m.

Cascade Bicycle Club
7400 Sand Point Way NE
(206) 522-3222
www.cascade.org

Bike riding doesn't get more organized than this. Cascade has several free bike rides a day every day of the year, all listed on the calendar on its website. The listings include terrain, pace, and ride description, as well as conditions for cancellation (some list steady rain and others list ice and snow). Participants should arrive at the meeting point 15 minutes before scheduled start and be ready to leave at the appointed time. They must also sign a waiver before the ride starts. If you have questions about a day's ride, contact the ride leader of the specific ride listed on the ride description.

Critical Mass
www.seattlecriticalmass.org

Locals either love or hate this controversial group. Considering that many of the members' goals include advocating biking as a healthy and fun alternative to driving, building community, and convincing more people to opt for two wheels rather than four, CM would seem to have its heart in the right place. The problem was in the execution. In its early years, its effort to assert bicyclists' right to the road through its Friday afternoon rides in downtown Seattle led to confrontations, when the group ended up blocking intersections during rush hour. Most rides have gone off without a hitch, however. The group meets at Westlake Center at 5:30 p.m. on the last Friday of the month.

Evergreen Tandem Club
www.evergreentandemclub.org

If you and your co-pilot have ever felt out of place at a regular group ride, the Evergreen Tandem Club has your back . . . well, both your backs, really, because it offers a ride almost every weekend for people who own bicycles built for two. Annual membership is $25.

Fleet Feet Sports
911 E. Pine St.
(206) 329-1466
www.fleetfeetseattle.com

Fleet Feet does three regular runs each week. On Tuesday and Thursday, the group meets at the store at 6 p.m. for a run with an urban flavor. The run goes for 5 to 6 miles on Tuesday and up to 6 miles on Thursday. The Tuesday gathering is a social 6-mile Fun Run that wends its way through the trails of Interlaken and the Arboretum in summer. Thursday's event is a 3- to 4-mile Pub Run that makes its way through the neighborhood and ends with drinks and food at Linda's. On the second Thursday of the month, there's also Pint Striders, which features a different sponsor each time, a chance to demo new gear, and discounted food and drinks at 95 Slide.

Niketown Running Club
Sixth and Pike
(206) 447-6453

Runners and walkers just do it on Tuesday at 6 p.m. The run starts at the store, is open to all levels and all paces, and goes for anywhere from 2 to 8 miles depending on participants. After the run, the store provides free refreshments including fruit and water.

Roadrunner Sports

Kent Station, 444 Ramsay Way, Kent; (253) 850-6200
7020 Woodlawn Ave. NE, Seattle; (206) 517-5100
www.roadrunnersports.com

The Kent branch of this national company offers a run at 6 p.m. every Tuesday and Thursday. The group welcomes people of all running abilities. The store also holds an adventure run every third Thursday at 6 p.m. complete with free raffle tickets, up to $3,000 in prizes given away, and a beer garden at the end. The Seattle store holds its adventure run on the first Thursday of the month.

Veloce Velo

2750 77th St. SE
Mercer Island
(206) 236-0123
velocevelo.com

The shop offers rides each Saturday at 8 a.m. In summer, the ride is a 27-mile South Lake Loop. In winter, it's a 14.5-mile loop around Mercer Island. Ride and pace adjusted based on the abilities of the riders.

West Seattle Running Club

(206) 938-2416
www.westseattlerunningclub.com

Running may be the main reason for getting together, but this running group for everybody also does potlucks, biking, and other activities. The group has three runs a week. Tuesday and Thursday runs start at 6 p.m. and Sunday runs begin at 8:30 a.m. All meet near the Statue of Liberty at Alki Beach Park, 1702 Alki Ave. SW. On Thursday, the group ends the run with pizza at Spiro's Pizza and Pasta. The Sunday group finishes off with coffee and baked goods at Tully's Coffee.

THRIFT STORES:
ONE MAN'S TRASH IS
ANOTHER MAN'S FURNITURE

*"My heart starts to palpitate when I see an open
sign at a thrift store. Especially, an uncharted
one I've never seen before."*
—Elizabeth Mason,
owner of The Paper Bag Princess

Let's face it, Seattle is a recycling kind of town. Where in some cities you'd have to drive around the night before garbage day looking for a great piece of furniture, here people just leave it out with a Free sign on it, hoping it will go away. Most items are garage sale rejects, but there have been some good values. Not long ago, my wife and I found ourselves considering a large dining room cabinet with marble counters that someone had left on the curb in front of the house they had just moved into.

We changed our minds when it started to rain, however.

During my 22 years in Seattle, I have seen the following items left on the sidewalk by owners who are either looking for good homes for their old stuff or just want to get it out of their houses. Heck, I've even left some of this stuff myself:

Barstools	Desks/desk chairs	Potted plants
Baskets	Diaper changing table	River rocks
Bookcases (man, they looked great)	End tables	Sofas
Building materials	File cabinets	Television
Chairs	Lamps	Tires
Computer monitors	Microwave oven	Wood
	Movie posters	Vanity (bathroom)

The better the neighborhood, the better the quality. Sure, curbside stuff is plentiful in the Central District, the University District, and Capitol Hill, but if you want better castoffs, you have to go to the same areas to which kids travel across town to go trick-or-treating during Halloween and for which garage salers make a beeline early on Saturday mornings. That's why I like Mercer Island, Kirkland, and Madison Park.

If you can't find it on the street for free, though, I know some really great places to get stuff for free or next to nothing.

Craigslist
seattle.craigslist.org/bar/
seattle.craigslist.org/zip/

Apparently, there are some things that the ubiquitous list won't sell, but that's only because it's helping people give them away via the free and barter categories under the "for sale" section. The free section is self-explanatory.

If you can pick it up and take it with you, these folks are more than happy for you to have it for absolutely nothing. Zero. Zilch. Zippo. Nada. Recent Seattle listings have included an Army surplus cabinet, a used picket fence, two toilets, a piano, goat manure, and even what one called a "very spicy amazing pot of curry." The barter category features an equally eclectic mix with a catch. Although many of the sellers will take money, they're also just as willing to take something in trade. One seller wanted to trade a tattoo for medical marijuana. Another wanted to trade a fly-fishing outfit for a handgun

Buffalo Exchange
4530 NE University Way
(206) 545-0175

2232 NW Market St.
(206) 297-5920
www.buffaloexchange.com

It isn't the cheapest thrift store in town, but the clothing selection is a little more stylish than at other stores. That's especially true at the University District location where many of the clothes are purchased from students.

Freecycle
www.freecycle.org

If you have something you want to get rid of and are just a little bit worried about Craigslist, there's always this green option to list the things you're trying to move out of your house, but don't want to sell. Even more fortunately, it takes absolutely no know-how to go to the site and sign up for the Seattle/Mercer Island group (there are also groups for other King County cities). Before you know it, you'll find out about more freebies than you ever wanted, and others that make you scratch your head in wonderment. During a recent weekend on the Seattle group, postings included someone looking to give away a finicky paper shredder, 12 pounds of Instant Ocean Saltwater mix, as well as drinks from China and offbrand lemonade mix. Of course, there were also more standard items like kitchen gadgets, books, and furniture. And if you're not finding what you're looking for, you can always do a wanted listing.

Goodwill Outlet

1765 6th Ave. S
Seattle
(206) 957-5516

2208 W. Casino Rd.
Everett
(425) 263-8540
www.seattlegoodwill.org

The bins! The bins! Considering that this is where Seattle Goodwill sends all of the merchandise that hasn't sold in any of its regular thrift stores, it's the type of place where only the serious need apply. If you've got a great eye for values that other people miss, this is the place for you. New bins filled with merchandise are rolled out frequently throughout the day, and shoppers are required to stay behind the blue line until all the bins have been secured and store employees have reached a safe distance. Then, shoppers lunge for their shot at the next round of bargains. The place is also good for people on an extremely tight budget as most items are sold by the pound. Clothes and linens sell for $1.49 a pound. If you buy more than 50 pounds, the price drops to $1.09. Over 100 pounds, it's 89 cents. Small electronics sell for 49 cents a pound.

Kookaburra Kids

3432 NE 45th St.
(206) 525-0619

It may be under new ownership, but one thing hasn't changed. It still has that "just-so" feel about it while other kids' thrift store and consignment shops specializing in kids' clothes look like my kids' playroom after they've been stuck inside on a rainy day. The clothing is gently used, and the prices are surprisingly low. It now also focuses on locally produced, handmade goods, gifts for newborns, and books.

Labels

7212 Greenwood Ave. N
(206) 781-1194
labelsseattle.com

Labels has been operating at the same spot for more than 30 years for a good reason: good value. It's neat and tidy, it's relatively easy to find what you want, and it charges a third of the original price for designer clothing. It also sells maternity clothes and clothes for kids and specializes in purses. A writer friend I know is still bragging about a Kenneth Cole purse she got for under $20 in early 2009. With prices like these, it's no wonder the store has had a loyal following since the 1980s.

Seattle Goodwill
Ballard, 6400 8th Ave. NW, Seattle; (206) 957-5544
Bellevue, 14515 148th Ave. NE, Bellevue; (425) 649-2080
Burien, 1031 SW 128th St., Burien; (206) 957-1020
Seattle, 1400 S Lane St., Seattle; (206) 860-5711
Shoreline, 14500 15th Ave. NE, Shoreline; (206) 631-8454
Southcenter, 1174 Andover Park W, Tukwila; (206) 575-4944
South Lake Union, 411 Westlake Ave. N, Seattle; (206) 812-6625
www.seattlegoodwill.org

All Goodwill shops have good bargains, but some are better than others. It may be because of its eastside location, but the Bellevue Goodwill has a reputation for having a better class of merchandise at unbelievably good prices. The Seattle store is known for its Glitter Gala (an off-site fundraiser) and its Glitter Sale in mid-November when it sells jewelry, formal wear, and high-end accessories. Although I'm not fashion-savvy enough to buy clothes at thrift shops, a friend who is assures me that the Ballard Goodwill has a good selection of stylish clothes. "People in Ballard know how to dress," she says. Who knew?

Value Village
Capitol Hill, 1525 11th Ave., Seattle; (206) 322-7789
Crown Hill, 8532 15th Ave. NW, Seattle; (206) 783-4648
Lake City, 12548 Lake City Way NE, Seattle; (206) 365-8232
Burien, 131 SW 157th St., Burien; (206) 246-6237
Totem Lake, 12515 116th Ave. NE, Kirkland; (425) 821-7186
Redmond, 16761 Redmond Way, Redmond; (425) 883-2049
www.valuevillage.com

The idea of a chain of thrift stores doesn't seem right, somehow, but Value Village seems to have just about everything you'd need in its huge stores— you just have to be willing to do a bit of work to find what you want. And isn't that what being a cheap bastard is all about? The best time to get great bargains is on holidays like Labor Day and Memorial Day when the store is open and everything's on sale. If you drop off your castoffs on the day you shop, you can save even more because the store gives you a coupon for a percentage off your next purchase. You can also get a Super Savers Club Card and save even more.

BUILDING **SUPPLIES**

Habitat for Humanity Home Improvement Outlet
21 S. Nevada St.
(206) 957-6914
habitatskc.org

The Habitat outlet sells used building materials at a discount, and also has new merchandise. That's because local contractors often donate appliances and other materials purchased for projects that ended up not being used. The store also sells a small selection of furniture and other odds and ends. All of the proceeds go to Habitat for Humanity, which uses the money to build houses for needy families.

The Re Store
1440 NW 52nd St.
(206) 297-9119
www.re-store.org

If you can't find the building supplies you need on the street, the ReStore is the next best thing. The store sells salvage building materials and more. The store accepts drop-offs of old building materials from contractors and everyday do-it-yourselfers and even has a field crew that will go out to a demolition site and collect usable used materials, then turn around and sell it for up to half the original price. That not only means cheap molding and doors, but also inexpensive antique lighting, door pulls, tubs, and a lot of stuff you didn't know you needed. If you bring in a donation, you'll get a store credit for 25 percent of the resale value of the item you donated. So, if the ReStore believes it can resell your item for $50, you'll get $12.50 off your next purchase.

Second Use Building Materials
3223 Sixth Ave. S
(206) 763-6929
www.seconduse.com

Second Use salvages and sells old building materials for less than new, allowing contractors and DIYers to save money while keeping perfectly usable supplies out of the dump.

Not Exactly a Thrift Store, but . . .

Yes, I know the Friends of the [Seattle Public] Library Book Sale isn't exactly a thrift store, but the prices are worthy of a thrift shop. CDs, DVDs, and paperback books all sell for $1 each, hardbacks $2, and the selection is large enough to take up an entire airplane hangar at the former Sand Point Naval Air Station. The sale is so popular that people start lining up outside the building around 5 a.m., at least four hours before the sale starts, sometimes earlier, no matter what the weather. Even owners of used bookstores stake out places in line.

The sale was held twice a year until construction on the hangar forced the Friends to have sales at locations around town. The sale was expected to return to Magnuson in late 2013, but there was some question about whether it would continue to be held semi-annually. Until they figure it out, they will be doing smaller sales around town.

If you don't mind going on the road to save money, there are a few other annual sales worth checking out. Packwood holds two annual flea markets Memorial Day and Labor Day so big that the booths cover an area three-quarters of a mile long by a quarter-mile wide, and it takes three days to see it all. In addition, the Long Beach Peninsula holds what it bills as The World's Longest Garage Sale on Memorial Day weekend, stretching 28 miles. Don't forget to bring your smartphone so you can check eBay or Amazon to see how good the deals are—unless you're like the cheap bastard and you're too thrifty to have one. At least, not yet anyway.

FURNITURE

Goodwill and Value Village are great places to get ridiculously cheap furnishings, but when you reach a point where you want to go to the next level, you may want to consider this place:

Armadillo Consignment
12421 Greenwood Ave. N
(206) 363-6700
www.armadilloconsignment.com

Armadillo isn't a thrift store; it's a consignment shop where people bring their goods to be sold hoping to get some money back. What makes Armadillo stand out is its discount pricing policy. Since the store prefers to clear items within 60 days, it cuts prices three times to keep things moving. At 30 days, the discount is 15 percent. After 45 days, it drops 20 percent, and at 60 days, it's 25 percent off, which can make for a great bargain. Even the price tags in the store show the discount, with each tag listing the current price as well as what the price will be lowered to if the item is still on hand and the date each markdown will occur. While it's a great policy, it's also important for shoppers to have what my wife calls a "Moscow mentality." If you see it, like it, and can't live without it, don't wait. Otherwise, it could be gone. If it's something you're not sure about and you think is just a little too expensive, you can take the chance, but there's no guarantee it will be there when you come back. Most of the furniture is modern, mid-century, and contemporary. The store also has a Spring Cleaning Sale, a Parking Lot Sale in mid-July where vendors give a percentage of their proceeds to charity, and an Anniversary Sale in November right before Thanksgiving.

SPORTING **GOODS**

Play It Again Sports
19513 Hwy. 99, Lynnwood; (425) 670-1184
17622 108th Ave. SE, Renton; (425) 227-8777
1304 Stewart St., Seattle; (206) 264-9255
13210 NE 175th St., Woodinville; (425) 481-8676
www.playitagainsports.com

Although there never seems to be any shortage of golf clubs or baseball mitts stacked amongst the stuff people pile curbside, they seem to disappear when you finally decide to take up golf or join a softball team. Some would call this a used sporting goods store. Me, I call it an equipment thrift shop. While all of the shops carry the standard mix of golf clubs and baseball bats, each store seems to have a specialty. Seattle's focus has been on specialty bikes, and it rents bikes in summer and fall. It's also a ski and snowboard shop with equipment rentals in winter. The Lynnwood location is said to be one of the biggest hockey stores in the state. Woodinville also specializes in skis, snowboards, and scooters and does scooter repair as well. Renton has weight and fitness equipment.

FOOD

No, we're not talking about previously used food. We're talking about a few select outlets where you can get really good deals on stuff you know you want anyway.

Brown & Haley
Factory Outlet, 110 E. 26th St., Tacoma; (253) 620-3067
Warehouse Outlet, 3500-C 20th St., Fife; (253) 620-3030
www.brown-haley.com/outletstores.php

What self-respecting Northwesterner doesn't love Almond Roca? Or Hazelnut Roca? Or Mocha Roca? And what self-respecting Northwesterner wouldn't love to save money on those and chocolate-covered graham crackers and

Brown & Haley Mountain Bars? It's a bit out of the way, but if you're headed down south, it's worth the trip. In fact, I think I'll go have a Mocha Roca right now.

Chocolati Factory Outlet
7708 Aurora Ave. N
(206) 784-5212
www.chocolati.com

Many of the truffles at this tiny shop on Aurora are the same price as those found in Chocolati's cafes, but there's at least one small tray filled with rejects and seconds that sell for a substantial discount. You may also be able to find old holiday candy for half off.

Oh Boy! Oberto Factory Outlet
1715 Rainier Ave. S
(206) 322-7524
www.oberto.com

It's no exaggeration to call this place a real sausagefest because that's what it is, as well as a celebration of inexpensive, locally produced dried meat in all its splendor. Jerky, salami, sausage, you name it, it's all here at lower-than-retail prices.

Seattle Chocolates Retail Outlet
1180 Andover Park W.
Tukwila
(877) 427-7915
www.seattlechocolates.com

Seattle Chocolates is known for its truffles, but most stores stock only a limited selection. The factory store not only sells the entire line, it also has samples out and sells factory seconds. What's available on the factory seconds shelf depends on what's being produced at the time of your visit, and also what mistakes have been made. No matter what the seconds are, you can usually get them for about $5 a pound. Other prices are close to what you'd find in regular retail stores. Open 10 a.m to 5 p.m. Monday through Friday; closed weekends.

SECTION 3:

Exploring Seattle

WALKING TOURS:
A CENTS OF PLACE

"Anywhere is walking distance,
if you've got the time."
—Steven Wright

The Ballard Locks. *The Seattle Times.* Benaroya Hall. The Washington Park Arboretum. These local institutions have been part of our lives so long that we feel we know them like the backs of our hands. We take all our out-of-town guests to see the fish ladder and watch boats go from Puget Sound to the Ship Canal and back again. We read the Times every day. Whenever we want a dose of high culture, the home of the Seattle Symphony is one of our favorite go-to places. And when we want to go out for a nice walk on a pretty day, the Arboretum is the natural choice. But can you name most of the flowers you see during your walk? Did you know there are organ concerts at Benaroya? Were you aware that the Seattle Times isn't printed in Seattle? And do you know how the locks work or why they're even necessary? Many of the free tours available in the Seattle area not only help out-of-towners learn more about the local culture, they also help locals understand many of the things they take for granted.

CITY **TOURS**

Seattle Free Walking Tours
2000 Western Ave. at Victor Steinbrueck Park
www.seattlefreewalkingtours.org

The name says it all. Founded in 2012, Seattle Free Walking Tours takes people on tours of the city and shows them cool stuff they might have otherwise missed. Unlike other tour companies, SFWT charges absolutely nothing for the service. It asks only that you tip the guides what you feel it was worth. Suggested tip is $15. No reservations necessary. Just show up. Its one-hour Pike Place Market tour meets daily at Victor Steinbrueck Park at 9:30 a.m. Its two-hour Seattle Experience tour meets there at 11 a.m. The company also does a weekly Sunday tour of Ballard that meets at 2:30 at Bergen Place Park, 5420 22nd Ave. NW.

GOVERNMENT **BUILDINGS** & OTHER **FACILITIES**

Hiram M. Chittenden Locks Visitors Center
3015 NW 54th St.
(206) 783-7059
www.nws.usace.army.mil/Missions/CivilWorks/LocksandDams/ChittendenLocks
.aspx

While it's always fun to take your children or out-of-town visitors to the Ballard Locks and the fish ladder, it always leaves so many questions. How were the locks built? Why are they necessary? And how do you train a fish to use a ladder, anyway? When those questions finally get the better of you, you can take this hour-long, ranger-led tour that covers the history of the locks and how they work and answers all the questions you've always had, but only your children were brave enough to ask. There are tours at 1 and 3 p.m. daily from May to the end of September. In October and November, there's one tour at 2 p.m. every day except Tuesday and Wednesday when the Visitors Center is closed. No tours December through February. In March and April, there's one tour daily at 2 p.m. except Tuesday and Wednesday.

Klondike Gold Rush National Historic Park
319 2nd Ave. S
(206) 220-4240
www.nps.gov/klse/index.htm

When most people think about national parks, they think nature and wildlife, not the gritty urban neighborhood of Pioneer Square. Unless you count pigeons, squirrels, and late-night bar patrons, there's not much wildlife, few trees, and no open space. Yet somehow, there's still a guided tour given by a national park ranger. Although the summer tour had long been offered on a daily basis at 2 p.m. June through Labor Day, the schedule and frequency were expected to change in 2013. Little information was available at deadline, however.

Port of Tacoma

Fabulich Center
3600 Port of Tacoma Rd
Tacoma
(253) 383-9463
www.portoftacoma.com

Go ahead, joke all you want about the aroma of Tacoma, but the city happens to be home to the ninth busiest port in the country (Seattle is number eight). The port's monthly bus tour shows you why with a glimpse into what it is that they actually do down there all day. The tour is free, but reservations are required because space is limited and fills fast. For dates, check the website at www.portoftacoma.com/tours.

Seattle Public Library

1000 Fourth Ave.
(206) 386-4636
www.spl.org

Just the thought of a tour of a public library is enough to make your eyes roll into your head from boredom, but the Seattle Central Library isn't your average library. Dutch architect Rem Koolhaas designed the building with a variety of cool architectural features including a reference library section called the Mixing Chamber, and the Book Spiral, which is essentially a gently sloping spiral ramp that takes people through the book stacks, following the Dewey Decimal System from bottom to top. Don't take my word for it, though. The best way to see all the Koolhaas cool is to schedule a free tour. You can also do a self-guided tour.

FACTORY **TOURS**

Boehm's Candies

255 NE Gilman Blvd.
Issaquah
(425) 392-6652
www.boehmscandies.com

At this candy factory and retail store in a chalet, you not only get your choice of a variety of confections including truffles, peanut brittle, and seasonal sweets, you also can choose your tour experience. You can take a self-guided window walking tour of the factory where you'll see workers produce pounds and pounds of the company's products, or you can get up close and personal on a guided tour. The windows on the self-guided tour give a glimpse of the kitchen, the hand-dipping area, and the factory where clusters are made. The guided walking tour costs $4, but if you want fresh samples, it's worth it. The factory typically runs until 3:30 p.m. You can't stop in and do a guided tour at the last minute, though. You need to have a confirmed reservation before you go.

Mighty O Donuts
2110 N. 55th St.
(206) 547-0335
www.mightyo.com

A tour at this doughnut production facility may be small, but it's mighty. That's because the factory floor where these organic doughnuts are made is a cramped space at the back of Mighty O's retail bakery in Seattle's Tangle-town neighborhood. Folks who go on the half-hour field trip get to handle some of the equipment used in the process, see the batter being mixed, and watch the mini-doughnuts being fried and dipped in cinnamon sugar before they eat them. Tours must be arranged at least a week in advance and are usually conducted on Wednesday, Thursday, or Friday between 9 and 11:30 a.m. Minimum tour size is 3; maximum tour size is 12.

Seattle Times Printing Plant
North Creek Facility
19200 120th Ave. NE
Bothell
(425) 489-7000
www.seattletimescompany.com/operations/tours.htm

Did you ever wonder how a newspaper comes together, but were afraid to ask? I'm not talking about how the stories get in there. Heck, you can see old episodes of Lou Grant to figure that out, but if you've ever wondered how a paper was actually printed and put together, this is the tour for you. You can see the process from the beginning when robots move the rolls of newsprint onto the presses through to when it's loaded on the trucks. The tour is free, but is only available on Thursday afternoons because that's the day the Times prints the non-news sections of the Sunday paper. There's room for up to 35 people on a tour. You don't have to be part of a group to take the tour, but you do have to call Kate Palmer to make reservations. Children under the age of 8 are not allowed.

BUILDING **TOURS**

Benaroya Hall
200 University St.
(206) 215-4800
www.seattlesymphony.org/benaroya/tour/

No matter how hard we try, whenever my wife and I go to the Seattle Symphony, we get there so late that we barely have time to find our seats much less really get to enjoy the place. Which is why a tour of the hall sounds like such a great idea. Now, all we have to do is find some free time at noon or 1 p.m. on Friday when the tours begin. The tour meets at Benaroya's Grand Lobby Entrance at the corner of Third Avenue and University Street and is appropriate for ages 10 and up. Some tours may also feature recital demonstrations of Benaroya Hall's Watjen organ. For dates of the organ recitals, check the website.

5th Avenue Theatre
1308 5th Ave.
(206) 625-1900
www.5thavenue.org

This grand 1926 movie house, which was saved from a wrecking ball in the 1970s, has a range of impressive Chinoise-style architectural features that you might miss when you're focused on the show on stage. That's why the beautifully restored theater offers a 20-minute tour of the building at noon on Monday. The tour is quite popular with silent movie fans. It's best to register in advance so the 5th Avenue can contact you if a tour is cancelled.

Moore Theatre
1932 2nd Ave.
(206) 682-1414
www.stgpresents.org

The Moore is one of Seattle's oldest theaters and well worth a behind-the-scenes look. Tours are on the second Saturday of the month, start at 10 a.m. at the theater's main entrance, and last 90 minutes.

Paramount Theatre
911 Pine St.
(206) 682-1414
www.stgpresents.org

Originally called the Seattle, the Paramount was a movie palace built by the movie studio of the same name in 1928. Although it fell on hard times and was eventually reduced to showing second-run films, a $20 million restoration in 1995 returned it to its original glory. Theater buffs can take tours of the movie house where Frances Farmer and Bruce Lee once ushered (but not at the same time). Tours take place on the first Saturday of the month at 10 a.m. and last about 90 minutes; meet at the Paramount's main entrance. The Paramount also has opened a Historic Theaters Library featuring old memorabilia, documents, and posters. It's open 10 a.m. to 3 p.m. Tuesday and Thursday.

NATURE TOURS

Mercer Slough Nature Park
1625 118th Ave. SE
Bellevue
(425) 452-6885
www.bellevuewa.gov/mseec.htm

Mercer Slough is an oasis within the city of Bellevue. The 320-acre park near downtown is the longest-standing preserved open space in the area and is on a major migratory path for birds. As a result, the park is often filled with wildlife, whether it be blue heron, green heron, or beaver and river otters, just to name a few. Every Saturday afternoon at 2 p.m., Mercer Slough offers a guided ranger walk that starts at the environmental education center and continues into the park where visitors learn about the freshwater wetland ecosystem.

Seward Park Environmental and Audubon Center
5902 Lake Washington Blvd. S
(206) 652-2444
sewardpark.audubon.org

Learn about the natural history of the park and all the things that grow there during this 90-minute walk in the park. Along the way, you'll find out stuff you never even considered when it comes to salamanders, salmon, and the area's many other inhabitants. Third Saturday of the month; toddler to age 4 free, youth to age 14 $2, and adults $4.

Washington Park Arboretum
Graham Visitors Center
2300 Arboretum Dr. East
(206) 543-8800
depts.washington.edu/uwbg/visit/tours.shtml

If you feel like you can't tell the players without a program whenever you go to an arboretum, the Washington Park Arboretum has a tour for you. Every Sunday, there's a 90-minute tour at 1 p.m. that covers some aspect of the park and should help you learn what you're seeing so you can impress your friends and neighbors on their next visit.

GALLERY WALKS:
FREE-FORM FETES

"Artists ought to walk a mile in someone else's pants. That way you're a mile away and you have their pants."
—Joseph P. Blodgett

In the beginning, there was the first Thursday of the month in Seattle, and it was good because it was the night before Friday. And then an artist or organizer or someone looking to make a buck came up with the idea of turning it into a night to go from art gallery to art gallery in Pioneer Square devouring art with our eyes and maybe having some free wine and cheese along the way. And it was very good. And then it came to pass that some enterprising soul decided to expand it to other parts of downtown and to museums, restaurants, and other non-arts-related businesses and it was even better. Soon, one art walk begat another and another and another and before we knew it, it seemed like there was a different gallery walk in a different part of the city almost every night of the month. And it was very, very good.

Here's a quick look at one of the best ways to enjoy high culture at no cost in neighborhoods throughout the city all while going out for a walk to get a little exercise.

GALLERY **WALKS**

Art Up Greenwood-Phinney
Second Friday
From Greenwood Avenue North and 87th Street south to Phinney Avenue and 65th Street

This fledgling effort boasts a mix of art exhibitions, live music, and restaurants and businesses either displaying artists' work or offering special Art Up discounts. About half of the venues are art galleries in their own right. The event runs from 6 to 9 p.m. There's now also a two-day art event in May called The Big One.

The Art Walk on Park Lane
Downtown Kirkland
(425) 893-8766

Artsy little Park Lane in downtown Kirkland closes to traffic from 6 to 9 p.m. on the second Friday of the month and its art galleries, boutiques, and restaurants get in on the act, displaying the work of local artists. The event runs May through October.

Ballard Art Walk

Second Saturday
Corner of NW Market Street and Ballard Avenue NW
(206) 784-9705
www.ballardchamber.com

Many of the galleries participating in this art walk aren't galleries at all. Instead, the ever-changing cast of characters includes restaurants, boutiques, salons, a wine shop, and, yes, even a few galleries. It is possible to walk the entire route between 6 and 9 p.m., but it's a bit of a hike from the heart of the event to the East Ballard participants. Fortunately, there are a few bars and even a grocery store along the way to fortify you for the trip. Print out a map of the month's route at the Ballard Chamber website before you go.

Capitol Hill Art Walk

Second Thursday
www.blitzcapitolhill.com

Capitol Hill has always been a bit edgy, so there should be no surprise that one of the art venues participating in its monthly art extravaganza is Babeland, an adult sex shop, but you don't have to go there if you don't want to. The rest of the event is similar to most other art walks, if not a little bit racier. It runs from 5 to 8 p.m. and also features live music as well as a literary component. For a complete list of venues and a map, go to Blitz's website.

Edmonds Third Thursday Art Walk

Edmonds
(425) 776-3778
www.edmondsartwalk.org

With more than 40 businesses participating in this monthly event north of Seattle, Edmonds claims it is one of the biggest art walks in the state. While I can't speak to that issue, there are several reasons to venture north for this art event, including live music and live artist demonstrations.

First Thursday

Pioneer Square and throughout downtown Seattle
www.firstthursdayseattle.com

When it comes to holding a big art event, the organizers of one of the country's first gallery walks don't mess around. It runs from noon to 8 p.m.—which allows plenty of time to cover the distance between Pioneer Square and the Seattle Art Museum—involves 80 venues, includes street musicians and art in the park, and even prompts museums to offer free admission. The event itself is in its late 40s, but it's still going strong and doesn't look a day over 39.

Fremont First Friday Art Walk
fremontfirstfriday.blogspot.com

The one-time artsy bohemian area that calls itself the Center of the Universe may have gone so upscale that the artists who made its reputation can no longer afford to live there, but its penchant for the odd lives on. This walk goes on from 6 to 9 p.m. and takes place under the watchful eyes of a Ukrainian statue of Vladimir Lenin and a sculpture of a Volkswagen Beetle–eating troll. In early 2013, there were 18 participants and the boundaries of the art walk went from Stone Way West to 2nd Avenue NW and from N. 34th Street to N. 36th Street.

Georgetown Second Saturday Art Attack
www.georgetownartattack.com

I love industrial art districts because they're filled with surprises. Once the original businesses that inhabit many of the warehouses have moved out, shut down, or gone belly up, artists often move in and change the way we see everything. And then they become victims of their own success by making an area so desirable that they can no longer afford it. This monthly event is part art show, part extended public relations effort to make the public aware of the community in order to save it from gentrification. While it has a mix of art, Art Attack could well be the only art walk in the city with a comic shop as a participant. And yes, it does comic art. The venues are spread out enough that this art walk also has a bus that runs along Airport Way South every 15 minutes from 6 to 9:30 p.m.

Wallingford Art Walk
First Wednesday
(206) 547-5177
www.wallingfordartwalk.org

Now in its fifth year, Wallingford's event runs along North 45th Street east from Stone Way North to I-5 with the heart of the event at Wallingford Center Plaza. The event features live music, artist demonstrations, restaurant discounts, and . . . art. The walk goes from 6 to 9 p.m. May through September.

West Seattle Art Walk
Second Thursday
westseattleartwalk.blogspot.com

Many of the businesses in this event feature the works of talented employees. The event goes from 6 to 9 p.m. with many of the venues centered in the Junction, a shopping district with a friendly neighborhood feel. The best time to go is when the event coincides with the area's annual art festival in July because the street is closed to traffic and there's more room to spread out. Participating businesses include a coffeehouse and an insurance office.

GETTING AROUND SEATTLE:
FREE RIDES & FREEWAYS

*"Why do they call it rush hour when
nothing moves?"*
—Robin Williams *from* Mork & Mindy

It seems like traffic in downtown Seattle is always a mess. If it's not a baseball game at Safeco Field, a football game at Qwest Field, or a concert at the Seattle Center, there seems to be some other inexplicably odd occurrence that messes up the traffic pattern. We've had a truck driver lose control of his vehicle and take out a historic landmark, Critical Mass rides blocking intersections during Friday afternoon rush hours, and the annual running of the anarchists every May Day. And that doesn't even include the random construction projects the city throws up without warning just to keep us on our toes.

And things may be about to get a whole lot worse before they get better. Thanks to the decision to replace the Alaskan Way Viaduct with an underground tunnel, Seattle will have its own version of the Big Dig for years to come, altering traffic patterns for what will seem like the rest of our lives.

While this isn't justification for avoiding downtown altogether, it is reason enough to start rethinking your options when you have to head into the heart of parkinglessness. Suddenly, transit is starting to look good again. While many of the options aren't necessarily free, most of them are a heck of a lot cheaper than paying the ever-increasing cost of parking. And that doesn't even include the wear and tear on your jangled nerves. Or your car. Thanks to rush hour express buses and Metro transit tunnels that allow Metro vehicles to avoid some of downtown's busiest streets, there are times when busing it really is the fastest option. Either that or finding a carpool so you can use the high occupancy vehicle (HOV) lanes on local highways. So sit back, relax, enjoy the ride, and maybe even bring a book (like this one) while you take advantage of one of these options.

Craigslist
Craigslist.com

It really makes more sense for people seeking longer rides to Portland or San Francisco, for example, but carless souls do advertise here to carpool from Bellevue, Seattle, or wherever their work life takes them. Ads are free, but you should offer to kick in a few dollars for gas. Even splitting fuel cost is still cheaper than paying full freight for parking. Remember, you are doing this at your own risk, though, so play it safe. If it doesn't feel right, look for another ride.

Erideshare.com

Where Craigslist's rideshare category seems to lean more toward long-distance trips than carpooling and commuting, this site tries to do both by matching those requesting rides with car owners offering same. Potential passengers and drivers alike join the site, then list their neighborhood or city, desired destination, when they need to go, and whether they are offering a ride, seeking one, or want to take turns. The information posts to a table listing what everyone is looking for in hopes that they will find a match. Although the public can see the table, you have to be a member to respond and the only way to contact a member is through the site, so there is some identity protection built in.

King County Water Taxi
Pier 50, Seattle
Seacrest Dock, 1660 Harbor Ave. SW, West Seattle
www.kingcounty.gov/transportation/kcdot/WaterTaxi.aspx

At $8 round-trip, the ferry from downtown Seattle to West Seattle may not sound all that cheap, but what it saves you in time and money is priceless. All it takes is a minor accident on the one route to West Seattle to cause a lengthy backup. And that doesn't include the difficulty of finding parking. It's also a great way to get out on the water on a sunny day during the ferry's daily April through October run. (It runs commuter hours only November through March.) The water taxi also operates two free shuttle buses that take people to the area's most popular spots, including the Admiral District and the Junction.

There's an interesting reverse catch when it comes to fares for the water taxi. If you have an ORCA card or other regional transit pass, your fare goes down to $3.50 each way. If the value of your pass exceeds $3 (which it would if you rode Light Link Rail from downtown for over $4, for example), you won't have to pay to board the water taxi. The water taxi also operates a run from Seattle to Vashon Island, but it's mostly a commuter route and travels only during rush hour. The water taxis run late on nights when the Seattle Mariners or Seattle Sounders play. Ticket vending machines accept Visa and MasterCard.

Metro
(206) 553-3000
metro.kingcounty.gov

Metro Transit runs a full schedule of bus and trolley service in Seattle and King County. The regular fare is $2.25 (one and two zones during off-peak hours), but increases to $2.50 for rides within the city of Seattle (one zone) and $3 (within King County/two zones) during peak hours from 6 to 9 a.m. and 3 to 6 p.m. on weekdays. While the city is considered one zone and all areas of King County outside Seattle city limits two zones, any time a trip starts or ends on a zone line, it is still considered a one-zone fare. The fare for ages 6 to 18 is $1.25; ages 65+ and individuals with disabilities ride for 75 cents. Up to four children age 5 and under ride free with a person paying an adult fare. Exact change is required, and passengers pay as they board. For more information about Metro fares, visit metro.kingcounty.gov/tops/bus/fare/fare-info.html. (Keep in mind that the rates were current at press time, but are subject to change.)

Fares for travel throughout central Puget Sound, including Washington State Ferries, can be paid using ORCA smart cards; just tap your ORCA at the card reader and your fare is paid. ORCA is accepted on Community Transit, Everett Transit, King County Metro Transit, Kitsap Transit, Pierce Transit, Sound Transit, and Washington State Ferries. For more information about ORCA, visit www.orcacard.com.

Sound Transit
(206) 398-5000
www.soundtransit.org

Sound Transit light rail may cost a bit more than Metro Transit, but it also has to cover more territory. A one-way adult trip from Tacoma to Seattle is $4.75, and one-way from Everett to Seattle is $4.50, with reduced fares for kids. Service is limited. There are only nine trains on the run between Tacoma and Seattle and four trains from Seattle to Everett. The best way to save money is to buy a monthly pass.

Washington State Ferries
Colman Ferry Dock
801 Alaskan Way
(206) 464-6400
www.wsdot.wa.gov/ferries

More Than Just Buses

When most people think of Metro, they just think about buses. The agency also offers other transportation services as well.

Carpool creator: Using the website rideshareonline.com, Metro helps people looking for rideshares and carpools to hook up and find a more economical, environmentally friendly way to their destination, whether it be the office, the big game, the blockbuster concert, or the kids' school. Yes, you saw that right, Metro/Rideshare's Schoolpool can even help you find a carpool for your kids or line you up with another season ticket holder to ride with all season long.

Vanpool maker: Heck, if there's enough interest and enough people wanting to go your way, you might even be able to start a vanpool. You need at least five people to create a vanpool. There are even vanshares if you just need to carpool on one leg of your commute— between the ferry dock and train station, for example. There's even metropool, a fleet of all-electric, no emission Nissan Leafs. For more information, go to metro.kingcounty.gov/commutervans.

Slugging facilitator: No, I'm not talking about a new baseball position or boxing coach. Instead, I'm referring to a practice now popular on the East Coast that allows car drivers to find riders at the last minute so they can drive in the HOV lanes. It's like going to the Home Depot to find a day laborer except that it involves going to a Park-and-Ride lot and picking up additional passengers on an informal basis. Now, Metro has formalized the practice with dynamic ride matching, only you won't have to wait out in the cold. Now you can do it via cellphone.

Airport shuttle service: Making the dreaded phone call to a friend to ask for a ride to the airport could become a thing of the past if you travel light enough. Instead of spending $50 on a town car or around $25 on a shuttle, depending on where you live, you could pay as little as $2.75 each way to ride a bus Sounder train.

Why spend $17 on an hour-long cruise around the harbor to see Elliott Bay when you could spend $7.70 for ferry rides back and forth across Puget Sound to Bainbridge Island? You won't get the narration about what you're seeing as you pass by, but you won't have to listen to the jokes that the tour guide thinks are funny, either. On the flip side, you'll get to see the city skyline coming and going and you'll even get a nice day trip to a small, walkable town on the other end for almost nothing. If you just want a cheap, roundtrip ferry ride, you can save even more by hopping the Vashon Ferry in West Seattle. Without a car it's $5 per person. A possible fare increase was expected in October 2013.

GETTING **OUT** OF **TOWN**

Ridester
www.ridester.com

If you want to put a lot of distance between Seattle and yourself for not a lot of money, this is a good place to start. It's a site where people planning trips longer than 20 miles can look for riders and riders can look for drivers. There's no charge to register with the site and the only fee a rider has to pay is a $2 service charge plus the amount the driver requests for the trip, which usually covers gas costs. Recent listings featured an odd mix of rates. A driver looking for riders from Seattle to Anchorage, for example, was asking $187 while a driver from Redding, California, to Seattle wanted only $30. Riders pay Ridester and the money is forwarded to the driver. Ridester charges drivers a 9.5 percent processing fee based on the asking price for the ride. Maybe that's why Mr. Tennessee only wanted to charge $1. The service is available in cities all over the country.

GARDENS & GARDENING:
FREE RANGE

"A perfect summer day is when the sun is shining, the breeze is blowing, the birds are singing, and the lawn mower is broken."

—JAMES DENT

One of the main reasons we put up with winter's gray, rainy days is that we know what they lead to: beautiful blooms in the spring and summer. Seattle has been named the Emerald City for a reason, and this is it. The area is so green and the temperatures so pleasant that more than a few visitors have been fooled into moving here because they think it's this beautiful all year. It's not. Summer quickly gives way to fall and fall quickly fades into winter and the dark months. That's why we all rush up north to see the first tulips in bloom in April and scramble to area gardens to see flowers as quickly as possible because we know they won't be around long. The displays at many public gardens are so impressive that we just can't help but be inspired to start a garden of our own, even if we don't have the foggiest idea of what we're doing. Fortunately, there's plenty of support for people like us, much of it is free, and none of it requires us to stand up and say, "My name is David . . . and I'm a plant-aholic."

GARDENS

Bellevue Botanical Gardens
12001 Main St.
Bellevue
(425) 452-2750
www.bellevuebotanical.org

Just because eastsiders have a reputation for shopping doesn't mean they don't appreciate a good garden. And this one is a great one. Not only is it known for its annual holiday display, Garden d'Lights, when its collection is festooned with lights, but it also includes a Waterwise Garden where water conservation is emphasized, an Alpine Rock Garden, and a 19-acre Botanical Reserve. It also offers free Living Laboratory classes for children from kindergarten to fourth grade in spring and early summer. The garden recently added the Ravine Experience, a suspension bridge over a ravine where you can see forest undergrowth and tree canopy.

Carl S. English Jr. Botanical Garden

3015 NW 54th St.
(206) 783-7059
www.nws.usace.army.mil/Missions/CivilWorks/LocksandDams/Chittenden-Locks/BotanicalGarden.aspx

How many times can you possibly go to the Ballard Locks and the fish ladder and not stop and smell the roses? For me, it took 10 visits before I finally succumbed to its charms. Before horticulturist Carl English laid his hands on it, the seven-acre plot featured the types of lawns you might expect at a military installation, as the government intended. Over 43 years on the job, English remade it into a garden in English landscape style. By the time he finished, the garden featured 500 plant species and 1,500 varieties from all over the world. Despite all the effort, most Seattleites are so focused on taking visiting friends and family to see ladder-scaling salmon and boats rising and falling that they barely notice it. You can make up for that oversight by taking a free guided tour.

The Center for Urban Horticulture

3502 NE 41st St.
(206) 543-8616
depts.washington.edu/uwbg/visit/cuh.php

The center and the Washington Park Arboretum are the two individual parks that make up the gardens that comprise the University of Washington Botanical Gardens. The center focuses on issues surrounding the use and growth of plants in cities, including pollution and the unusual natural conditions flora face in an urban environment. It's more than just a dry academic setting, though. The center itself is the first "green" building on the UW campus and includes the Soest Herbacious Display Garden, the Otis Douglas Hyde Herbarium, and the Seattle Garden Club Fragrance Garden, all of which are open to the public. It's also home to the 74-acre Union Bay Natural Area, a public wildlife area that not only has 4 miles of shoreline, but is also believed to be the city's best place for bird-watching. Numerous environmental and garden groups meet here as well, and it's home to the King County Master Gardener Foundation.

Kubota Garden
9817 55th Ave. S (Rainier Avenue South and 55th Avenue South)
(206) 684-4584
www.kubotagarden.org

Originally the headquarters of a well-loved, family-owned gardening company, Kubota was such a neighborhood institution that residents lobbied for historic landmark status and pushed the city to purchase it when it looked like condos would be built on the site. The 20-acre park combining Japanese technique with Northwest plants is filled with streams, waterfalls, bridges, and a wide range of mature plants and makes for a nice retreat. There's a free public tour at 10 a.m. on the fourth Saturday of the month and free docent-led tours for groups of at least eight.

Olympic Sculpture Park
2901 Western Ave.
(206) 654-3100
www.seattleartmuseum.org/visit/osp

As the name would suggest, there are plenty of sculptures in this nine-acre outdoor park on a bluff overlooking Elliott Bay. There are more than a dozen larger-than-life artworks ranging from the park's iconic painted steel *Eagle* by Alexander Calder to *Typewriter Eraser, Scale X* by Claes Oldenburg set along a Z-shaped path that runs from the glass and steel Paccar Pavilion's greenhouse down to the waterfront along Elliott Bay. There are four distinct landscapes with sculptures to match. As odd as it sounds, despite the artworks being out in the open, touching them is not allowed. The park is open every day from 30 minutes after sunrise to 30 minutes after sunset. The Paccar Pavilion is open 10 a.m. to 4 p.m, Tuesday through Sunday in winter and early spring and from 10 a.m. to 5 p.m. daily from May 1 to Labor Day.

Seattle Chinese Garden
6000 16th Ave. SW
(206) 934-5219
www.seattlechinesegarden.org

A combination garden and cultural center, the 2-year-old garden is one of the largest Chinese gardens outside China and features traditional plants as well as traditional structures built by artisans from Chongqing. It's open from 11:30 a.m. to 5 p.m. Wednesday through Sunday from April to November 1 with free guided tours at 1 p.m. on the first Saturday of the month. Open only on Saturday in winter. The garden also offers free basic Chinese language classes and other courses throughout the year.

Seattle Waterfall Garden
219 2nd Ave. S

The Catch: Copyrighted photography/video is strictly prohibited.

In much the same way that the Klondike Gold Rush Museum is a national park in an urban setting, the waterfall garden is an unexpected bit of nature in an urban setting. The 22-foot waterfall is located at the original headquarters of United Parcel Service. Workers come here for lunch, some visit for reflection, and others even get married here. (Cheap bastard alert: There's no charge to hold a party here other than the hourly rate charged by the security firm.)

South Seattle Community College Arboretum
6000 16th Ave. SW
(206) 764-5300
www.southseattle.edu/arboretum

No, not that arboretum. This is the one few Seattleites even know exists. Situated next to the Chinese Garden, the six-acre campus park was designed by students in the school's Landscape Horticulture program and essentially serves as a living classroom where they can learn about plant identification, landscape construction, and a variety of other issues within their field of study. Open 10 a.m. to 7 p.m.

Washington Park Arboretum
2300 Arboretum Dr. E
(206) 543-8800
depts.washington.edu/uwbg/gardens/wpa.shtml

There are times when it seems like this is Seattle's biggest park, especially when you're driving from Montlake to Madison Park and are stuck in slow-moving traffic on the two-lane road that cuts through the park, but it's not quite. Fortunately, at least the view is nice and helps calm jangled nerves, especially in a city where honking your car's horn is frowned upon. The 230-acre park has 40,000 trees and shrubs, 139 endangered species of plants, and plenty of space to walk among trees, flowers, and shrubs. The Arboretum has a

Horticultural Tourism

There was a time when garden shops and nurseries were just places you went to buy seeds and plants and the odd bit of specialized equipment not available in your local hardware store. All that changed when nurseries began expanding, specializing, and offering more than just the standard range of stuff. Some added furniture into the mix, others gifts, a few even opened restaurants. Before they knew it, some became so well known that people were coming from all over the region to visit, some to buy, others just to enjoy the experience. Although the area has a number of locally owned nurseries that fit the description, there are three that come up in conversation again and again.

It may be located about an hour out of town in Woodinville, but **Molbaks Garden + Home** (13625 NE 175th St., Woodinville; 425-483-5000) seems to be the best known. The big draw here is the total package, from plants and gear to decorative touches for inside the house as well including linens, tableware, and candles. It also has free gardening seminars and a cafe that serves sandwiches, beer, and wine. All of which adds up to the perfect way to spend a Saturday morning or afternoon, just wandering the aisles. Be careful, though, or you just might be tempted to buy something.

visitor center with a gift shop and a conference room for meetings and classes. It's also a pretty place to walk during the colder months when the Winter Garden is a popular stop. Although it's not free, the park also has a Japanese Garden (admission: $6) where there's a formal tea ceremony each month.

Swansons Nursery (9701 15th Ave. NW, Seattle; 206-782-2543) is a bit more modest. It doesn't have indoor furniture or accessories, but it does have free classes, a gift shop, cafe, and a koi pond where kids and adults can hang out and watch fish frolic. It's also a popular spot during the holiday season because it has reindeer and a camel. There's also a fall festival with a pumpkin patch and activities for kids. Not many people know this, but it's also where Molbaks got its start because Egon Molbak got his training here before he went off and founded his own nursery. If you're in a buying mood, the store prides itself on its deep selection of perennials and unusual varieties of plants.

Sky Nursery (18528 Aurora Ave. N, Seattle; 206-546-4851) is even more modest as its slogan, "the gardener's gardening store," might attest. Its focus is on the meat and potatoes of the business. The real attractions are its new 35,000-square-foot retail greenhouse, its classes, and its high level of customer service. If you're in the market for gardening items, it tends to have lower prices than the other two and is quick to admit that the family-owned store isn't "a fru fru experience." Where the other destination nurseries are good places to spend the day, Sky would easily classify itself as a shorter, get-and-go type of destination.

Woodland Park Rose Garden
750 N. 50th St.
www.zoo.org/visit/rose-garden

An often-overlooked 2.5-acre splash of color near the Woodland Park Zoo's south entrance, the Rose Garden features 280 rose varieties on 5,000 individual plants and sees about 200,000 visitors every year. In addition to being a beautiful summertime retreat for rose lovers, it's also a popular spot for weddings. On the last Sunday of February or first Sunday in March, the park holds a free rose-pruning demonstration run by the Seattle Rose Society.

GARDENING

Has seeing all those gardens got you itching to start one of your own? These organizations will help you scratch that itch.

King County Extension Master Gardeners
3501 NE 41st St.
(206) 685-5104
kingcountymg.org

What's that you say? Your plant has developed some sort of rot and no longer looks like its happy self? You've heard that a particular shrub would look great in your backyard, but you'd like to see what it looks like in a variety of settings before you buy it? Thanks to the master gardeners' program, you're not alone and you are in luck. This cadre of trained volunteer horticulturists stands ready to diagnose problems with your favorite flora and address your concerns about other gardening-related issues. And the best part is, you don't have to go all the way to their office to find them. Instead, they host 38 plant clinics throughout the county and have six demonstration gardens. They're also happy to dispense garden-variety advice to neophytes. To find the location of the clinics where you can take samples of your ailing plant, go to the website.

MUSEUMS:
FREE TO SEE
IN YOUR FREE TIME

"One time I went to a museum where all the work in the museum had been done by children. They had all the paintings up on refrigerators."

—STEVEN WRIGHT

It's amazing what people will dedicate a museum to. Over the years, the Seattle area has had museums that focus on gas stations, bananas, and even potatoes. While those are long gone, they make a museum centered on doll art, another dedicated to the weird, and a national park in the heart of Pioneer Square sound somewhat tame in comparison. Although most of the city's best museums aren't free day in and day out, many of them offer free admission at least once a month. And some of the ones that you've never heard of are free year-round. Although some favorite local museums may not be free, there is one other way to get in without paying—volunteering.

ALWAYS **FREE**

The Center for Wooden Boats
1010 Valley St.
(206) 382-2628
www.cwb.org

Now that the Museum of History and Industry has moved next door, parking has become a bit more difficult to find, but it's well worth the trip on a sunny day because most of the exhibits here are outside, not indoors. It makes perfect sense considering that its mission is to preserve wooden boats while teaching landlubbers and new salts an appreciation of the history of the boats and the skills necessary to sail them. The facility also rents boats and offers free boat rides on Lake Union every Sunday from 10 a.m. to 2 p.m. It's also the home to the annual Wooden Boat Festival around July 4th. As an added bonus, if you volunteer for three hours, you can take a boat out for an hour for free.

Children's Bug and Reptile Museum
1118 Charleston Beach Rd. W
Bremerton
(360) 373-7691
www.bugmuseum.com

There comes a time in every child's life when he or she wants to know more about bugs. Perhaps they want to play with the critters or maybe even eat them. While they don't make great playmates and aren't all that tasty, bugs are always fun for kids to look at and get grossed out by, especially when they're in a museum behind glass and you know that neither child nor bugs will get hurt. The museum also recently added a reptile room. On weekends, the reptile handler takes out some of the critters so that kids can see them up close and personal. Admission is free.

Coast Guard Museum of the Northwest
Pier 36
1519 Alaskan Way S
(206) 217-6993

If you haven't heard of this museum, you're not alone. It's so far south on the waterfront that most people never make it that far. The collection includes a piece of the USS Constitution and a Coast Guard flag that went into space on the first space shuttle. There are also 25 models of Coast Guard ships, displays on World War II, and a wide range of uniforms. You will need a photo identification to get in. Open from 9 a.m. to 3 p.m. Monday, Wednesday, and Friday.

Frye Art Museum
704 Terry Ave.
(206) 622-9250
fryemuseum.org

You've got to love a museum that believes that art is so important that it should always be free to the public. Much of the collection focuses on European paintings from the late 1800s and early 1900s. And did I mention that it's always free? So's the parking in the parking lot. I love this place already.

Hiram M. Chittenden Locks Visitors Center
3015 NW 54th St.
(206) 783-7059
www.nws.usace.army.mil/Missions/CivilWorks/LocksandDams/ChittendenLocks.aspx

It's always fun for kids and adults alike to watch vessels be raised or lowered as they pass between the Lake Washington Ship Canal and Puget Sound, but

I'm Not a Museum, But I Could Play One on TV

Two of Seattle's best and cheapest museums aren't really museums at all, but they should be.

While most visitors see **Ye Olde Curiosity Shop** on the waterfront as just another tacky souvenir stand, many locals know better. Of course, it sells all the standard memorabilia that you'd find at any tourist shop including Seattle key chains, snow globes, pens, and postcards, and you could run in and run out without giving the shop a second thought. If you look a little closer, you'll see a collection of oddities that would easily rival those found in many small museums. There's a walrus *oosik* (penis) hanging from the ceiling, a two-headed calf, a collection of shrunken heads, a walrus skull with three tusks, fleas in dresses, a collection of Northwest native art, and even the Lord's Prayer engraved on a grain of rice. If anyone could be said to be a mascot for this strange conglomeration, it would have to be Sylvester, a mummy who was said to have been found sticking out of the sand in an Arizona desert in 1895 and who has been at the store since 1955. Or it could be Sylvia, his mummified female counterpart. Believe it or not, there's no admission fee to all this wonderful kitsch.

The other, more frequently overlooked collection is **The Giant Shoe Museum** at the Pike Place Market. Not only does it have some of the largest shoes you'll ever see, it's likely one of the world's few coin-operated museums (which prompted the *Seattle Post-Intelligencer* to call it a "peep shoe"). The odd accumulation features 20 ginormous brogans, including a size 37 shoe that once belonged to Robert Wadlow, considered to be the world's tallest man (at 8 feet 11 inches), and the Colossus, a 90-year-old, 5-foot-long wingtip shoe. It's not free, but it's close enough. You can see the entire collection through several windows for about $1 in quarters. The whole shebang is found Down Under at the market next to Old Seattle Paperworks.

the operation is even more impressive when you understand all of the effort that went into making this engineering feat an everyday experience. The Visitors' Center details the history of the project and the concepts behind the engineering that makes it work. Add to that a visit to nearby Golden Gardens Park and a stop at a nearby ice cream stand and you've got the makings of a great day.

Klondike Gold Rush National Historic Park
319 2nd Ave. S
(206) 220-4240
www.nps.gov/klse/index.htm

Pioneer Square may not be the first place people think of as being ideal for a national park, but this park isn't about huge tracts of land. Instead, it commemorates the turn-of-the-20th-century rush for gold in the Great White North and Seattle's role as outfitter to the masses in the very area where prospectors stopped to get their supplies. Admission is always free. The park also offers guided walking tours of the Pioneer Square area and gold-panning demonstrations during the summer. Demonstrations are limited to 30 people, walking tours to 25. For more details, check the website.

OCCASIONALLY **FREE**

Bellevue Arts Museum
510 Bellevue Way NE
Bellevue
(425) 519-0770
www.bellevuearts.org

You can't ask for a better location for an eastside museum than a place that's right across the street from a shopping mall. BAM's focus is on art, craft, and design. Admission is free on the first Friday of the month.

Burke Museum
University of Washington Campus
Corner of 17th Avenue NE and NE 45th Street

See Museums Free . . .
Through Your Local Library

Many library cardholders may not know this, but both the King County and Seattle Public Library Systems offer patrons free passes to select museums; they just have to know where to look. And no, the Dewey Decimal System can't help you with this one. Instead, you'll have to head to each organization's website.

The King County Library offers free passes to the Bellevue Arts Museum, the KidsQuest Childrens Museum, and the Washington State History Museum. You simply go to the museum passes page (www.kcls .org/programs/museumpasses.cfm), select the museum you want to see, select the date you want to visit, and print your e-mail confirmation if a pass is available. Each museum has restrictions on how many people the pass covers and how often you can get a pass from the library.

The Seattle Public Library's selection at www.spl.org/library-collection/museum-pass includes the Burke Museum, EMP, the Children's Museum, and the Seattle Art Museum. The process is similar to that of the King County Library, but requires your library PIN. In addition to restrictions from each museum, cardholders are limited to one pass per card per week and can only get a pass for the same museum every 30 days.

Even so, it's hard to beat free.

(206) 543-5590
www.washington.edu/burkemuseum

Parents of dinosaur-loving children beware! This much-loved natural history museum has free admission on the first Thursday of the month. It features collections of cultural artifacts from indigenous peoples of Washington state and the Pacific Rim. Plus the only real dinosaur fossils on display in the state.

Experience Music Project and Science Fiction Museum

Seattle Center
325 5th Ave. N
(877) 367-7361 (EMP-SFM1)
www.empsfm.org

EMP has opted out of the First Thursday art walk and no longer offers free admission. So the only way to get into the museum for free is to get a free pass from the Seattle Public Library. Volunteers also get in free. The only other bargain to be had here is the Thursday 2 for $10 Teen Tix deal, but it comes with a lot of conditions. For starters, you have to know someone who is a member of Teen Tix. If they're interested, they can get in for $5 and get you in for an additional $5 even if you are too old to be a Teen Tix member. So you may want to start being nice to your kids again, not only because that means a substantial savings over regular admission, but also because they'll be choosing your nursing home.

Henry Art Gallery

15th Avenue NE and 41st Street
(206) 543-2280
www.henryart.org

Not every museum can claim to be one of the first in the state, but the Henry can. Its initial focus was on 19th- and early-20th-century paintings, but it has since expanded to include photography from the mid-1800s to multi-disciplinary art from the 21st century. Admission is free on the first Thursday of the month.

Kidsquest Museum

4091 Factoria Mall SE
Bellevue
(425) 637-8100
www.kidsquestmuseum.org

Until this eastside kids' museum takes over the former home of the Rosalie Whyel Museum of Doll Art in 2015, it will remain at Factoria Mall (are you detecting a theme here?). Kidsquest is a hit with kids for its imaginative hands-on exhibits. I love the Backyard exhibit because it is a large enclosed area in the middle of the museum for toddlers to play in with plenty of room to roam. My kids enjoy putting things in the water at Central Stream and watching them head downstream. Admission is free from 5 to 8 p.m. on the third Thursday of the month.

Last Resort Fire Department
301 2nd Ave. S
(206) 783-4474
www.lastresortfd.org

Most Seattle residents know all about the Great Seattle Fire, but aren't as aware of the Cedar Mill or Grand Trunk fires. The Last Resort not only features a display on all three, it also has some of the equipment that was used in fighting those conflagrations and other fires dating back to the 1800s. Admission is free, but hours are limited to 11 a.m. to 3 p.m. on Wednesday and Thursday in summer and just Wednesday in winter. There's no signage, so you'll have to watch for the address or you'll miss it. Curiously, some of the best stuff—including 12 antique fire engines—isn't on display because there's not enough room. Instead, it's in a storage and maintenance facility in Ballard that you can tour for free, but by appointment only. For more details, go to www.lastresortfd.org/facilities.htm.

Microsoft Visitor Center
15010 NE 36th St.
Microsoft Campus
Building 92
Redmond
(425) 703-6214
www.microsoft.com/about/companyinformation/visitorcenter/default.aspx

The once and former Microsoft Museum has become the Microsoft Visitor Center. Where the museum provided a look back at the early days of Microsoft and the origins of the personal computer, the center shows where the software firm is heading while showcasing its latest offerings. There's an Xbox Theater with a 13-foot screen and surround sound, a gaming area, and a section detailing Microsoft research. Open 9 a.m. to 7 p.m. Monday through Friday. Call before visiting as the center does close for private events. It's also located near the Microsoft company store. The center and the store are the only two areas on campus that the public can visit.

Museum of Flight
9404 E. Marginal Way S
(206) 764-5720
www.museumofflight.org

The museum's collection may include the Airpark where you can see Air Force One and the Concorde; the problem is, it's not always open on the first Thursday evening of the month when the museum is free from 5 to 9 p.m. You can always see the Personal Courage wing and try out the flight simulator (for an additional charge), though.

Museum of Glass
1801 Dock St.
Tacoma
(866) 4-MUSEUM (468-7386)
www.museumofglass.org

The roof of the hot shop auditorium is such a prominent part of the Tacoma skyline that it seems like the 11-year-old museum has always been there. It features the work of Dale Chihuly and other glass artists. Admission is free from 5 to 8 p.m. on the third Thursday of the month.

Museum of History and Industry (MOHAI)
860 Terry Ave. N
(206) 324-1126
www.mohai.org

After years of being on the edge of the University of Washington campus, MOHAI moved and opened splashy new digs in the Naval Reserve Building at Lake Union Park in 2012. The old, hands-on displays showing how salmon canneries worked before automation have been replaced by cool, new higher-tech exhibits including an opportunity to help build a railroad, a fun movie on the Great Seattle Fire, and a Maritime Gallery periscope that offers a 360-degree view of the park. It's free from 10 a.m. to 8 p.m. on the first Thursday of the month and free to children under 14 every day. You can also park for $4 for the entire day in the AGC lot with validation from the museum.

Northwest African American Museum
2300 S. Massachusetts St.
(206) 518-6000
www.naamnw.org

Admission to this former community school turned history museum is free on the first and second Thursday of the month.

Seattle Art Museum
300 First Ave.
(206) 654-3100
www.seattleartmuseum.org

The Catch: *If you only make a suggested donation, you might not be able to see the latest special exhibit.*

What you pay to get in the door at the Seattle Art Museum isn't called an admission fee; it's a suggested donation of $20. Did you notice the word "suggested" there? Since it's a donation, you can actually give what you want, even if it's only $1. Heck, you might even be able to get in for free, but most Seattleites are too polite to try. Most simply wait until one of the museum's many days when admission is free. The Permanent Collection Galleries and special exhibitions are free all day on the first Thursday of every month in conjunction with the First Thursday Gallery Walk. A discount is sometimes offered for special exhibits. The museum is also free to people 62 and over on the first Friday of the month and to teens age 13 to 19 from 5 to 9 p.m. on the second Friday of the month (ID required).

Seattle Asian Art Museum
Volunteer Park
1400 E. Prospect St.
(206) 654-3100
www.seattleartmuseum.org/visit/visitsaam.asp

This sister of the Seattle Art Museum is located across town in a popular Capitol Hill park with lots of parking. It's free all day on the first Thursday of the month and in conjunction with the Capitol Hill art walk on the second Thursday of every month from 5 to 9 p.m. Seniors also get in free on the first Friday of the month and families get free admission on the first Saturday of the month. Kids 12 and under get in free.

Soundbridge
Benaroya Hall
200 University St.
www.seattlesymphony.org/soundbridge

The musical education component of the Seattle Symphony isn't exactly a museum as much as it is a chance for kids to learn about musical instruments and an excuse to make as much noise as they want without being shushed. Fridays are pay-what-you-can days and also feature a music-focused story time at 1:45 p.m. that can feature dancing, rhythm, and clapping. Soundbridge also offers classes in instrument making, film scoring, and other subjects for $10 per session.

Volunteer Park Conservatory
Volunteer Park
1400 E. Galer St.
(206) 684-4743
www.seattle.gov/parks/parkspaces/volunteerpark/conservatory.htm

The classic Victorian Greenhouse dating back to the days of 19th-century urban planners Frederick Law Olmsted and John Charles Olmsted has gone from asking for a suggested donation to charging $4 for adults and $2 for 13- to 18-year-olds. Admission is free on the first Thursday and Saturday of the month.

Wing Luke Museum of the Asian Pacific American Experience
719 S. King St.
(206) 623-5124
www.wingluke.org

This International District museum details the Asian-American experience in Seattle and includes a tour of a historic hotel. Admission is free all day the first Thursday and third Saturday of the month. It's close enough to Safeco and Qwest Field stadiums that it also has a cool deal for sports fans. When the sign is out, people who have ticket stubs from a recent Sounders, Mariners, or Seahawks game can buy one admission and get one free. While the stub doesn't have to be from the previous night's match, it does have to be from the current season.

APPENDIX A:

ADDITIONAL RESOURCES

One of the few frustrating things about writing a book like this is that there's no way to list every bargain because new ones pop up every day and other ones go away without warning. And any cheap bastard worth his or her salt is always looking for the latest freebies and bargains. That's why I continue to track deals on my Cheap Bastard Seattle blog at cheapbastard seattle.com

Here are the places I turn to to keep current.

DEALS AT LOCAL SUPERMARKETS & OTHER STORES

Coupon Connections Northwest
www.couponconnections.com

The Coupon Project
www.thecouponproject.com

Frugal Living Northwest
www.frugallivingnw.com

This blog may be based in Portland, but many of the deals are also available in Seattle.

Hip2Save
hip2save.com

My favorite national deal site, it's a great resource to find out about upcoming deals involving national chains.

The Krazy Coupon Lady
thekrazycouponlady.com/blog

A good site for national deals that are often available in Seattle.

Queen Bee Coupons
queenbeecoupons.com

This site features tabs that will take you to the latest grocery store deals. In addition, the blogger who runs it often teaches classes on how to use coupons.

Seattle Moms Deal Finder
www.seattlemomsdealfinder.com

Thrifty and Thriving
www.thriftyandthriving.com

Thrifty Northwest Mom
www.thriftynorthwestmom.com

DISCOUNTED **PERFORMANCES**

Goldstar.com
Sports, concerts, and plays are just some of this site's offerings.

ODDS & **ENDS**

Freeattle
www.freshpickedseattle.com/free-event-calendar

This page on the Fresh-Picked Seattle site lists free events around town every day. Although the main Fresh-Picked Seattle page lists the same free events, it also lists a wide range of events that have an admission charge, some inexpensive, others not. Both calendars are good resources for finding out what's coming up around town. It includes everything from meditation classes and author readings to lectures and travel workshops.

Seattle Free School
www.seattlefreeschool.org

As the name suggests, the school offers free classes on a variety of subjects depending on the interests and passions of its instructors.

DAILY DEAL SITES

Although there's been an explosion in the popularity of sites like Groupon and Living Social since the first edition of this book came out, there's some question about whether the business model really works all that well for all involved. Restaurants get more business in the short run, but they end up losing money on food and the customers they attract rarely return when the deals end. Companies that provide services like haircuts, handyman services, and lawn mowing may do better because they don't lose money on stock sold below cost, but they can become overwhelmed with the spike in demand.

And then there are the buyers. Sure, the group buying deals are great, but only if we remember to use them. The cheap bastard can't tell you how many times he's found himself buying a Groupon, and then scrambling to use it the day before it expires. Not only that, but the fine print can be frustrating. Yes, Company x did have a great deal on its duct-cleaning services, but it charged extra for some of the things that should have been included.

The cheap bastard doesn't mean to be a downer, here. Nor is he predicting the end of daily deal sites as we know them, even though he has noticed that truly good deals are often harder to find—unless you want your fat suctioned, your teeth whitened, your skin bronzed, or something like that. When he finds deals that are too good to pass up, he will continue to use them; he's just reminding you to let the buyer beware.

Oh, and don't forget to tip your server on the basis of what the bill would have been before the discount.

Here are some of the CB's favorite deal sites:

AAA Member Deals
memberdealsusa.com/seattle

Membership has its privileges and these deals are open only to members of AAA Washington. One additional hint: If you have an AAA card and are at a tourist attraction, don't forget to ask if they offer AAA discounts. You'd be surprised how often the answer is yes.

Amazon Local
local.amazon.com

The online retailer brings its muscle and purchasing power to the daily deal site world. The advantage here is that you can track your vouchers along with your other Amazon purchases.

Groupon
www.groupon.com

If any site can be said to be the granddaddy of them all after only four years, Groupon would be it. Couponing and social networking come together on this site that offers a variety of deals every day with one little catch. The only way for the deal to work is if a minimum number of people sign up and pay up. Minimums vary from deal to deal.

Living Social
www.livingsocial.com

Like Groupon, this site offers a wide range of deals every day.

Travel Zoo Local Deals
www.travelzoo.com/local-deals/Seattle-Tacoma/deals

Offers a wide range of mostly travel- and entertainment-related deals, including sporting events, hotels, and day trips.

APPENDIX B:

LIBRARY BRANCH LOCATIONS

SEATTLE **PUBLIC** LIBRARY

Ballard Branch, 5614 22nd Ave. NW; (206) 684-4089

Beacon Hill Branch, 2821 Beacon Ave. S; (206) 684-4711

Broadview Branch, 12755 Greenwood Ave. N; (206) 684-7519

Capitol Hill Branch, 425 Harvard Ave. E; (206) 684-4715

Central Library, 1000 Fourth Ave.; (206) 386-4636

Columbia Branch, 4721 Rainier Ave. S; (206) 386-1908

Delridge Branch, 5423 Delridge Way SW; (206) 733-9125

Douglass-Truth Branch, 2300 E. Yesler Way; (206) 684-4704

Fremont Branch, 731 N. 35th St.; (206) 684-4084

Green Lake Branch, 7364 E. Green Lake Dr. N; (206) 684-7547

Greenwood Branch, 8016 Greenwood Ave. N; (206) 684-4086

High Point Branch, 3411 SW Raymond St.; (206) 684-7454

International District/Chinatown Branch, 713 Eighth Ave. S; (206) 386-1300

Lake City Branch, 12501 28th Ave. NE; (206) 684-7518

Madrona-Sally Goldmark Branch, 1134 33rd Ave.; (206) 684-4705

Magnolia Branch, 2801 34th Ave. W; (206) 386-4225

Montlake Branch, 2401 24th Ave. E; (206) 684-4720

New Holly Branch, 7058 32nd Ave. S; (206) 386-1905

Northeast Branch, 6801 35th Ave. NE; (206) 684-7539

Northgate Branch, 10548 Fifth Ave. NE; (206) 386-1980

Queen Anne Branch, 400 W Garfield St.; (206) 386-4227

Rainier Beach Branch, 9125 Rainier Ave. S; (206) 386-1906

South Park Branch, 8604 Eighth Ave. S at South Cloverdale Street; (206) 615-1688

Southwest Branch, 9010 35th Ave. SW; (206) 684-7455
University Branch, 5009 Roosevelt Way NE; (206) 684-4063
Wallingford Branch, 1501 N. 45th St.; (206) 684-4088
West Seattle Branch, 2306 42nd Ave. SW; (206) 684-7444

KING **COUNTY** LIBRARY

Algona-Pacific, 255 Ellingson Rd., Pacific; (253) 833-3554
Auburn Library, 1102 Auburn Way S, Auburn; (253) 931-3018
Bellevue Library, 1111 110th Ave. NE, Bellevue; (425) 450-1765
Black Diamond Library, 24707 Roberts Dr., Black Diamond; (360) 886-1105
Bothell Library, 18215 98th Ave. NE, Bothell; (425) 486-7811
Boulevard Park Library, 12015 Roseberg Ave. S, Seattle; (206) 242-8662
Burien Library, 400 SW 152nd St., Burien; (206) 243-3490
Carnation Library, 4804 Tolt Ave., Carnation; (425) 333-4398
Covington Library, 27100 164th Ave. SE, Covington; (253) 630-8761
Des Moines Library, 21620 11th Ave. S, Des Moines; (206) 824-6066
Duvall Library, 15508 Main St. NE, Duvall; (425) 788-1173
Enumclaw Library, 1700 1st St., Enumclaw; (360) 825-2045
Fairwood Library, 17009 140th Ave. SE, Renton; (425) 226-0522
Fall City Library, 33415 SE 42nd Place, Fall City; (425) 222-5951
Federal Way Library, 34200 1st Way S, Federal Way; (253) 838-3668
Federal Way 320th Library, 848 S. 320th St., Federal Way; (253) 839-0257
Foster Library, 4060 S. 144th, Tukwila; (206) 242-1640
Greenbridge Library, 9720 8th Ave. SW, Seattle; (206) 762-1682
Issaquah Library, 10 W. Sunset Way, Issaquah; (425) 392-5430
Kenmore Library, 6531 NE 181st St., Kenmore; (425) 486-8747
Kent Library, 212 2nd Ave. N, Kent; (253) 859-3330
Kingsgate Library, 12315 NE 143rd St., Kirkland; (425) 821-7686
Kirkland Library, 308 Kirkland Ave., Kirkland; (425) 822-2459
Lake Forest Park, Lake Forest Park Towne Centre, 17171 Bothell Way NE, Lake Forest Park; (206) 362-8860
Lake Hills Library, 15590 Lake Hills Blvd., Bellevue; (425) 747-3350
The Library Connection at Crossroads, inside the Crossroads Mall, 15600

NE 8th St. (near QFC), Ste. K-11, Bellevue; (425) 644-6203

Library Express@Redmond Ridge, 10735 Cedar Park Crescent NE, Redmond; (425) 885-1861

Maple Valley Library, 21844 SE 248th St., Maple Valley; (425) 432-4620

Mercer Island Library, 4400 88th Ave. SE, Mercer Island; (206) 236-3537

Muckleshoot Library, 39917 Auburn Enumclaw Rd. SE, Auburn; (253) 931-6779

Newcastle Way Library, 12901 Newcastle Way, Newcastle; (425) 255-0111

Newport Way Library, 14250 SE Newport Way, Bellevue; (425) 747-2390

North Bend Library, 115 E. 4th, North Bend; (425) 888-0554

Redmond Library, 15990 NE 85th, Redmond; (425) 885-1861

Renton Highlands Library, 2902 NE 12th St., Renton; (425) 277-1831

Renton Library, 100 Mill Ave. S, Renton; (425) 226-6043

Richmond Beach Library, 19601 21st Ave. NW, Shoreline; (206) 546-3522

Sammamish Library, 825 228th Ave. SE, Sammamish; (425) 392-3130

Shoreline Library, 345 NE 175th, Shoreline; (206) 362-7550

Skykomish Library, 100 5th St., Skykomish; (360) 677-2660

Skyway Library, 7614 S. 126th St., Seattle; (206) 772-5541

Snoqualmie Library, 7824 Center Blvd. SE, Snoqualmie; (425) 888-1223

Southcenter Library Connection @ Southcenter Westfield Shoppingtown, 1386 Southcenter Mall, Tukwila; (206) 242-1640

Valley View Library, 17850 Military Rd. S, SeaTac; (206) 242-6044

Vashon Library, 7210 Vashon Hwy. SW, Vashon Island; (206) 463-2069

White Center Library, 11220 16th SW, Seattle; (206) 243-0233

Woodinville Library, 17105 Avondale Rd. NE, Woodinville; (425) 788-0733

Woodmont Library, 26809 Pacific Hwy. S, Des Moines; (253) 839-0121

APPENDIX C:

POOLS & RECREATION CENTERS

This list was current at press time, but is subject to change. I did not list hours as budget cuts may lead to reductions in service. In 2010, many centers were already taking at least one furlough day every month.

SEATTLE

Community Centers

Alki Community Center, 5817 SW Stevens St.; (206) 684-7430
Ballard Community Center, 6020 28th Ave. NW; (206) 684-4093
Belltown Community Center, 415 Bell St.; (206) 684-7245
Bitter Lake Community Center, 13035 Linden Ave. N; (206) 684-7524
Delridge Community Center, 4501 Delridge Way SW; (206) 684-7423
Garfield Community Center, 2323 E. Cherry St.; (206) 684-4788
Green Lake Community Center, 7201 E. Green Lake Dr. N; (206) 684-0780
Hiawatha Community Center, 2700 California Ave. SW; (206) 684-7441
High Point Community Center, 6920 34th Ave. SW; (206) 684-7422
International District/Chinatown Community Center, 719 8th Ave. S; (206) 233-0042
Jefferson Community Center, 3801 Beacon Ave. S; (206) 684-7481
Laurelhurst Community Center, 4554 NE 41st St.; (206) 684-7529
Loyal Heights Community Center, 2101 NW 77th St.; (206) 684-4052
Magnolia Community Center, 2550 34th Ave. W; (206) 386-4235
Magnuson Community Center, 7110 62nd Ave. NE; (206) 684-7026
Meadowbrook Community Center, 10517 35th Ave. NE; (206) 684-7522
Miller Community Center, 330 19th Ave. E; (206) 684-4753
Montlake Community Center, 1618 E. Calhoun St.; (206) 684-4736
Northgate Community Center, 10510 5th Ave. NE; (206) 386-4283
Queen Anne Community Center, 1901 First Ave. W; (206) 386-4240

Rainier Beach Community Center, 8825 Rainier Ave. S; (206) 684-4075
Rainier Community Center, 4600 38th Ave. S; (206) 386-1919
Ravenna-Eckstein Community Center, 6535 Ravenna Ave. NE; (206) 684-7534
South Park Community Center, 8319 8th Ave. S; (206) 684-7451
Southwest Community Center, 2801 SW Thistle St.; (206) 684-7438
Van Asselt Community Center, 2820 S. Myrtle St.; (206) 386-1921
Yesler Community Center, 917 E. Yesler Way; (206) 386-1245

Weight Rooms
Garfield Community Center, 2323 E. Cherry St.; (206) 684-4788
Loyal Heights Community Center, 2101 NW 77th St.; (206) 684-4052
Magnuson Community Center, 7110 62nd Ave. NE; (206) 684-7026
Meadowbrook Community Center, 10517 35th Ave. NE; (206) 684-7522
Northgate Community Center, 10510 5th Ave. NE; (206) 386-4283
Rainier Community Center, 4600 38th Ave. S; (206) 386-1919

Indoor Swimming Pools
Ballard Pool, 1471 NW 67th St.; (206) 684-4094
Evans Pool, 7201 E. Green Lake Dr. N; (206) 684-4961
Helene Madison Pool, 13401 Meridian Ave. N; (206) 684-4979
Meadowbrook Pool, 10515 35th Ave. NE; (206) 684-4989
Medgar Evers Pool, 500 23rd Ave.; (206) 684-4766
Queen Anne Pool, 1920 1st Ave. W; (206) 386-4282
Rainier Beach Pool, 8825 Rainier Ave. S; (206) 386-1944
Southwest Pool, 2801 SW Thistle St.; (206) 684-7440

Outdoor Swimming Pools
Colman Pool, 8603 Fauntleroy Way SW; (206) 684-7494
Lowery C. "Pop" Mounger Pool, 2535 32nd Ave. W; (206) 684-4708

Wading Pools and Sprayparks
Ballard Commons Park, spraypark, 5701 22nd Ave. NW
Beacon Hill Playground, wading pool, 1902 13th Ave. S
Bitter Lake Playfield, wading pool, 13035 Linden Ave. N
Cal Anderson Park, wading pool, 1635 11th Ave.
Dahl Playfield, wading pool, 7700 25th Ave. NE
Delridge Playfield, wading pool, 4458 Delridge Way SW
E.C. Hughes Playground, wading pool, 2805 SW Holden St.

East Queen Anne Playground, wading pool, 1912 Warren Ave. N

Georgetown Playfield, spraypark, 750 S. Homer St.

Gilman Playground, wading pool, 923 NW 54th St.

Green Lake Park, wading pool, 7201 E. Green Lake Dr. N

Hiawatha Playfield, wading pool, 2700 California Ave. SW

Highland Park Playground, spraypark, 1100 SW Cloverdale St.

John C. Little, Sr. Park, spraypark, 6961 37th Ave. S

Judkins Park and Playfield, spraypark, 2150 S. Norman St.

Lake Union Park, spraypark, 860 Terry Ave. N

Lincoln Park, wading pool, 8011 Fauntleroy Way SW

Miller Playfield, spraypark, 330 19th Ave. E

Northacres Park, spraypark, 12718 1st Ave. NE

Peppi's Playground, wading pool, 3233 E. Spruce St.

Powell Barnett Park, wading pool, 352 Martin Luther King Jr. Way

Pratt Park, spraypark, 1800 S. Main St.

Ravenna Park, wading park, 5520 Ravenna Ave. NE

Sandel Playground, wading pool, 9053 1st Ave. NW

Soundview Playfield, wading pool, 1590 NW 90th St.

South Park Playground, wading pool, 738 S. Sullivan St.

Van Asselt Playground, wading pool, 7200 Beacon Ave. S

View Ridge Playfield, wading pool, 4408 NE 70th St.

Volunteer Park, wading pool, 1247 15th Ave. E

Wallingford Playfield, wading pool, 4219 Wallingford Ave. N

Warren G. Magnuson Park, wading pool, 7400 Sand Point Way NE

BELLEVUE

Community Centers

Crossroads Community Center, 16000 NE 10th; (425) 452-4874

Highland Community Center, 14224 Bel-Red Rd.; (425) 452-7686

North Bellevue Community Center, 4063 148th Ave. NE; (425) 452-7681

Northwest Arts Center, 9825 NE 24th St.; (425) 452-4106

South Bellevue Community Center, 14509 SE Newport Way; (425) 452-4240

Fitness Center
South Bellevue Community Center, 14509 SE Newport Way; (425) 452-4240

Swimming Pool
Bellevue Aquatic Center, 602 143rd Ave. NE; (425) 452-4444

KIRKLAND

Community Centers
North Kirkland Community Center, 12421 103rd Ave. NE; (425) 587-3350
Peter Kirk Community Center, 352 Kirkland Ave.; (425) 587-3360

Swimming Pool
Peter Kirk Pool, 340 Kirkland Ave.; (425) 587-3335

REDMOND

Swimming Pool
Redmond Pool, 17535 NE 104 St.; (425) 233-3031

PWYC PERFORMANCES

You spend hours searching the Internet for inexpensive airfare, and travel a few extra miles to save money at the outlet malls, so why pay full price to see a play when there's a chance you can spend a little less and still see the same show as everyone else? If you don't mind taking a bit of a gamble on an evening's entertainment, there are many theaters that offer reduced-price tickets. Some are unsold rush tickets released just minutes before a show, while others are slightly less risky **pay-what-you-can (PWYC)** performances. Regardless of which you choose, remember to get there early to increase your odds of getting in, and have a backup plan handy just in case you don't. After all, just getting in is half the fun. The following theaters offer a variety of discounts. If you don't see your favorite, you might want to call and ask, check its website or its Facebook page, or join its e-mail list to learn about unadvertised specials or receive special offers.

For detailed information on the theaters listed here, see the Theater: Free Speech chapter starting on page 2.

A Contemporary Theatre: Why save the best for last? Apparently, almost every mainstage performance and many Central Heating Lab performances are pay what you can—if there are still tickets left. You must buy the tickets in person on the day of show starting at 1 p.m. Certain special engagements not included. Teen Tix members pay $5, full-time students can get advance tickets for $15 except on Saturday nights, and patrons under 25 can get advance tickets for any performance for $20, depending on availability. Who said there were no benefits to going back to school? Now, if I could just be 25 again. Seniors get 25 percent off of regular-priced tickets, and hospitality industry workers pay $15.
Annex Theatre: All Thursday shows are PWYC. Student tickets $5.
ArtsWest: Presents a PWYC preview on the night before opening night; suggested donation $5. People under 25 pay $15 for all performances; seniors get a 10 percent discount on tickets.
Balagan Theatre: PWYC performance on one Monday night of a play's run.

Copious Love Productions: PWYC performances on two Thursday nights during a play's run.

Eclectic Theater Company: PWYC the Thursday before opening night. Free dress rehearsals; $12 tickets for students, seniors, and union members.

5th Avenue Theatre: Patrons 25 and under get day-of-show tickets for $20 for most local productions.

Ghostlight Theatricals: PWYC performances every Monday and Thursday during a play's run.

Harlequin Productions: Offers PWYC shows the Wednesday evening after opening weekend.

Intiman Theatre Festival: Offers PWYC on the first preview night of each show.

Kirkland Performance Center: Check center's website and e-mail for PWYC performances.

Mirror Stage: Ten PWYC tickets are available at the box office an hour before each performance. Minimum cost $1. Half off for students and seniors.

New Century Theatre Company: The first preview of a run is a PWYC performance.

Phoenix Theatre Edmonds: PWYC shows on the Thursday before opening night.

Printer's Devil Theater: Offers PWYC performances the first two Thursdays of a show's run.

ReAct: Features one or two PWYC performances per run, depending on show. Call theater for details.

Redwood Theatre: Has two PWYC shows. The first is an actor's benefit on the first Saturday matinee where all of the money raised goes to the actors. The second PWYC is the first Sunday matinee.

Seattle Musical Theatre: PWYC previews the Thursday night before a Friday night opening.

Seattle Public Theater: PWYC dress rehearsal the Wednesday before the start of a show's run.

Seattle Repertory Theatre: Does a PWYC preview at the Bagley Wright the Tuesday before opening night; minimum suggested donation $1. Patrons 25 and under pay $12 at all performances for best available seat. Rush tickets $22. Teen Tix are $5.

Seattle Shakespeare Company: Holds a PWYC show early in play's run, usually on Tuesday or Wednesday. Rush tickets available to a group called Groundlings on day of show for $10.

Seattle Theatre Group (the Moore and the Paramount): Some traveling shows offer student rush tickets. For more information, sign up for eNews at STGPresents.org.

Second Story Repertory: Offers a PWYC preview the Thursday before opening night.

Sound Theatre Company: Offers PWYC performances most Thursday nights of a play's run.

Stone Soup Theatre: All Thursday night shows are PWYC, and a show's final dress rehearsal is half off. Stone Soup also sends two-for-one deals to members of its mailing list.

Tacoma Little Theatre: This one's a little confusing, but here goes. The company has a preview the Thursday before a play's opening night. While that one isn't a PWYC performance, the Thursday night performance a week after the preview is PWYC.

Taproot Theatre Company: Holds one PWYC performance per production with a minimum suggested donation of $5. Students and seniors have $4 discount on tickets, which usually sell for $20 to $35. Patrons 25 and under get tickets for $15.

Theatre22: Every Thursday night performance of a show's run is PWYC.

Theater Schmeater: All Thursday night performances are PWYC. If you're under 18, you can get into any show free, but must reserve a seat in advance.

UPAC Theatre Group: Offers a PWYC performance the first Thursday of the mainstage show's run and a two-for-one matinee for seniors on the second Saturday.

Village Theatre: Rush tickets are available to students and members of the military 30 minutes before curtain.

WARP: Students and seniors get half-price tickets to WARP productions.

Washington Ensemble Theatre: PWYC shows are sporadic.

APPENDIX E:

ADDITIONAL **SEATTLE** MUSIC **FESTIVALS**

The musical offerings at local festivals aren't as extensive as those at the various summer concerts throughout the area, but almost all of them have a concert's worth of free live music.

FEBRUARY

Tet Festival
Observe Vietnamese New Year's with music, arts, performance, and food.

MARCH

Irish Festival
Seattle Center
www.irishclub.org/center.htm

Enjoy music, singing, stepdancing, and all things Irish at this annual festival that includes the obligatory St. Patrick's Day Parade.

Seattle's French Fest
Seattle Center
fenpnw.org

Don't get upset over the cancellation of the Bastille Day Festival. Instead, take the Seattle Center by storm at this new celebration of French-speaking cultures.

APRIL

Seattle Cherry Blossom & Japanese Cultural Festival
Seattle Center

An opportunity to hear the roar of Taiko drums and all things Japanese.

World Rhythm Festival
Seattle Center
www.swps.org

A celebration of drumming and dance with a wide range of musical workshops.

MAY

Asian Pacific Islander Heritage Month Celebration
Seattle Center
www.seattleapi.com

Drill teams and dragon dances are among the highlights of this festival honoring China, Japan, the Philippines, and other South Pacific islands.

Chinese Cultural and Arts Festival
Seattle Center
www.chinaartandculture.org

Enjoy a glimpse into the traditions of one of the world's oldest cultures through a variety of arts including dance and performance.

University District Street Fair
University Way from NE Campus Parkway to NE 50th Street
www.udistrictstreetfair.org

Neighborhood festival featuring crafts, street performers, and several music stages.

JUNE

Edmonds Art Festival
9th Avenue and Main Street
Edmonds
www.edmondsartsfestival.com

An event built around a juried art show, the gathering has something everyone can love, including activities for the younger set, performers, and a wine bar that looks out over Puget Sound.

Festival Sundiata
Seattle Center
www.festivalsundiata.org

A celebration of African-American cultural heritage featuring music from all over Africa, including drumming, dance, gospel, jazz, and hip hop.

Fremont Fair
From Fremont Avenue West between North Canal and North 36th Streets
www.fremontfair.org

Seattle's only festival that comes complete with a parade featuring nude bikers. Three music stages and many buskers.

HONK! Fest West
honkfestwest.com

Feel the beat at this three-day celebration of "anything acoustic and mobile that makes a ruckus" including samba lines, marching bands, and maybe even a few drum and bugle corps for good measure.

Pagdiriwang Philippine Festival
Seattle Center
www.festalpagdiriwang.com

Observe Filipino independence from Spanish rule at this event featuring the islands' art and culture.

Pride Fest
Seattle Center
www.seattlepridefest.org

A celebration of Seattle's gay and lesbian community.

JULY

Ballard Seafood Festival
Downtown Ballard
www.seafoodfest.org

A celebration of the Scandinavian heritage of an area Garrison Keillor once called "the only ghetto in the world with hydrangeas."

Bellevue Arts Museum Arts Fair
Bellevue Arts Museum
510 Bellevue Way NE
Bellevue
www.bellevuearts.org/fair

Arts demonstrations, live music, kids' events, and the opportunity to buy the works of top artists are all part of the draw at this event near the Bellevue Arts Museum.

Bite of Seattle
Seattle Center
www.biteofseattle.com

Sample food from many of the city's favorite restaurants all in one place at this annual food-focused event.

Seafair Indian Days Pow Wow
Discovery Park (Magnolia Hill)
Daybreak Star Indian Cultural Center
Park entrance: 3801 W. Government Way
www.unitedindians.org/powwow

Native American gathering featuring drum and dance contests and traditional singing.

Vashon Island Strawberry Festival
17200 Vashon Hwy. SW
Vashon
www.vashonchamber.com

Strawberries may not be the king crop they once were when this festival started in 1909, but there are still plenty of them and that's as good a reason to celebrate as any.

West Seattle Summerfest
West Seattle Junction (the corner of California Avenue SW and SW Alaska Street)
wsjunction.org/summerfest

A community street fair complete with live music in one of Seattle's nicest out-of-the-way neighborhoods.

AUGUST

Brasilfest
Seattle Center
www.brasilfest.com

The samba and the bossa nova are just the beginning at this festival focusing on all things Brazilian ranging from soccer to Feijoada stew.

Central Area Community Festival Association
Garfield Community Center
2323 E. Cherry St.
www.cacf.com

Salute the culture and community of the city's Central District through art, food, and music.

Lake City Pioneer Days
Lake City Way

Enjoy the city's second longest running festival in Lake City of all places. Who knew?

South Lake Union Block Party
101 Westlake Ave. N
www.slublockparty.com

Celebrate one of Seattle's newest neighborhoods with one of the city's newest festivals. Events include a wine tasting, live music, and a burger grilling challenge.

Tibet Fest
Seattle Center
www.washingtontibet.org/TAW

Learn about the ancient traditions of Tibet through art, dance, and discussion during this annual event.

SEPTEMBER

Festa Italiana
Seattle Center
www.festaseattle.com

Stomp on grapes, take in cooking demonstrations, view movies, and learn everything you wanted to know about Italian culture but were afraid to ask.

Korean Cultural Celebration
Seattle Center
www.koamartists.org

Korea's annual harvest day is observed through folk music, native food, and film.

Oktoberfest
Fremont neighborhood
www.fremontoktoberfest.com

No one's really quite sure why Oktoberfest is traditionally held in September, but beer is just a small part of Fremont's interpretation of the celebration, which includes a Brew Ha-Ha 5K Run and Texas Chainsaw Pumpkin Carving.

Seattle Fiestas Patrias
Seattle Center
seattlefiestaspatrias.org

The Seattle Latin-American community's observance of Independence Day.

OCTOBER

Arab Festival
Seattle Center
arabcenterwa.org

Roam a traditional bazaar, learn about all things Arab, and even dance the night away at this annual gathering.

Croatia Fest
Seattle Center
www.croatiafest.org

Get serenaded by the music of the tamburitza while soaking up the culture of this often overlooked corner of Europe.

Issaquah Salmon Days
Downtown Issaquah
www.salmondays.org

San Juan Capistrano can have its swallows, but nothing beats a festival designed to celebrate a homecoming of creatures that make for good eating.

Turkfest
Seattle Center
turkfest.org

Observe the creation of the Republic of Turkey with dance, music, and art.

NOVEMBER

Hmong New Year Celebration
Seattle Center

Learn about the cultural roots of the hill people of China, Laos, and, Thailand through performance, music, and art.

DECEMBER

Seattle Center Winterfest
Seattle Center

Six weeks of celebrating the end of the year with music, lights, performance, and a train village.

INDEX